History, heritage and tradition in contemporary British politics

MANCHESTER
1824

Manchester University Press

History, heritage and tradition in contemporary British politics

Past politics and present histories

Emily Robinson

Manchester University Press

Published by Manchester University Press
Altrincham Street, Manchester M1 7JA, UK
www.manchesteruniversitypress.co.uk

British Library Cataloguing-in-Publication Data is available

Library of Congress Cataloging-in-Publication Data is available

ISBN 978 1 7849 9384 9 *paperback*

First published by Manchester University Press in hardback 2012

This edition first published 2016

The publisher has no responsibility for the persistence or accuracy of URLs for any external or third-party internet websites referred to in this book, and does not guarantee that any content on such websites is, or will remain, accurate or appropriate.

Printed by Lightning Source

Contents

Acknowledgements	*page*	vii
Introduction		1
1 Ideology and temporality		18
2 Structures of memory: parties and their pasts		47
3 Against the tide of history: conservatism in the 1980s and 1990s		88
4 Negotiations with Labour's past: the SDP and New Labour		122
5 New times, new politics: the collapse of the CPGB's historical narrative		153
Conclusions		181
Bibliography		186
Index		205

For my parents, Irene and David Robinson

In memory of my grandmother, Dorothy Lewis

Acknowledgements

I have incurred many debts in the writing of this book, the first and greatest of which is to my PhD supervisor, Richard Grayson, who has been exceptionally generous with his time and his insights. His support made the process of completing both my thesis and this book far easier and more pleasant than it might have been. Thank you also to Jim Martin for his sound advice and timely interventions. My two examiners, Steven Fielding and Andrew Flinn, have both been extremely encouraging and made many wise suggestions for the improvement of this study, as did Lawrence Black. I only hope I have done them justice.

I remain grateful to the Politics Department at Goldsmiths College for awarding me a PhD studentship and providing a supportive and stimulating environment in which to develop my ideas. The School of Political, Social and International Studies at the University of East Anglia awarded me a Postdoctoral Lecturing Fellowship to complete this manuscript and my colleagues there, and also in the School of History, made me very welcome. I would also like to thank everyone at Unlock Democracy (formerly the New Politics Network), who sparked my interest in political parties, and particularly Peter Facey, who not only gave me a job (twice), but also introduced me to the machinations of the SDP–Liberal merger and the dissolution of the CPGB.

I am grateful to the staff at all the archives and libraries I have used: the British Library at St Pancras and Colindale, the Liddell Hart Centre for Military Archives at Kings College London, the London Metropolitan Archive, the Marx Memorial Library, the Raphael Samuel Archive at the Bishopsgate Institute and the UCL Special Collections, but particular thanks must go to Nigel Cochrane at the Albert Sloman Library, Sue Donnelly at the LSE, Jeremy McIlwaine at the Conservative Party Archive, Andrew Riley at the Churchill Archives Centre and Darren Treadwell and Helen Roberts at the Labour History Archive and Study Centre, who all provided advice and suggestions in addition to files and folders.

Another debt is owed to the individuals who gave up their time to be interviewed both for this text and for the thesis which preceded it: Bill Barritt, Tony Belton, Stephen Bird, Duncan Brack, Nigel Cochrane, Penelope J. Corfield, Iain Dale, Sue Donnelly, Jim Garretts, John Grigg, Dianne Hayter, Graham Lippiatt, Jeremy McIlwaine, Joan O'Pray, Tessa and Derek Phillips, Jeanne and Dave Rathbone, Anne Reyersbach, Andrew Riley, Helen Roberts, Greg Rosen, Rachel Shawcross and Sheridan Westlake.

Many friends and colleagues have encouraged and helped me during the process of writing this book. As well as those listed above, I would particularly like to thank Mark Bevir, Bernadette Buckley, John Charmley, John Greenaway, Jon Lawrence, Alastair Reid and Sanjay Seth, who have not only been particularly encouraging but have also read and commented on sections of the text and provided many helpful suggestions for its improvement. I have also benefited enormously from conversations with Catherine Alexander, Sally Alexander, Lewis Baston, Duncan Brack, Kate Bradley, Siv Gøril Brandtzæg, Valentina Cardo, Sophia Deboick, Thomas Dixon, Cathy Elliott, Elizabeth Evans, David Gill, James Graham, Simon Griffiths, Rhodri Hayward, Imogen Lee, Alun Munslow, Ian Parker, Greg Rosen, Olivia Swift, Ted Vallance and Jon Wilson. Alastair Bonnett was kind enough to send me a copy of *Left in the Past* before it was published and Dianne Hayter allowed me to borrow from her collection of local Labour Party histories. I am especially grateful to those (who know who they are!) who have acted as my referees over the past few years – I know this has been a laborious and seemingly endless task. And also to James Smith for his monumental act of friendship in proof-reading my thesis. More recently, Tony Mason and Sarah Hunt at MUP have been patient, helpful and encouraging editors, and Fiona Thornton did a wonderful job of copy-editing.

Finally, a huge thank you to my parents for all their help, support and love over the years; without them I would not be doing this. Also to Jon, who is a constant source of encouragement and inspiration. He sets an admirable example of commitment and creativity and – even more importantly – never fails to raise both my mood and my confidence. I value his partnership above all else.

Introduction

On 23 November 2010, Nick Clegg announced a new division in British politics: between 'new progressives' and 'old progressives'. The first of these categories encompassed Conservative and Liberal Democrat supporters of the new coalition government but explicitly excluded the Labour Party, who, Clegg warned, were 'at risk of ... becoming the conservatives of British politics'.[1] More than a striking piece of wordplay, this was also an explicit attempt to redraw the dividing lines of British politics. 'Old progressivism' became, by implication, new conservatism; old conservatism was nowhere to be seen.

While Clegg's words were part of an immediate political strategy of justifying the Conservative–Liberal Democrat coalition, they also indicate a wider shift in political positioning. For over a year before this speech, Cameron's Conservatives had been describing themselves as 'a new generation of politicians', to whom the 'torch of progressive politics' had been passed.[2] But although both Clegg and his Conservative coalition partners were laying claim to a very specific tradition of progressivism in British politics, they have also made efforts to dissociate themselves from the social democratic policies conventionally associated with this tradition. Instead, their 'new progressivism' seems above all to be a statement of temporal orientation, indicating an emphasis on optimism over pessimism and reform over conservation. This is indicative of a significant shift in the British political landscape, which began long before 2010.

In 1979 Henry Drucker set out his analysis of the ethos of the Labour Party (as distinct from its doctrine) under the chapter heading 'The Uses of the Past'.[3] This choice of words indicates the importance of the past to political positioning. It is generally accepted that Labour Party activists have, in the words of a more recent scholar, 'always had an especially strong sense of their party as a historic "movement", which must know its past in order to envisage its future'.[4] Socialists' use of the past as a political resource is frequently set against Conservatives' veneration of the past for its own sake. Furthermore, while the right have claimed the *whole* past and attempted to speak for English (if not British[5]) history itself, the socialist left have carved out a particular niche, an oppositional, self-consciously 'alternative' narrative to set against this all-encompassing hegemony.

However, Drucker also noted a competing strand of thought within Labour: that of social democracy, which ignored the past in its struggle to appear '"modern", "up-to-date", "*au fait*"' and to present Labour as 'a party of the future'. Drucker felt that this attitude was 'in harmony with the dominant time-perspective of our age'.[6] The contention of this book is that since Drucker wrote this in 1979, this attitude has come to dominate not only the Labour Party but the Conservative Party as well. However, far from ignoring the past, such an attitude seeks to use it as a way of affirming the present. Contrary to the conventional wisdom which presents contemporary party politics as ahistorical, it is clear that history remains an ever-present point of reference in political discourse, providing a source of lessons, warnings and precedents. This is in line with wider social attitudes towards history in late twentieth- and early twenty-first-century Britain, which think less in terms of betraying or honouring the past and more in terms of adapting and adopting it as a form of (often individualised) identity affirmation.

Previous understandings of the political past emphasised its capacity to make demands upon the present – for conservatives a duty of continuity and tradition; for progressives an obligation to right past wrongs. Both of these traditions were able to offer powerful critiques of the present, yet both have now been sidelined in favour of a present-focused view of the past as 'heritage', which can be embraced or rejected as politically expedient. 'History' is no longer viewed as a political force – providing deliverance, conveying inheritance – instead, it is a tool to be mastered. This leaves contemporary politicians unable to speak of radically different futures. By imagining the present as 'the same old thing', they also imagine 'making history' (i.e. making the future) as making *more of the same*.

As will be clear throughout this study, this convergence in the parties' attitudes to time should be understood as part of a wider shift in their political positioning and particularly in the way in which they conceive their roles within national politics and national history. The division between the Conservatives and Labour can no longer be characterised as the party of 'national' versus 'sectional' interest, of 'elite' versus 'marginalised' history. Both parties now compete for the same place in the national story and both have consequently adopted a similar approach to the past. However, the parties' narratives of their histories are increasingly becoming the preserve of an interested minority of partisans who have more in common with one another than with the wider population.

Both of these observations have their parallels in the studies of political scientists. In 1966, Otto Kirchheimer suggested that in the post-war years mass parties began to play down their sectional class appeal and instead aimed to be national 'catch-all' parties, which could appeal across the social spectrum.[7] More recently, Katz and Mair have argued that Kirchheimer's catch-all parties have now become 'cartel parties', which are entrenched in the state but distant from civil society. According to this model, the political elite from all parties colludes in order to protect their own privileged position within the state.[8] In our story, this could be transposed to the parties' positions within a rarefied historical narrative of parliamentary politics, perpetuated across the political spectrum. Lawrence Black has shown that in the late 1950s and 1960s party politics became an increasingly marginal activity, estranged from popular culture and treated with cynicism and derision when not ignored altogether. The parties responded by attempting to utilise and ape popular culture, using celebrity supporters, market research and modern advertising techniques.[9]

History as culture

There is a close relationship between ideology and history. At the most obvious level, this plays itself out in politically slanted inter-pretations of the nation's past. At its most profound, it shapes beliefs about the historical process. However, in the period under scrutiny in this volume, history and heritage have also become increasingly important components of popular culture, part of the cultural landscape which politicians must negotiate. As Raphael Samuel noted, the late twentieth century was marked by an increasing public interest in the past – from 'retrochic' to the 'heritage industry'.[10] More recently Jerome de Groot has added TV historians, historical re-enactments and history-themed computer games to this list.[11] However, this very interest has also been seen to be a symptom of decreasing 'connection' with the past.

These arguments were particularly explicit in France, around the bicentenary of the 1789 Revolution and in the seven-volume discussion of public memory organised by the historian Pierre Nora.[12] In Britain, they coalesced around questions of the conservation of historic buildings and the consequent growth of a commercialised 'heritage industry', with a particular emphasis on industrial heritage. Commentators such as Robert Hewison saw this as a desperate and disingenuous search for meaning in a seemingly meaningless post-modern world. Desperate because it was associated with the sense that the past as a living memory was disappearing and must be caught and fixed before it did; disingenuous because this was a sanitised past of quaint interiors and supposedly traditional values, in which hardship, poverty and misery became little more than tourist attractions.[13] The fear was that memory was becoming 'historicised' and the living past was becoming 'heritage' – closed off from the present and of interest only as a reminder of 'the way we were'.

Such critiques have been particularly associated with the left. The debates over the 'heritage industry' were sharpened by its association with the Thatcher governments' commercialising approach to culture and political mobilisation of narratives about the national past. Patrick Wright's text *On Living in an Old Country* is a wonderful example of this genre.[14] However, the complaint that Labour was losing touch with traditions of working-class solidarity dates back almost as long as the labour movement itself, and became particularly prevalent in the post-war years, when Labour-in-parliament seemed to replace Labour-in-society. Running alongside the narrative of modernisation and popularisation was the perennial lament that popular culture was not what it had been and that left politics, working-class identity and indigenous culture had lost out in the process.

More recently, Martin L. Davies has discussed the 'historicisation' of society, whereby history has become the dominant mode of thinking, yet because it encompasses everything, it also means nothing.[15] This historical attitude can be seen in British party politics. The past is called upon to provide lessons (was Brown following Callaghan's mistake in not calling an election in autumn 2007?), to confer legitimacy (monetarism as 'Victorian values') and to demonstrate continuity (abandoning Marxism as itself 'Marxian' in spirit). Yet, by its very malleability, and its ubiquity, the political past has ceased to exist as either a radical or a conservative force. Instead, a rather general sense of continuity is invoked in the service of the present. In a culture in which antiquity is coded as authenticity – from estate agents' brochures to vintage clothing boutiques[16] – a link with the past is a valuable political commodity.

British political parties provide a particularly interesting study in this respect because they are relatively stable as mnemonic groups – as communities bound together by a sense of collective memory. The procedures and processes of parliament positively encourage a sense of lived continuity with the past and the parties themselves remain recognisably consistent as political institutions. Moreover, unlike pressure groups and social movements, the subject of a great deal of academic interest in recent decades, parties are also unusually interested in the means by which they will *become History* (emphatically with a capital H). As we will see in Chapter 2, parties occupy an unusual position between top-down elite history and bottom-up collective memory. Whilst high-politics parliamentary narratives remain firmly lodged in the 'official' story of British history, it is also clear that as levels of party affiliation continue to decline, parties' institutional pasts become further removed from the mainstream cultural memory of the nation. Neither trade union banners nor Primrose League pins now resonate with large sections of the population. Indeed, it is not fanciful to suggest that in terms of narrative memory, the parties have more in common with one another than with the wider public. Although party political interpretations of the past are often in direct competition with one another – both between and within parties – it is also clear that they (mostly) function within an overarching mnemonic framework; they are retellings of the same stories from different perspectives.

It is striking that what we might call the emotional side of political identity – both personal and collective – is often expressed through discourse about the past. History is used as a proxy for emotion. The flipside of this, as we will see in relation to New Labour, is that references to the past can be interpreted and presented as intrinsically emotional, sentimental and hence irrational, even when they are part of a conversation about policy and ideology, focused on the options for the future. Whilst parties and politicians are expected to remain 'true' to their pasts – thus demonstrating continuity, integrity, authenticity – they must also demonstrate that they are of their time, in tune with time and have time on their side. The awkwardness of this juggling act is demonstrated by the title of an event held in June 2009 by New Labour pressure group Progress: 'Focus on the fourth term: where have we come from and how can we get there?'[17] In many ways, the particular pasts to which parties and individuals must be 'true' matters less than a general sense of rootedness. In popular culture, discovering one's roots has become a means of self-authentification almost (it seems) regardless of what those particular roots are.[18] Peter Mandler suggests that tracing a connection to even 'very remote ancestors provide[s] a more individualised form of identity, better suited to a highly individualised society than the traditional markers of identity, class, religion or nation'.[19] This rarely, if ever, imposes obligations upon the descendant but is instead a means of enhancing their sense of self.

Mandler suggests that the appeal of such history is rather different from its older, nationalist forms, which relied upon establishing a linear narrative with ourselves as (he quotes Richard Evans), 'the end product of a process of becoming'. Instead, 'The new appeal of history has more to do with people rejecting their "place", seeing themselves as artists of their own becoming, and using history imaginatively to assist in that process'.[20] As we will see throughout this study political approaches to the past are rather caught between these two forms. On the one hand, individual politicians and activists may be interested in establishing 'connections' with their forbears, picking and choosing from a range of possible inspirations and political identities; on the other, the political present is also imagined as part of a rather more whiggish linear historical narrative. It is, in other words, continually constructed as 'historic'.

Politics as history

While for the historicised society *everything* is history, it is also the case that some things are seen to be more 'historic' than others. Parliamentary politics is resolutely one of those things, as seen in E.A. Freeman's maxim that 'history is past politics, and that politics are present history', from which the sub-title of this book is drawn. This view may be outmoded among academic historians, to the extent that proponents of the 'new political history' have had to defend their decision to study politics at all,[21] yet it forms the staple of public and political conceptions of 'the historic'. The everyday language of parliamentary politics revels in declarations of historic missions – whether to tackle climate change, bring democracy to Eastern Europe or eradicate child poverty.[22] It is not enough to make a political pledge to reduce child poverty; it must, instead be an 'historic commitment' – even if the particular target is unachievable.

These could be seen as attempts to pre-empt history, to project the present moment into a history not yet written. But the present can only be presented as historic if it is set within a temporal framework, leading from a receding past towards a still malleable future. To be historic is to be part of an ongoing historical narrative. There is also a powerful sense that *marking* history is somehow historic in and of itself. For instance, Margaret Thatcher declared the fiftieth anniversary of Churchill's appointment as Prime Minister as itself one of the many 'historic events' to have taken place in 10 Downing Street.[23]

Political memory also operates with a keen regard for the formalities and authority of professional history. Political actors are not only aware of their role in history as *what has happened*, they are also intensely aware that they will be part of history as *what is written about what has happened*. We will see in Chapter 2 that party archives are maintained through a general sense of obligation to historians of the future, rather than as a practical aspect of political operations or even as a mode of identity affirmation. At the same time, however, a large number of politicians have engaged in historical research, most often biographies of their political forebears, and the party history groups are well attended. By these means political actors set themselves in the context of an ongoing, familiar, narrative. Moreover, Oliver Daddow describes the way in which political actors attempt to write the 'first "cut" of history' by publishing 'retrospective justifications of their opinions, decisions and policies, in the form of diaries, memoirs and autobiographies' during the time in which official documents remain closed to scholars. Daddow believes that this puts historians 'on the back foot' as 'the texture and shape of scholarly debates' has already been determined by the way in which policy-makers are able to 'foreground' particular events and 'forget' others.[24]

Within the wider mnemonic activities of the parties (history groups, written histories, commemorative projects), great respect is accorded to professional historians. For instance, Dianne Hayter felt that in order for her history of Labour's right wing in the 1970s and 1980s to be authoritative, it needed to be a PhD project.[25] Similarly, Professor Penelope J. Corfield described the way in which members of Battersea Labour Party's centenary DVD project were happy to allow her to shape the narrative of the party's history because they trusted her skills as a professional historian. This is all discussed in greater detail in Chapter 2. It is, however, worth noting that at an event discussing the Battersea DVD, Corfield asked Tony Belton, veteran leader of the Wandsworth Labour Group, how it felt seeing himself 'rendered into history on film' and thus *becoming* 'an historical personage'.[26] This is a particularly explicit statement of the complicated interaction between politics as present-action and politics as future-history: it is through becoming enshrined in narrative that politics becomes 'historical'. Looking at this from the other direction, Edwina Currie has justified publishing her diaries which reveal her affair with John Major on the grounds that 'It is history; it is a part of history.'[27] The implication is that the leaders of national parties are necessarily 'part of history'; they are part of a historical narrative which is already in progress and have the advantage of attempting to shape it as they go through.

Re-using the mould?

The principal focus of this study is the period from 1979 to 2010, dominated by the Thatcher and Blair governments. This period was marked by its claims to novelty. The late 1970s and early 1980s were constructed by contemporaries as a break with the past, from Stuart Hall's assessments of the new terrain of Thatcherism to the feeling of some right-wingers that changes in the politics and procedures of the Labour Party justified the founding of a new Social Democratic Party (SDP). The subsequent period is seen to mark the end of post-war Keynesianism, the rise of neo-liberalism and the collapse of communism; all of the major political parties in Britain underwent substantial organisational and political change and the Communist Party of Great Britain (CPGB) disbanded completely. None of these events should be understood as self-contained, but rather as much longer-term processes with roots in the 1950s and – ultimately – in the early decades of the twentieth century.[28] It is striking how often debates about 'the past' in this period revolve around the period at the end of the First World War, when the Labour's Party Constitution was drawn up, the Communist Party of Great Britain was established and the Lib-Lab alliance of the Edwardian period came to an end. The other 'past' is the post-war settlement, seen variously as the founding moment of modern Britain, the cementing of the Labour Party as a serious national force, an unrepeatable moment of popular socialism, a lost opportunity for genuine radicalism and a dreadful mistake.

The wider context of the book therefore stretches back into the earlier twentieth century. However, as will be clear from the arguments presented below, it is in the years after 1979 that these longer-term changes became solidified. This is when the new right strain of Conservative thought, visible from the 1950s, came to dominate not only the party but also the country. It is when Labour revisionism became (New) Labour orthodoxy. And it is when the 'history boom' of the later twentieth century reached saturation point. It is also clear that the relationship between people and politics shifted in this period. The alignment of voters along class and partisan lines broke down in the 1970s and while concerns about public disengagement from the political process were audible in earlier periods, it was in the 1990s and 2000s that they became deafening.

The causality of the relationship between cultural and political changes is opaque and it is likely that the work of unpicking the interraction between the two will continue for some time yet. What is clear, however, is that political actors in this period were self-consciously constructing themselves, their actions and their circum-stances as novel, historic and unprecedented. The declared intention to 'break the mould' of politics was particularly common in the late 1970s and early 1980s. Stuart Hall used the phrase in relation to Thatcher in 1978 and it was later adopted by the SDP.[29] This speaks of a desire to break out of the existing narrative of political history, to take a new course. The rhetoric of 'new politics' was evident as well, used by the CPGB modernisers and Tony Blair, long before Cameron and Clegg.[30] Yet, at the same time, efforts were made to convey the historical roots of these supposedly radical departures – witness the convoluted attempts to place Thatcher within either the traditions of conservatism or liberalism (or both!). Even New Labour, though explicitly devised to demonstrate discontinuity with Labour's past, was quick to claim the legitimacy of the 1945 government and to portray itself as a return to an older form of socialism, based on the co-operative movement and the 'historic progressive consensus' with radical liberalism.

Davies' analysis of the historicised society shows how it inevitably reduces new events to 'the same old thing' by setting them in a historical framework and showing that this is really a story we already know.[31] Thus, the 2010 General Election was proclaimed to be 'an historic moment', or rather, an extended series of historic moments: from the first televised leaders' debate[32] right through to *that* handshake outside Number 10.[33] At the 'historic' press confer-ence in the Rose Garden, the new Prime Minister announced that he would be taking the country in 'a historic new direction' as leader of the 'historic Liberal Democrat–Conservative administration'.[34] Yet, for all the attempts to proclaim 2010 as a wholly new departure, media reports were also saturated with historical comparisons. Thus, we had the first hung parliament *since 1974*, the first coalition government and first Liberals in government *since 1945*, the Conservatives' largest gains *since 1931* and Labour's lowest share of the vote *since 1983*. The BBC's election coverage involved Jeremy

Vine literally measuring the leaders' performances against the portraits of their predecessors on a virtual recreation of the staircase inside Number 10 (itself the ultimate symbol of the historicity of the office).

Portrayals of Nick Clegg were particularly affected by notions of history and the historic. As his popularity grew after the 'historic' leaders' debates, Clegg was perceived to be capable of making history by supporters who were primarily concerned that they should be part of the moment when he did. As Richard Reeves explained in the *Guardian*, a group of high-profile individuals had written a letter supporting Clegg because they couldn't bear to 'sit out this historic, democratic moment'. Politics was about to change and 'When our grandsons and granddaughters ask – "so what did you do in May 2010?" – we want to be able to say that at this moment, at the potential birth of a new democracy, we tried to play our part.'[35] However, speculations that Clegg's party was about to 'break the mould' of two-party politics were inevitably also reminders that we had been here before, that after similar claims of novelty and unexpected public acclaim, the SDP/Liberal Alliance had failed to do just that.

In the months following the coalition agreement, it was the Thatcher governments which provided the most obvious historical comparison. Although Clegg, in particular, insisted that proposed cuts did not signify a return to the politics of the 1980s,[36] the opponents of the coalition's policies made much use of this trope, slotting the student protests of winter 2010 into a comfortable narrative of Conservatives in Number 10 and riots on the streets. This was not, however, history as constraint. It was, rather, history as safe and comforting repetition, reinforced by the announcement of a royal wedding, allegations of Russian espionage and heavy snowfall. This was self-aware, self-parodying history, which revelled in its own referential structure. The 1980s provided a simple point of reference for a political situation which seemed otherwise to be alarmingly fluid and unpredictable.

Structure of the book

Chapter 1 examines political approaches to the past, particularly the contested and often misleading distinction between conservatism and progressivism. It is suggested that this division has been particularly powerful because of the way that it defines itself with regard to the historical process, above and beyond political commitments or ideological assumptions. However, the relationship between the explicit temporal and implicit political meanings of these terms is highly ambiguous. 'Conservatives' and 'progressives' cannot simply be characterised as looking backwards and forwards, respectively. Both positions involve nostalgia and obligation but this has different implications for right and left. However, it is also suggested that the parties' attitudes to the past are becoming less distinct from each other and that the dominant attitude of contemporary party politics might be better characterised as one of presentism. Rather than progress towards a promised future or historic destiny, it is based in an eternal, liminal present. It is always *becoming* history, becoming historic.

Chapter 2 is a study of the structures of memory within the parties, including party archives, history groups, commemorative events, written histories, biographies and memoirs. It examines how ideological approaches to the past, explored in the previous chapter, are instituted within the parties in practice: their structures, limits and gatekeepers. Although these mainly offer a picture of the present status of party political memory, this is set in historical context, in order to assess how the parties' structures of memory have changed over the twentieth century. Again, the story is of convergence, with the key features of memory remarkably similar across the three main parties. This is a relatively recent development and differs from the first half of the twentieth century when Labour's mnemonic culture was markedly different from the other parties'. Unsurprisingly, the parties have converged more closely at national than at local level, where differences are more clearly visible. Across the three parties, formal memory activities are undertaken by a small group of interested individuals rather than as a part of an official programme. Even the directors of the party history groups admit that there isn't always time to learn from history, due to the business of *making* history, making the political present.

Chapters 3, 4 and 5 examine the uses of the past during moments of political re-positioning. In order to make comparisons across the parties, I have chosen to look at a number of moments of political crisis, when identities were called into question and imagined futures collapsed. In looking at the parties' institutional positioning, my focus inevitably falls disproportionately on leaders and national figures rather than the wider ambit of activists, organisational structures and affiliated bodies at both national and local level. I have sought to mitigate this by making use of letters sent from grassroots members to party leaders and to the letters pages of the internal and national press. Whilst this is a self-selecting sample of members' views, it does give an idea of the internal conversations within the parties and enables me to present a nuanced story of internal contestation and uncertainty, rather than a monolithic view of the elite position. This strategy inevitably means that I am dependent on the traces left by parties and individuals in the historical record even as I seek to understand the means by which those records (both physical and imaginary) have been constructed. Nevertheless, this approach has allowed me to get a sense of the way in which the debates were set within historical narratives and conceived as 'historic' at the time, rather than through the retrospective prompting of oral history interviews.

It is important to note here the difference between the parties' organisational structures. While the parties of the left have traditionally emphasised the role of members in feeding policy from branch level to national conferences, Conservative policy has officially emanated from the leader's office. However, all of the parties studied here went through significant changes in structure during the period in question. Beyond the obvious processes of dissolution (CPGB) and merger (SDP–Liberal) we also see important changes in the status of individual members within the major parties. The Conservatives' 1997 *Blueprint for Change* programme, for instance, fundamentally altered the status of party members, who for the first time could join a centrally administered Conservative Party, rather than a local Conservative Association. They also gained more formal power within the party, including voting for the leader. Similarly, the Labour Party's more gradual adoption of institutional change in the 1980s and early 1990s had important implications for relations between the party and its members, largely at the expense of the culture of branch and conference resolutions. This enabled the New Labour leadership to appeal to the whole (largely passive) membership on Clause IV via a direct mail consultation exercise and one-member-one-vote ballot, thereby diluting the contribution of grassroots activists. Therefore the responses of the members of each party to the changes initiated by their leaderships have differed not only in type but also in intensity. While, for instance, the CPGB's 'transformation process' generated vigorous debate in internal party newspapers, the Conservative Party do not have the same culture of debate and dissent, and therefore the analysis in this case is based much more heavily on the views of the political elite.

Chapter 3 focuses on the Conservative Party in the 1980s and 1990s. As we see in Chapter 1, the Conservative Party has prided itself on being a national party, with a special affinity with the British (or more properly the *English*) past. Yet in the decades after 1945 this position was undermined by changes in history teaching as well as by the Labour Party's increasingly confident claims to national status itself. In the wake of the 1997 General Election, it became unsustainable. Chapter 3 examines the ways in which the Conservative Party responded to these challenges, both by attempting to reassert its own historical narrative (most notably through the wrangling over the National Curriculum for History) and by developing more of a sense of its institutional past. In particular, the intense debates over Thatcher's relation to 'traditional Conservatism' indicate both the ambiguity of her own temporal positioning and the desire of many Conservatives to define the party's identity through a relationship to its own past.

The book then looks at the different ways in which the founders of the SDP and the self-proclaimed architects of New Labour presented their negotiations with the Labour Party's past and particularly with revisionism, which was by this stage a tradition in its own right. Despite the emphasis on novelty and on starting a new historical narrative outside the traditions of 'left' and 'right', both of these re-positionings also depended on reworking Labour's past. Whilst Blair used Labour's tendency to focus on its history against his opponents by presenting them as simply nostalgic for a dead past, he also tried to portray himself as the figure who could reach back to the party's older and therefore more authentic pre-1918 past. Whilst the narrative of a historic 'progressive consensus' with liberalism had long been an important strand of social democratic revisionism, it gained fresh meaning in the context of the SDP's merger with the Liberals. However, it is argued that there was a significant difference in the way that the SDP and New Labour positioned themselves in relation to this past. Most of the founders of the SDP (with the exception of Roy Jenkins) were determined to demonstrate that they remained loyal to Labour's heritage, justifying their re-positioning as a necessary response to the direction the Labour Party had taken in the recent past. For them, the social democratic narrative was a means of maintaining a sense of personal continuity as they broke with Labour and eventually merged with the Liberal Party. New Labour was far less of a genuine break with the party's past but was deliberately constructed as a statement of a new temporal attitude, valorising novelty and presentism for their own sake. Yet its spokes-people used the alternative historical narrative of the 'progressive consensus' to position themselves within a legitimating historical framework and as a further claim to *national* status – to reaching past the Labour Party and speaking for the country beyond.

Finally, we turn to the collapse of the CPGB's historical narrative in 1989–91. While communism has remained electorally marginal in Britain, the Marxist interpretation of history has influenced and shaped British politics across the political spectrum. It is the ever-present 'other' in this period, whether we are looking at social democratic revisionism, Conservative fears that Marxist views of history were undermining patriotism or neo-liberal declarations of the 'end of history'. Some of the themes of this chapter are reminiscent of those in Chapter 4 – the clash between modernisers and their opponents who feared betraying the past and losing their ideological bearings in the process. What made these negotiations different was that, first, Marxism had placed far more faith in the redemptive 'march of history', so abandoning this notion was more painful than for Labour members. And second, the changes were necessitated by the loss of a stable past in the wake of revelations about Soviet communism. This was not a new development and had been in progress since 1956, but the fall of the Eastern European regimes made the process both unavoidable and urgent. This was fundamentally a historical and mnemonic crisis. But not only the past was under revision – the future also looked incredibly uncertain: if communism had failed, how much of Marxism and Marxist historical theory could be salvaged? The only options were to adopt a presentist approach towards the future – finding ways to progress socialism without relying on a discredited grand narrative – and to take advantage of the new freedom to bring the light of 'history' to bear upon what had too often been a politically delineated 'past', despite the efforts of the Communist Party Historians' Group.

The dominance of this presentist trend across all the parties indicates more than a 'betrayal' of roots or of traditional temporal positioning. It is a cultural shift, informed by popular approaches not only to time and progress, but also to high politics, national heritage and historical narrative. This contradicts the received wisdom of an ahistorical political sphere and instead suggests that the very idea of history continues to operate as a powerful source of legitimation, within both political and popular culture. This is dependent on an understanding of history as linear and knowable, which sets present action (and particularly high-political action) in a longer context, giving it a 'place' in history and in the unfolding national story. At the same time a cultural and political premium is placed on novelty, modernity and timeliness and the taint of anachronism or being 'stuck in the past' is to be avoided at all costs. The play of these competing strands within contemporary party politics is the subject of this book.

Notes

1 Nick Clegg, Hugo Young Lecture, London, 23 November 2010.
2 George Osborne, 'Progressive reform in an age of austerity', speech to Demos, 11 August 2009. Available at: www.demos.co.uk/press _releases/george-osborne-progressive-reform-in-an-age-of-austerity. Accessed 06.09.2010.
3 H.M. Drucker, *Doctrine and Ethos in the Labour Party* (London: George Allen & Unwin, 1979).
4 Jon Lawrence, 'Labour: the myths it has lived by', in Duncan Tanner *et al.* (eds), *Labour's First Century* (Cambridge: Cambridge University Press, 2000), p. 342.
5 Throughout this book the matter of 'national' identity is somewhat questionable. As I am dealing with the parties' own conceptions of 'national history' I have tended to follow their Anglo-centrism. By and large, Conservatives have more of an affinity with English than with British history, although, 'Britain' is often used to refer to outward-facing questions of national identity and constitutional matters of national unity. Where emotional questions of culture, tradition and heritage are at stake, the invocation is more often of 'England', or at least a very English version of Britain. The other parties have a more heightened sense of Britain and its constituent nations, yet invocations of 'Britain' still tend towards Anglo-centrism. All of these debates should be seen against a backdrop of increasing uncertainty over the future and status of the Union and also about the nature of Englishness, considerations of which have ranged from Simon Heffer's plea for a more assertive Englishness in *Nor Shall My Sword: The Reinvention of England* (Weidenfeld & Nicolson, 1999) to Billy Bragg's attempts to 'reclaim' English patriotism for the progressive left in his *The Progressive Patriot: A Search for Belonging* (London: Bantam Press, 2006). These debates intensified in the late 1990s with the Euro '96 England/Scotland Game and the 1999 referenda on devolution. It is this uncertainty, rather than the optimism of a united 'Cool Britannia' which seems to be the legacy of the Blair years.
6 Drucker, *Doctrine and Ethos*, p. 35.
7 Otto Kirchheimer, 'The transformation of the western European party systems', in Joseph LaPalombara and Myron Weiner (eds), *Political Parties and Political Development* (Princeton: Princeton University Press, 1966).
8 Richard S. Katz and Peter Mair, 'Changing models of party organization and party democracy: the emergence of the cartel party', *Party Politics*, 1:1 (January 1995), 5–28.
9 Lawrence Black, *Redefining British Politics: Culture, Consumerism and Participation, 1954–70* (Basingstoke: Palgrave Macmillan, 2010).
10 Raphael Samuel, *Theatres of Memory, Vol. I: Past and Present in Contemporary Culture* (London and New York: Verso, 1994); Raphael Samuel, *Island Stories:*

Unravelling Britain: Theatres of Memory, Vol. II, ed. Alison Light with Sally Alexander and Gareth Stedman Jones (London and New York: Verso, 1998).

11 Jerome de Groot, *Consuming History* (London: Routledge, 2008).

12 Pierre Nora (ed.), *Realms of Memory: Rethinking the French Past* (New York: Columbia University Press, 1996), English language edn edited by Lawrence D. Kritzman, tr. Arthur Goldhammer.

13 Robert Hewison, *The Heritage Industry: Britain in a Climate of Decline* (London: Methuen, 1987).

14 Patrick Wright, *On Living in an Old Country: The National Past in Contemporary Britain* (Oxford: Oxford University Press, 2008 [Verso, 1991]).

15 Martin L. Davies, *Historics: Why History Dominates Contemporary Society* (Abingdon: Routledge, 2006).

16 See Samuel, *Theatres of Memory*.

17 http://theprogressive.typepad.com/the_progressive/2009/06/event-report-focus-on-the-fourth-term-where-have-we-come-from-and-how-can-we-get-there.html. Accessed 02.10.2009.

18 The most explicit example of this trend is the BBC TV series *Who Do You Think You Are?* (2007–).

19 Peter Mandler, *History and National Life* (London: Profile Books, 2002), p. 3.

20 Ibid., p. 108.

21 Steven Fielding, 'Political History'. Available at *http://www.history.ac.uk/makinghistory/resources/articles/political_history.html*. Accessed 20.02.2011.

22 See, for instance, Gordon Brown, speaking to the Major Economies Forum, 19 September 2009. Available at: www.number10.gov.uk/Page21030. Accessed 23.10.2009; Margaret Thatcher, Speech to International Democrat Union Conference in Tokyo, 22 September 1989. Available at: www.margaretthatcher.org/speeches/displaydocument.asp?docid=107773. Accessed 23.10.2009; Tony Blair, Beveridge Lecture, Toynbee Hall, 18 March 1999. Available at: www.bris.ac.uk/poverty/Publication_files/Tony%20Blair%20Child%20Poverty%20Speech.doc. Accessed 15.08.2011.

23 Margaret Thatcher, 10 Downing Street, 9 May 1990. Available at: www.margaretthatcher.org/speeches/displaydocument.asp?docid=108085. Accessed 23.10.2009.

24 Oliver Daddow, 'Playing games with history: Tony Blair's European policy in the press', *British Journal of Politics and International Relations*, 9 (2007), 583.

25 Interview with Dianne Hayter, Chair of the 1906 Centenary Group, 22 May 2009.

26 Penelope J. Corfield, speaking at Social History Society Southern Region Postgraduate and Early Career Workshop, 'History and Image', Goldsmiths College, University of London, 28 November 2009.

27 Edwina Currie speaking on *Dear Diary*, Sharon Adam (dir.), BBC4, 18 January 2010.

28 See E.H.H. Green, *Ideologies of Conservatism: Conservative Political Ideas in the Twentieth Century* (Oxford: Oxford University Press, 2002) and Steven Fielding, *The Labour Party: Continuity and Change in the Making of New Labour* (Basingstoke: Palgrave Macmillan, 2003).

29 Stuart Hall, 'The great moving right show', *Marxism Today*, December 1978.

Reprinted in Stuart Hall, *The Hard Road to Renewal* (London and New York: Verso in association with *Marxism Today*, 1988), p. 44).

30 See Labour History Archive and Study Centre, People's History Museum, Manchester (hereafter LHASC), Communist Party of Great Britain Papers (hereafter CP), CP/CENT/EC/24/08, Nina Temple, *'New* times, *new* politics', Report to CPGB Executive Committee (January 1990); Tony Blair, *The Third Way: New Politics for the New Century* (London: Fabian Society, 1998); David Cameron, New Year Message 2009/10, 27 December 2009. Available at: http://conservativehome.blogs.com/thetorydiary/2009/09 /do-you-receive-conservativehomes-daily-email.html. Accessed 05.01.2010.

31 Davies, *Historics*, p. 4.

32 See for instance BBC News, 'Three way clashes in historic leaders' debate', 15 April 2010. Available at: news.bbc.co.uk/2/hi/uk_news/politics /election.../8621119.stm and Martin Kettle, 'Nick Clegg was the winner in this historic leaders' debate', *Guardian*, 15 April 2010. Available at: www.guardian.co.uk/commentisfree/2010/apr/15/leaders-tv-debates-brown-cameron-clegg. Both accessed 08.06.2010.

33 See for instance Phillipe Naughton, 'Cameron and Clegg get to work at No 10', *The Times*, 12 May 2010, which begins with the words 'An historic handshake marked the start of a new era in British politics today'. Available at: www.timesonline.co.uk/tol/news/politics/article7123920.ece. Accessed 08.06.2010.

34 David Cameron, Rose Garden Press Conference, 10 Downing Street,12 May 2010.

35 Richard Reeves, 'Our Clegg-backing letter is one for the grandchildren', *Guardian: Comment is Free*, 28 April 2010. Available at: www.guardian.co .uk/commentisfree/2010/apr/28/our-clegg-backing-letter-grandchildren. Accessed 10 May 2010.

36 Andrew Rawnsley, 'Nick Clegg interview: "We're not going to do it the way we did in the 80s"', *Observer*, Sunday 6 June 2010. Available at: www.guardian.co.uk/politics/2010/jun/06/nick-clegg-interview-coalition-cuts. Accessed 07.06. 2010.

1
Ideology and temporality

This chapter focuses on political approaches to historical time. In particular, it examines the distinction between conservatism and progressivism, which is often understood as one of temporal perspective, with conservatives looking backwards and progressives forwards. This characterisation is contested and it is shown that both conservatism and progressivism involve nostalgia and obligation to the past but that this has different implications within each tradition: inheritance and preservation on the one hand, action and justice on the other. Moreover, it is shown that both attitudes are in decline, having been predicated on a division between the parties' views of their place in British politics which no longer holds true. The Conservative and Labour parties can no longer be characterised as the representatives of 'national' versus 'sectional' interest, of 'elite' versus 'marginalised' history. Both parties now compete for the same place in the national story and both have consequently adopted a similar approach to the past. This approach can best be described as 'presentist'.

The politics of the past

There is a close relationship between ideology and history. At the most obvious level, this plays itself out in politically slanted interpretations of the nation's past. At its most profound, it shapes beliefs about the historical process. This has important implications for the narrative form of history-writing. In his seminal study of this topic, Hayden White allied nineteenth-century modes of history-writing with narrative forms drawn from literature. Yet he made clear that this also has ideological implications. Drawing on Karl Mannheim's *Ideology and Utopia*, White distinguished between anarchist, radical, conservative and liberal modes of historical thinking, which have elective (but not exclusive) affinities with romantic, comic, tragic and satirical modes of emplotment, respectively. Each ideology is distinguished by its temporal orientation – its projection of the utopian moment into either the remote past, imminent future, present or remote future.[1]

It is clear that such considerations can also shed light on British political practice. It is no accident that the labels Whig, Tory, Socialist and Marxist are applied to philosophies of history as well as to party political orientations. However, these philosophies are no longer stable, either in terms of political ideology or academic history. The 'end of history' moment of the early 1990s was most obviously seen to be an argument for the 'end of socialism'. It was heralded not only as the culmination of a Hegelian narrative but also as its triumph over the alternative historical model offered by Marxism. Yet this millennial moment affected the centre-left as well as the new right. The election of centre-left governments in the USA (1992), the Netherlands (1994), Italy (1996), the UK (1997), France (1997) and Germany (1998) was taken to indicate a possible 'political realignment in the advanced capitalist world', an international third way.[2] This was itself seen as a product of the collapse of the USSR which had freed the left 'from the straightjacket of the cold war and the long division of the socialist movement between state collectivists and social democrats'.[3] In 1999, Michael Freeden noted that New Labour had departed from the traditional progressive conception of 'open-ended' social evolution and instead displayed a belief 'that the future has already arrived, that the millennium (courtesy of new Labour) virtually signifies the end of history and the final attainment of modernity'.[4]

Progressivism and conservatism

British politics is often characterised as dividing into two camps: conservatives and progressives. The Conservative Party supposedly stands alone on the first side of the line, with Labour and (most) Liberal Democrats clustering on the other. This division has been particularly powerful because of the way that it defines itself with regard to a position on the historical process, above and beyond particular political commitments or ideological assumptions. That is not to say that conservatism and progressivism are not strongly associated with positions on social justice, civil rights and law and order; they are. But these are implied rather than stated. Above all, the words 'conservative' and 'progressive' express distinct attitudes towards time, with progressivism being forward-looking and conservatism backward-looking.

There are, however, some distinct problems with these categories. The first and most obvious is that they conceal some very important political distinctions, within as well as between political parties. The Labour Party, for instance, is often held to contain three different strands, each dating to the late nineteenth century: Fabianism, ethical socialism and Marxism. The Liberal Democrat Party divides most obviously into 'classical' liberals, 'social' liberals and social democrats. The Conservative Party, with its aversion to ideological labels, is the most difficult to classify but certainly contains adherents to a wide range of political traditions. In his 1974 study of the party, Andrew Gamble identified three strands of post-war conservatism: 'the right progressive, the diehard (which had two wings – whig and imperialist) and the new right'.[5] The historical thinking of each of these traditions is rather different, from the 'gradual improvement' of the Fabian tradition to the historical stages of Marxism and from the sceptical pessimism of Toryism to the interventionism of the new right.

Second, the relationship between the explicit temporal and implicit political meanings of these terms is highly ambiguous. For instance, at the 2010 General Election, all three main parties presented themselves not only as 'progressive' but also as the rightful heir to an historical tradition of Lib-Lab progressive politics, dating back to the late nineteenth century. It was unclear whether this was predicated on a supposed commitment to social justice, equality and civil liberties or whether it was a reference to a rather more general sense of optimism, forward movement and belief in the possibility of progress. Given both the cuts agenda (described as 'regressive' by the Institute for Fiscal Studies) and the decidedly pessimistic presentation of Britain's current state and future possibilities, neither seems particularly apt. The ambiguity of 'progressivism' conceals these difficulties.

Third, the opposition between 'conservatism' and 'progressivism' is itself inherently 'progressive', seeing time as a linear construct, along which we must either progress or make a futile attempt to retreat. By this reckoning, the dice is always loaded in the progressive's favour: historical time moves on and we must move with it or be left behind. Unsurprisingly, many conservatives express scepticism towards this kind of progressive reasoning, which suggests that there is a pattern to history, from which it is possible to take comfort. This connects with the conservative tendency towards pessimism, to viewing 'the progress of civilisation not as something certain and inevitable, guaranteed by any law, natural or divine, for they know that the process can be reversed'. Any progress that can be discerned in human history should therefore be viewed as 'miraculous' rather than 'automatic'.[6] This attitude leads to a humbleness with regard to the past, a refusal to accept the progressive assumption that the present is (or even should be) better and more enlightened. The onus should therefore be on reformers to prove that change is necessary, rather than the other way around.

These objections notwithstanding, however, it is certainly possible to group political tendencies into rough 'progressive' and 'conservative' categories, but with rather different results depending on how the division is defined. There are perhaps three key features which could be used to distinguish progressivism from conservatism: a belief in social improvement, a desire to shape history and a left or centre-left political orientation. Dividing the British political scene along each of these lines produces rather different results, as we will see below.

Optimists and pessimists

First we could examine the idea of progress as advance, as a belief in the possibility of social improvement (regardless of how that 'improvement' is understood). The defining distinction here would be between optimism and pessimism and only the sceptical brand of old Tory would fall cleanly into the conservative camp. Neoliberals, social democrats, Marxists and classical liberals alike would clearly be on the side of optimism, convinced that progress *can* take place, even if the current political path is not the right one.

There are however, important distinctions here. For instance, Walter Benjamin identified optimism about progress as a characteristic which separated social democracy from socialism. In his *Theses on the Philosophy of History*, Benjamin complained that social democracy places its hope in the possibilities of progress and assigns 'to the working class the role of redeemer of future generations'. This was, Benjamin felt, 'cutting the sinews of its greatest strength': the hatred and sacrifice which 'are nourished by the image of enslaved ancestors rather than that of liberated grandchildren.'[7] This does not mean that socialists in Benjamin's mode are not optimistic about the future, but rather that they prefer to draw strength from the injustices of the past. While the conservative pessimist might view the nation in decline and wish to restore elements of the past, the socialist's dream remains on a distant horizon. Socialists remember the struggles and martyrs of the past precisely because they have not won, because they have not achieved their ends. They wouldn't want to return to the past but instead stress the need to bear it forward with them, to achieve what their forbears could not. History then carries a double obligation: to recover and remember past struggles and oppressions and to carry forward the outrage necessary to reshape the present and future. This is, as we will see, problematic for a left which has itself become the political establishment and which is concerned with generating a high-politics, monumental legacy.

Rather than the historicist attitude of conservatism, which seeks to understand the past on its own terms, the left's attitude to the past has traditionally been a political one, which uses past struggles as inspiration in the present. In the words of African-American anthropologist Michel-Rolph Trouillot, 'No amount of historical research about the Holocaust and no amount of guilt about Germany's past can serve as a substitute for marching in the streets against German skinheads today.'[8] The 1934 commemoration of the Tolpuddle Martyrs by the Trades Union Congress (TUC) is an interesting example here. Clare Griffiths has shown how, in common with the wider labour movement in the 1920s and 1930s, loyalty to trade unionism was justified on the grounds of duty to the past, rather than hopes for the present or the future: it was 'almost as if no argument could be found for membership other than the guilt that non-members should be enjoying, at no personal cost, conditions won by previous generations at enormous personal sacrifice'.[9] The TUC's attitude to history is particularly instructive. Griffiths explains that the organisers disapproved of myth and describes their attitude to the Martyrs' story as 'entirely forensic and thoroughly committed to authenticity'. However, 'the main function of history in the commemoration was to inspire, not to inform'. The intention was 'not only to host a few days of unity and celebration, but to provide more enduring resources of unity and celebration'. The organisers felt that 'history had a vital role to play in shaking the movement out of its apathy; that it was necessary to show the younger generation what had been fought for in the past, in order to awaken some response from them'.[10]

This concern with authenticity – in terms of *both* the historical record *and* the appropriateness of our response to it – has been a key feature of socialist history. For instance, Dave Renton has discussed the difficulties facing the professional historian in trying to maintain both scholarly standards and a political response to the subject. He describes his experience of working on a public history project on Liverpool's labour history. One of his co-authors was concerned that while the pamphlet had 'a role in documenting the unwritten history of liverpool's [sic] class struggle', its main focus should be to produce 'something we can use in order to organise workers now'. Renton, on the other hand, 'was more concerned to convey the totality of what happened'. He felt this was a matter of 'professional pride' which depended upon allowing readers 'access to a range of accounts'. Yet this did not diminish his political investment in the project.[11] Peter Glazer tells a similar story of the need to do justice to the past through action in the present. His study of Spanish Civil War commemoration in America led to him becoming a dedicated partic-ipant in commemorative events himself. He sees contemporary political action as a way to 'somehow avenge the loss in Spain by refusing to forget it'.[12] Glazer's central organising concept is the idea of 'radical nostalgia', which he believes 'revises what Jay Winter has called a "traditional vocabulary of mourning" by insisting on a concomitant language of politics'.[13]

The idea of 'radical nostalgia' feels counter-intuitive because, as David Lowenthal documents, much of the literature on nostalgia sees it as a wholly reactionary – or, at best, a regressive – activity.[14] More recently, Alastair Bonnett has examined the importance of nostalgia to radical politics. He has uncovered something of a secret history of nostalgia amongst even those parts of the left which have been most vocal in disavowing it.[15] There are however also plenty of examples of more overt forms of radical or progressive nostalgia, which stress the ideas of continuity and lineage as forcefully as their counterparts on the Tory right. For instance, participants at the 1985 History Workshop 20 national conference suggested that nostalgia involves a special way of being involved in the past through a connection such as kinship or class affiliation. It requires a sense that 'These were in some way *my* people and my present therefore was bound up in their past. Had they acted differently, then my present would be other than as it is now.'[16]

Eric Hobsbawm noted the paradoxical 'search for ancestors (Spartacus, More, Winstanley) by modern revolutionaries whose theory, if they are Marxists, assumes their irrelevance'. He added, 'Clearly the sense of belonging to an age-old tradition of rebellion provides emotional satisfaction, but how and why?'[17] Similarly, Barbara Taylor has described how 'in resurrecting the feminist aims of the Owenites [she] was giving [her]self back [her] own radical ancestry'. She described 'weeping bitterly' as she narrated the death of her subject and claimed, 'I *knew* Emma Martin, she was my Welsh communist grandmother or maybe even my mother … I claimed and mourned her, and wrote my book for her.'[18] Lowenthal suggests that nostalgia is not about 'the past as it was or even as we wish it were; but ... the condition of *having been*, with a concomitant integration and completeness lacking in any present'.[19] It is the very injustice of the 'having been', of the lack of opportunity for genuine redress which could be seen as the motivating feature of such 'radical nostalgia'. This is not only a vicarious experience, by which injustice is felt on behalf of the long-dead. As Hobsbawm, Glazer and Taylor all make clear, there is also an element here of 'emotional satisfaction' on the part of the nostalgic.

Svetlana Boym draws a distinction between 'restorative' and 'reflective' nostalgia, which might be useful here. The first 'stresses *nostos* and attempts a transhistorical reconstruction of the lost home'. It 'does not think of itself as nostalgia, but rather as truth and tradition'.[20] It is this type of nostalgia which lends itself to the creation of national and political identities. The second type 'thrives in *algia*, the longing itself, and delays the homecoming – wistfully, ironically, desperately'.[21] Boym's distinction has resonances with the distinctions between 'conservative' and 'progressive' nostalgia. However, Tory nostalgia is not wholly reactionary or restorative. While some conservatives may be attracted by the idea of turning back the clock,[22] it seems clear that it is the attractions of pastness itself, the distance, the exoticism of the past which underpins a great deal of conservative imagining in this area.

Enoch Powell once described his childhood and adolescent perception of England and Wales as 'always somehow in a fourth dimension, the dimension of time, as if they were the stage and scenery of the long epic of the English kings'. Although his political position on the monarchy and parliament changed in adulthood, Powell claimed that he never lost 'the old sense of the symbolic, numinous kingship'.[23] This sense of history as a terrifying but spiritual presence depends upon the past *as past*, not as a recoverable reality. The pessimism at the heart of Tory thought comes not from a fear of the future in itself, but a fear that these spiritual links with the past will be lost in the process. Tradition and heritage only have meaning within a concept of temporal change. Furthermore, we find that the obligation to do justice to the past can also be found in conservative as well as radical-left politics. An editorial in the first edition of the *Salisbury Review* following the 1997 General Election, remarked that those with a conservative mindset now had a duty to 'preserve for the future as much as they can of our nation's past – to keep alive the work of memory'. The author felt that 'Remembrance ... is indispensable to social continuity, and goes to the heart of our loyalty.'[24]

Progress as rupture

The second division could be drawn along the line which separates those who want to shape history – who want the future to be significantly different from the present – from those who are happy to be in step with history as it unfolds. This is a rather more complicated division and might, for instance, set Andrew Gamble's 'right progressives' on the side of conservatism and the new right on the side of progressivism, the former being prepared to accept and continue the post-war consensus and the latter being determined to unpick it and forge a different path.

In the third Keith Joseph Memorial lecture, John O'Sullivan defined conservatism as a 'system of ideas employed to defend established institutions' until they are fundamentally overthrown, whereupon the new status quo must be absorbed and should itself be preserved. Previous challenges to the status quo had included the Reformation, French Revolution and nineteenth-century campaigns for universal suffrage and the abolition of slavery.[25] An interesting account of conservatives' relation to their political inheritance was provided by Alasdair Morrison in a *Swinton Journal* article of 1969. He pointed out that many of the causes upheld by previous generations of conservatives had not only been losing causes – the medieval barons, the King's side in the Civil War, the opponents of the 1832 Reform Act and of universal suffrage – but were also not in tune with the principles of modern conservatives. History was, in his words, 'littered with dead issues, and also with the wreckage of conservative stands on those issues'. Yet, in contrast to the progressive veneration of lost causes and dead martyrs, Morrison counselled that conservatives must accept that 'one is on, after all, a sort of moving staircase in history – time passes, circumstances change'. And not only have circumstances changed before, but they will again. Conservatives then must 'remain confidently open to the possibilities of change, while at the same time treasuring continuity'.[26] This is, in many ways, the direct opposite of the traditional progressive (or socialist) view, which sees itself as fighting for the same causes in generation after generation, remembering and honouring its forbears whilst struggling to bring about radical change. The conservative, on the other hand, will jettison past causes once they are 'dead' for the sake of a more fundamental 'continuity'.

In the post-war period, Robert Eccleshall has shown that both Labour and Conservative politicians mobilised upbeat historical narratives of British exceptionalism to show how they could overcome its current malaise. The message was always that 'things could only get better', which would place them all on the 'progressive' side of the optimism/pessimism divide. However, in the case of post-war Conservatives, this meant finding the best way of continuing the 'comfortable direction' of British history, whereas for Thatcher it involved departing from this linear developmental view of British history.[27] As outlined in Chapter 3, Thatcher had a deep impatience with the notion of organically unfolding narratives. Daniel Wincott has suggested that her desire to enact change had resulted in a 'hyperactive' style of government, which would clearly place her on the progressive end of our scale.[28] As she declared in 1977: 'We see nothing as inevitable. Men can still shape history'.[29]

The question of modernity is crucial here. On the one hand, we see the attempt to adapt to the modern world, with the social and moral changes that it entails. On the other is the rejection of current reality and the attempt to forge a new type of modernity. Thatcher clearly fits into the second of these categories, as do the radical left. In the late 1950s and early 1960s both Labour and the Conservatives struggled to respond to the new political and social circumstances in which they found themselves. The Conservatives adapted themselves to modernity as they found it, accepting the post-war settlement and adopting social legislation which reflected rather than led changing social mores. Mark Jarvis argues that while Harold Wilson and Roy Jenkins have received much of the credit (or blame!) for the 'permissive society' legislation, their work was a continuation of their Conservative predecessors, Harold Macmillan and R.A. Butler. However, Jarvis also suggests that the Conservatives were rather ambivalent about the consequences of this social change. While happy to accommodate 'progress', they worried that the world of Sunday shopping, television and gambling might actually constitute social and moral regression.[30]

For Labour in the post-war years, the situation was rather more complicated. On the one hand it seemed clear, particularly following the 1959 General Election defeat, that Labour needed to update its image and appeal to the modern voter. It was necessary to overcome the party's 'conservative' commitment to its established policies, such as nationalisation. On the other was the fear that this meant accommodation with reality at the expense of genuinely radical progressive change. The far left has always worried that whiggish faith in gradual progress and consensual improvement would deflect workers' energies from the need for struggle and revolution. Here, as Lawrence Black has shown, a moderate left worried that the 'progress' of affluence did not represent progress at all.[31]

In later years, a version of this debate was characterised as one between 'Old' and 'New' Labour, between 'traditionalists' clinging to outmoded notions of social division and 'modernisers' adapting Labour's core principles to suit the late twentieth century. In 1959, however, it was not only the commercialised affluent society that spoke of progress, novelty and innovation; an alternative vision of modernity also existed. As Barbara Castle put it:

> What are the typical symbols of the modern age? Russia's nationalised sputnik now circling round the moon tracked at every stage by Britain's publicly owned radar telescope at Jodrell Bank. The Hovercraft – the most revolutionary development in transport – sponsored by the National Research Development Corporation which you and I own. Nimrod, the giant atom-smasher now being built next door to Harwell – another product of nationalised enterprise.[32]

Similarly Richard Crossman argued that Britain's mixed economy was 'intrinsically unable to sustain the competition with the Eastern bloc to which we are now committed'. He warned that if Britain did not keep pace with the model of public ownership, exemplified by the USSR, it would be left floundering in the wake of this new modernity.[33] Crossman's principal target was Tony Crosland, whose own argument was also predicated on the need to modernise, to overcome Britain's 'natural vice of conservatism' and to increase its productivity which was lagging behind the rest of Europe. For Labour traditionalists and revisionists alike, this was a matter of how best to compete in a new global order, how best to respond to the challenges of modernity. It is striking how often the charge of 'conservatism' was thrown from either side.

Tony Blair took a similar line in his 1999 conference speech, when he declared that 'the 21st century will not be about the battle between capitalism and socialism but between the forces of progress and the forces of conservatism'.[34] He referred seventeen times in this conference speech to the battle against the 'forces of conservatism', but made clear that this went beyond the familiar roll call of the opponents of female suffrage and the NHS and also included those members of his own party who opposed rewriting Clause IV of Labour's Constitution and reforming public services. His invocation of the Labour Party's 'historic mission' was now recast as a desire to 'liberate' the country from an imagined past, which seemed to be based in the values of 'old' Labour: 'the old class divisions, old structures, old prejudices, old ways of working and of doing things, that will not do in this world of change'.[35]

The notion that progress is inextricably tied to modernity and novelty is at the root of the near-universal embrace of the language of progressivism in contemporary politics. Modernity here is taken to be an uncontroversial good; the ambivalence on both right and left about the consequences of such modernity has been muted.

Progress as social justice

The counter-intuitive nature of any definition which places Thatcher on the side of progressivism indicates the extent to which the third, ideological, feature underpins understandings of progressivism: that any 'improvement' and any forward movement should be judged according to left or centre-left standards. Here the technical meaning of 'progressive taxation' as redistributive also comes into play. It is this reading of progressivism which is often applied to the kind of moderate conservatism associated with Macmillan's *Middle Way* and the Tory Reform Group, who were described as 'right progressives' by Andrew Gamble.[36] For such conservatives, who date their ancestry to Disraeli, gradual change was undertaken as the best means of maintaining a more fundamental continuity. While reaction could lead to stagnation, decline or revolution, consensual moves towards social justice, civil rights and personal liberty were likely to preserve and deepen national solidarity. This was progress as moderate consensus, not as radical rupture. Yet, as we saw above, it was not straightforwardly optimistic.

Cameron's use of the language of progressivism references *both* the social policy concerns of the Macmillan tradition and the radical rhetoric and activism of the Thatcherite right. These are contrasting traditions employing different uses of the language of progress. Unlike Thatcher, Cameron and Osborne have been happy to reference the centre-left associations of the progressive tradition while rejecting its traditional emphasis on an interventionist state. Even Conservative proposed budget cuts were justified with reference to the centre-left politics of Clinton and Chrétien long before the coalition necessitated such a shift in language.[37]

Osborne's claim that 'The torch of progressive politics has been passed to ... [the] Conservatives' was a clear attempt to lay claim to a specific historical tradition of progressivism in British politics – the Lib-Lab Alliance of the late nineteenth and early twentieth centuries.[38] Yet, even within this political context, 'progressivism' carries connotations of both moderation and left-wing radicalism. On the one hand, the Lib-Lab alliance speaks of cross-partisan co-operation. This was the ethos of the Rainbow Circle, described as 'a vital crucible of progressive thought' by Michael Freeden.[39] We might also think of the frequent calls for 'progressives of all parties' to work together in the 1970s. The meaning here was unequivocally one of moderation in the face of sharpening ideological divides between left and right. The 1977 Lib-Lab Pact seems to have been born more of this spirit than of a shared historic tradition between the Labour and Liberal parties. David Steel repeatedly emphasised that the offer he had made to Callaghan was exactly the same as that made by Jeremy Thorpe to Heath.[40] Moreover, he made clear that the same offer would be open to Margaret Thatcher on the same terms following the next general election, 'even though many current Tory policies are unacceptable to Liberals', on the grounds that 'Liberals are [as] capable of taming Tory excess as they are of controlling Labour lunacy'.[41] Steel also publicly made the abandonment of socialist policies a condition of his support for Labour. While he did describe the Pact as offering a chance for 'long awaited realignment in politics', this was not presented as the reunion of the two strands of progressive thought, as Steel later said of the SDP–Liberal merger. Instead he concentrated on the Pact's ability to 'signal the end to the politics of confrontation', strengthen the moderate centre of British politics, and, ultimately, to 'provide the basis for the return of a radical Liberal Government of the kind which this country has not seen since the early years of this century'.[42]

On the other hand, progressivism is often regarded as the exclusive property of the left and more associated with the struggles of the labour movement than with a particularly consensual style of politics. In the aftermath of the 2010 General Election and subsequent coalition, this tension was evident within the Labour Party, particularly, for instance, at the annual conference of pressure group Compass, held in early June 2010. While the official line was one of progressive pluralism, with the keynote speech given by newly elected Green MP Caroline Lucas, the mood in some of the breakout sessions was unmistakeably tribalist. Many Labour members insisted that only their party could be trusted to pursue progressive policies and angrily rejected proposals for electoral reform on the grounds that they might make clear-cut Labour victories more difficult and thus lead to less progressive outcomes, less social justice.[43]

Electoral reform is one of the key causes of Lib-Lab moderate progressivism, reflecting both the hope that the two 'progressive' parties together can command a majority of fairly allocated votes and also the consensual pluralist politics which proportional systems encourage. It is not only in the wake of the coalition of Liberal Democrats with Conservatives that this has become a step too far for many within the Labour Party, especially for the MPs elected by the First Past the Post system. Many of those MPs who have been known to oppose electoral reform – John Reid, David Blunkett, John Prescott – were also those who came out against the idea of a 'progressive rainbow coalition' between Labour, Liberal Democrats and smaller parties. While these politicians have not shied away from the language of progressivism altogether,[44] for them it is a Labour value, denoting a left-of-centre commitment to equality and social justice, not to pluralism. The tension is not limited to the centre ground of British politics and can be seen, for instance, in the Communist Party of Great Britain in the late 1980s and early 1990s. While the revisionist *Marxism Today* faction was urging the party towards a moderate, pluralist, progressive politics,[45] the left faction which broke away to form the Communist Party of Britain was attacking Kinnock's Labour Party for not being 'progressive' (i.e. socialist) enough.[46]

Whigs, Tories and Marxists

As we will see in Chapter 3, the relationship between the Conservative Party and liberalism has been rather tangled. Unlike the seemingly straightforward narrative of the Lib-Lab 'progressive alliance' examined in Chapter 4, conservatives have been split between those who embraced and those who shunned an accommodation with liberal principles and particularly with what they saw as an overly confident whiggish belief in progress and instrumental use of history. Resistance to such an attitude has, at times, resulted in a rather surprising alliance between Toryism and Marxism.

In a 1978 collection of essays intended to 'suggest respects in which Mrs Thatcher's stance might be open to improvement',[47] John Casey presented a defence of an active political engagement with the past. Importantly, Casey felt that his sense of the past was closer to Marxism than to liberalism as it 'avoid[ed] the view of customs and institutions as either on the one hand instrumental or on the other merely associative and nostalgic and hence irrational'.[48] Instead, he insisted that the past has 'authority' over the present. For the Marxist, this is established through 'general causal laws', whereas the conservative prefers 'tradition', expressed through customs and institutions.[49] It is these two attitudes to the past which seem to have been largely replaced with a presentist approach, similar to that which Casey links with liberalism.

It is instructive to compare Casey's views with those of Marxist theorist Fredric Jameson who argued (the following year) that 'it is not we who sit in judgement on the past, but rather the past ... which judges us'. For Jameson this seemed to be a radical departure because 'the very dynamics of the historical tribunal are unexpectedly and dialectically reversed'.[50] Yet for the pessimistic conservative this is the *natural* relation of past and present. For both, 'our concrete relationship with the past remains an existential experience, a galvanic and electrifying event'.[51] Yet while Jameson is concerned with 'disturbing and unsettling' the present through confrontation with 'the radical difference of other modes of production', Casey advocates an attitude of *'pietas'* towards the past whereby, 'individuals can be enlarged in their relation to customs, institutions and the state'.[52] Rather than the notion of justice, of righting past wrongs, the conservative obligation to the past could perhaps be more easily characterised as one of filial duty. Casey bemoaned the attempts of Conservatives to justify their attachment to the nation's historic institutions on the basis of rational judgements, such as the House of Lords' ability to scrutinise legislation. By disguising sentiment behind rationality, they undermined the very value of those institutions.[53] This amounts to a rejection of Whig teleology. The British state has not been developed as a result of rational judgements and progressive improvement; we do not owe allegiance because of its structural attributes. Rather it comes to us through the accidents of history and our allegiance should be unconditional, based on the power of tradition and heritage. This quintessentially Tory approach to the past is emotional and ineffable. By its very nature it can be neither effectively explained nor theorised. It is a structure of feeling, an inherited state.

It is the argument of this chapter that the parties have coalesced around a form of historical whiggism. Butterfield's exploration *The Whig Interpretation of History* emphasised the extent to which such an approach derives not only from a particular political narrative which favours the forces of progress (the Protestant radicals who formed parliament in its current shape) but is also the inevitable consequence of a history which works backwards from the present. This is a history which favours the winners, seeing the past as the means by which we arrived safely at the present moment. It is therefore not surprising that such an approach continues to shape party political perceptions of the past.[54] It is often argued that although the Liberals lost the electoral battle in the twentieth century, their ideas – from Keynesianism to the Beveridge Report – continue to shape the political scene.[55] It does not seem too much of a leap to suggest that the same analysis could be applied to the historical positioning of whiggism.

In 1969 J.H. Plumb expressed the liberal hope that 'history' would replace what he called 'the past'. This was, in Plumb's words, 'always a created ideology with a purpose, designed to control individuals, or motivate societies, or inspire classes'.[56] Henry Drucker was doubtful about Plumb's prediction, arguing that 'people whose identity is threatened by history-books do not cease believing as a result of what has been written'.[57] He felt that this was particularly true of the working-class communities upon which Labour politics were founded. As Drucker recognised, there is a clear connection between the institution of professional history, the development of public time (or 'clock-time') and the dominance of parliamentary politics. Moreover, he noted that Plumb's faith in the rational triumph of history was rooted in his own professional background as an eighteenth-century political historian. While Drucker's argument that the political 'past' is very far from being replaced by researched and authenticated 'history' holds true, it seems clear that there has been a clear shift in the kinds of 'pasts' which the parties remember. The parliamentary story of Labour as a political party has largely replaced that of labour as a movement and – albeit at a slower rate – the Conservatives are developing an institutional sense of self to compensate for their loss of status as the party of the national past. But this is not 'history' in Plumb's sense. As Plumb himself recognised, the progressive political narrative of the whig interpretation of history was itself a myth, which though '[m]ortally wounded, certainly dying ... still exists and still exerts force ... In the middle-class reading public of England it still provides support for their bruised and damaged egos.'[58] In the case of political parties, this is not necessarily connected to the idea of Britain as a Great Nation; more importantly it bolsters faith in the efficacy of parliamentary politics itself.

Party politics occupies an unusually privileged position with regard to historical time. As we have already noted, political discourse trades in the 'historic': monumental battles, epoch-changing decisions, great personalities. This discourse is a reflection of the way in which the nineteenth-century development of professional history was associated with the legitimation of the nation state. It is worth noting here the chronological conjunction of the professionalisation of politics and of history; indeed, from Clarendon to Acton, many of the same individuals were involved in both professions. Another way of thinking about this conjunction between 'the historic' and political action is that, as privileged public actors, politicians are able to take a major role in *making time*. As Bonnie G. Smith showed in her seminal work on the gendering of history, the professionalisation of history in the late nineteenth century was associated with an appropriation of time:

> Just as natural scientists produced a 'deep time' in their studies of the universe, earth, and species, historical scientists produced this time for the nation-state by filling its emptiness with the historical facts of great national events and great men's lives.[59]

The passage of time was 'signalled by the movement from one great (universal) individual man to the next' and depended upon 'details' in order to distinguish between them. The nature of this time was associated with whiggish ideas about 'the developmental man' and, according to Smith, this emphasis on the masculine 'weighted time as progressive'.[60] Although the gender bias of historical time has (arguably) been challenged, and both academic and public history have embraced social, working-class and women's history, it is clear that parliamentary politics is still governed by old historical time. For this reason, as we will see in subsequent chapters, histories produced by political actors continue to focus on individuals, on the passage from one leader to the next and on details to distinguish between them. Moreover, parliamentarians seem to see themselves as having a role as custodians of the national past. Speaking in a 1991 parliamentary debate on the proposed National Curriculum for History, Labour MP Gordon Oakes addressed the Deputy Speaker 'and all right hon. and hon. Members as 650 history teachers' with a particular role in transmitting the history of British democracy:

> We all take tourists around this place. We talk about Simon de Montfort and the row between the Lords and the Commons. We talk about the civil war and show them the painting with Mr. Speaker Lenthall. We then take them into the Chamber and out into Westminster Hall. When I take people round, I talk about the fight for democracy over hundreds of years – it did not happen overnight – and I tell them about events that have occurred in the past 20 years.[61]

Remembering 1688

The seventeenth century provides a recurring reference point in British political debate. On the one hand lies the foundation of modern constitutional monarchy; on the other floats the spectre of the unrealised republican future. It is striking that for modern conservatives the parliamentary narrative of 1688–9 has come to replace the monarchical-religious overtones of the doomed Restoration.[62] The 'Glorious Revolution' of 1688 has politically ambiguous connotations, speaking to both the progressive, Whig, narrative of reform, liberty and democracy and the Tory, Burkean, narrative of the defence of the status quo and preservation of political institutions. It is taken to be the foundation moment of the constitutional settlement, an emotional touchstone which deserves respect and preservation. James Vernon has shown how 1688 was very quickly absorbed into the Tory narrative and used to demonstrate that in fact nothing had changed.[63]

However, it is striking that the most high-profile tribute to 1688 came from the left. Crucially, it was not a memorial to things as they had been but a desire to channel the spirit of 1688 whilst demanding further reforms. What began as a petition organised through the *New Statesman* became the campaign organisation, Charter 88. Again, we see the emphasis on taking forward the radical spirit of the past, rather than simple commemoration of its achievements. The *New Statesman* article launching the Charter 88 campaign noted that there was no cause to celebrate the tercentenary at a time when 'In the name of freedom, our political, human and social rights are being curtailed while the powers of the executive have increased, are increasing and ought to be diminished.' More than simply noting a gap between the ideals of 1688 and the reality of 1988, Charter 88 laid much of the blame for the current situation on the failure of the Glorious Revolution to guarantee citizens' freedoms through a written constitution. Instead, it 'only shifted the absolute power of the monarch into the hands of the parliamentary oligarchy'. The current administration was thus able to 'exploit the dark side of a constitutional settlement which was always deficient in democracy'.[64]

The same feelings came to the fore in a parliamentary debate over the tercentenary of 1688. On 7 July 1988, Margaret Thatcher moved a Humble Address expressing:

> ... our great pleasure in celebrating the tercentenary of these historic events of 1688 and 1689 that established those constitutional freedoms

under the law which Your Majesty's Parliament and people have continued to enjoy for three hundred years.[65]

Thatcher not only presented this narrative as one of seemingly uninterrupted progression between past and present but also used it to tie together Tory and Whig interpretations of British history. The 'bloodless revolution' seemingly established respect for the law and for private property, it was 'the first step on the road' to parliamentary reform and universal suffrage and it created 'that renewal of energy and resourcefulness which built Britain's industrial and financial strength and gave her a world role'. However, the left of the Labour Party was not prepared to let Thatcher gloss over historic differences so easily. In a debate lasting over two hours, speakers including Tony Benn, Jeremy Corbyn, Eric Heffer and Bob Cryer sought both to discredit the 1688 Revolution itself and to use the legacy of the past to undermine the Thatcher government's policies on a host of contemporary issues.

Predictably, these issues included the powers of the Executive, the House of Lords, Anglo-Irish relations, civil liberties, the Oath of Allegiance, electoral reform and the need for a modern Declaration of Rights. More surprisingly the debate also covered nuclear weapons, the European Community, female priests, the miners' strike, trade union legislation, the abolition of the Greater London Council and the presence of US troops on British airfields. Tony Benn even drew a parallel between the Enclosure Acts and Thatcher's policies on privatisation. The very malleability of these historical symbols demonstrates the way in which they are used not in a historicist sense, for what they mean in themselves, but as a set of shorthand signifiers in a contemporary political context with its own web of meanings. These labels can be used to stand for a whole range of political positions.

One of the striking features of the debate was the way in which the critics of the motion tried to hold the government accountable for the injustices of the past. We see again the sense of temporal continuity and of the continuing political potency of the past. Eric Heffer turned on Julian Amery, declaring that 'The fight for democracy had to be wrung out of the class of which the right hon. Gentleman's party has been representative since the days of the 1640 revolution.' These speakers insisted on the need to honour the past through bearing forward its struggles, not closing it down with self-satisfied commemoration. In Graham Allen's words, it would be a travesty 'to pickle that Bill of Rights, to put it into aspic and to say, "It is a marvellous thing. We should have a drink and a bit of a sing-song.'' Instead, he stressed the need to assess the current state of civil liberties and to make plans for the future. Otherwise, 'in 300 years' time we may not be celebrating even those few rights that are enshrined in the 1688–89 settlement'.[66]

By treating the tercentenary as a simple historical commemoration, Thatcher tried to wrap herself in the colours of liberty, progress and also (crucially) heritage. Her opponents objected that this outfit didn't fit her, that she had no right to wear it and that it was not, in any case, something in which she should be proud to be seen. Yet while the debate was heated, it was far from evenly matched. The opponents of the address dominated the debate, yet gained just eighteen votes, compared with 139 in favour. This was an angry outburst from a small number of MPs who maintained a strong faith in the political power of the past. As Benn put it, 'If one blows on the embers of any old controversy, the flames come up quite quickly.' Yet the fire failed to ignite. The vast majority of both sides of the House were happy to endorse Thatcher's commemorative Humble Address.

Levelling the past

The English Civil War has been a constant feature of attempts to create an alternative, radical narrative of a British history. It was a key reference for Marxist historians, most notably Christopher Hill and A.L. Morton, in their attempts 'create the history of a popular democratic tradition in English history and culture'.[67] More recently, Tristram Hunt led a *Guardian* campaign to commemorate key moments in Britain's radical past, culminating in the exhibition and public events surrounding the 360th anniversary of the Putney Debates.[68]

In the recent past, this has been a source of deep contention between the parties. In 1976 Douglas Hurd fiercely opposed a commemoration of the Levellers taking place in his constituency and opened by Tony Benn, then Minister for Energy. Hurd wrote to the Labour Secretary of State for Education protesting both at Benn's presence and at the support of the publicly funded Workers' Educational Association (WEA) for a 'party political occasion'. He particularly objected to 'the use of a church for this political purpose [and] the curious reading of history which promotes these mutineers into martyrs'.[69] It is clear from Hurd's objection to the event that he felt the Levellers' deaths to be a still-contentious topic. There are echoes here of Hobbes' warning that learning of old rebellions could stir men to insurrection.[70] This discussion was revisited in 1988 during a debate on the Security Services. Benn used Hurd's objection to Levellers' Day against him, claiming that it showed that he was 'consistent in his opposition to dissent in any century by anybody'.[71]

But times have changed. In November 2007 Justine Greening, Conservative MP for Putney was rowed down the Thames to attend the 360th anniversary celebrations of the Putney Debates, with her Labour counterparts from neighbouring constituencies. As a post-Thatcher Conservative, Greening perhaps sees the Levellers as part of a libertarian, meritocratic line of 'freeborn Englishmen'. Indeed, in June 2007 Daniel Hannan MEP claimed the Roundheads for the right, arguing that although 'Many contemporary Tories imagine, without giving the matter much thought, that they would have fought for the King', they were 'almost certainly wrong. The causes they hold dearest: personal liberty, small government, parliamentary supremacy, patriotism, localism, Euro-scepticism would in fact have inclined them to Old Ironsides.'[72] But no matter how many alternative readings we can apply to seventeenth-century British history, the association of the Levellers with the communist histories of Morton and Hill and with the speeches of Benn and songs of Billy Bragg now seems irreversible. Indeed the latter two featured prominently in the displays inside St Mary's Church, Putney. Despite this, Greening attended.

No longer a freshly resurrected tradition designed to 'stir men to insurrection', the Levellers' story is now as quaint in its evocation of 1960s radicalism and 1970s class conflict as in its seventeenth-century associations. A similar tendency is observable in Dorset where Griffiths notes that while the annual Tolpuddle rally 'purports to commemorate an event in 1834, it is also in many ways a continuing memorial to the labour movement of the inter-war period'.[73] It seems that as narratives associated with 'socialist history' have become part of the political and historical mainstream they have lost their radical power. Levellers' Day has now become something of an institution itself, with a somewhat nostalgic, even 'small c' conservative atmosphere. In 2008, one member of the audience asked a question 'in memory of … the late Chair of the Witney Constituency Labour Party, who many of you will know and who always came to Levellers' Day and always asked a question, usually about land tax'.[74] This was greeted by warm laughter. Although the subject of the question may have been radical, the fact of its being asked seemed in many ways safe and comforting. It seems that Levellers'

Day not only commemorates events in the seventeenth century but also displays elements of nostalgia for more recent history, when the divisions between left and right were still clear-cut. This could be seen in the warm reception given to guest speaker Giles Fraser's joke that as a vicar, he 'may be the last member of a nationalised industry up here [on the platform]'.[75] The 'History' section on the Levellers' Day website revels in the tales of local Conservative opposition to the early events and finishes its account in 1990.[76] The narrative does not seem to have moved on to accommodate a time when Conservative MPs would attend events organised to commemorate the Levellers.[77]

In 2001, David Cameron, Hurd's successor as MP for Witney, spoke about the constituency in his maiden speech. He mentioned the birth and burial places of Winston Churchill, then cast his net a little wider:

> West Oxfordshire's political history extends to all traditions. The Levellers, who are now regarded as heroic early socialists, rebelled during the civil war because they believed that their leader, Cromwell, had betrayed the principles for which they fought. I am sure that Labour Members who might sometimes feel the same way do not need reminding that the leaders of that rebellion were rounded up and shot in Burford's churchyard. William Morris, the socialist visionary, lived and is buried at Kelmscott Manor in my constituency, and I have no hesitation in urging all hon. Members to visit that beautiful village on the banks of the Thames which time seems to have passed by.[78]

There are a number of layers to this statement. On the surface, it seems to be a simple piece of party-political humour. Cameron opens out the field apparently in the spirit of political generosity before making a joke at the expense of the Labour leadership. However, the way that Cameron leads from this immediately into his anodyne encouragement to visit the burial place of 'socialist visionary' William Morris, hints at something more complicated. In joining together Conservative luminaries and two separate parts of what are seen to be the Labour tradition, Cameron also makes an appeal to history *in general*. This has the effect of closing down the political potential of the particular pasts in question. The radical past becomes part of the national heritage, part of the unfolding national story which conservative historian John Vincent reminds us, 'cannot be undone', it can only be 'absorbed'.[79]

Socialist history

Socialist history is predicated on the hope of progress, but not necessarily the expectation of it. It has been the history of exclusion from high politics. So what are the implications when Labour history itself becomes high politics?

Take, for example, Aneurin Bevan's description of his arrival in parliament as an MP, at a time when Labour politicians still felt themselves to be excluded from the grand narrative of national life:

> Here he is, a tribune of the people, coming to make his voice heard in the seats of power. Instead, it seems he is expected to worship; and the most conservative of all religions – ancestor worship.
>
> The first thing he should bear in mind is that these were not his ancestors. His forbears had no part in the past, the accumulated dust of which now muffles his own footfalls. His forefathers were tending sheep or ploughing the land, or serving the statesmen whose names he sees written on the walls around him, or whose portraits look down on him in the long corridors. It is not the past of his people that extends in colourful pageantry before his eyes. They were shut out from all this; were forbidden to take part in the dramatic scenes depicted in these frescoes. In him his people are there for the first time, and the history he will make will not be merely an episode in the story he is now reading. It must be wholly different; as different as the social status which he now brings with him.[80]

It is worth noting that although Bevan disparages 'ancestor worship', his account is in itself suffused with nostalgia for 'his people'. It is the memory of these people which inspires his commitment to the future, his declaration that it must be 'wholly different'. Labour politicians no longer carry such an intense awareness of cultural and class difference, of the sense of being out of place which informed Bevan's politics. Since 1945 and particularly since 1997, they have been at home in Westminster, they have made it the site of their political action, of their own narrative of past and future. This project has been so successful that, as we will see in Chapter 3, Conservatives have come to doubt their own claim to the title of 'national party'. Doubts remain, however, about the extent to which Labour succeeded in bringing about a 'wholly different' type of history.

As we will see in Chapter 2, labour history groups, such as Labour Heritage or the Society for the Study of Labour History, have tended to concentrate on working-class and labour movement history. In contrast the newer Labour History Group, founded in 2002, purposely asserts a much more institutional Labour Party identity.[81] Rather than structures, processes and conflicts, it is focused on events, personalities and outcomes. Its meetings in the Palace of Westminster usually highlight aspects of the history of the parliamentary party and often include contributions from high-profile parliamentarians, from Denis Healey to Tessa Jowell. The group has borrowed from the methodology of social history by collecting oral history accounts on its website. Yet, to date, the group's oral history project includes only the accounts of high-profile politicians, speaking about their early inspirations.[82] While tribute is always paid to working-class roots, struggles and heroes, this is very much a 'high political' narrative, in which Bevan himself plays a key role. This is not a new trend. Rather, it marks the triumph of a particular strand of Labour thought: the Fabian tradition, with its emphasis on legislative action and faith in expertise, at the expense of a rather looser, extra-parliamentary labour movement.[83]

In many ways, this comes down to a debate about the role of the Labour Party within the nation. In the post-war years, critics including Ralph Miliband and Richard Crossman complained that the party has become too concerned with its parliamentary role and its participation in the alternating pendulum between government and opposition. They were concerned that Labour should not accept the role of government-in-waiting at the expense of upholding its particular sectional appeal. They insisted, in effect, that it should 'be wholly different'. However, the Labour Party is now unquestionably a national party of government, part of elite political history. Its heroes, including of course Bevan, are statesmen whose names are written on the walls and 'whose portraits look down ... in the long corridors' of Westminster. Labour's victory in the 1945 General Election reinforced its position within the political establishment and its programme in government sealed its place in national history.

The tension between an inward-facing, class-based, commitment to the past and an outward-facing, national, commitment to the future have long been visible in the Labour Party's internal culture. For instance, in 1962, as Labour prepared to challenge Macmillan's Conservatives, the London party staged a large 'Festival of Labour'.[84] As a party circular made clear, the theme was '"Labour in the 60's" – a forward looking movement.' Local parties and trade unions branches were warned that their tableaux should be mindful of this theme and that 'the historical aspects should be avoided unless they can be geared to the future'. The 'danger' as the party conceived it was that 'in the short time the public see an individual tableau, they might get the impression that the Labour movement is only concerned with the past and not the future'.[85] Great emphasis was placed upon modernity: a national competition was launched to encourage constituency parties to modernise their premises and publicity for an exhibition of 'New Art – 1962' boasted that although 'It might have been easier to stage a show of work by universally esteemed and established artists' their emphasis was on 'the *future* of art in Britain'. This exhibition was held in Congress House: 'one of London's most notable examples of modern architecture'.[86]

It could be argued that this was protesting too much, that the need to warn local parties and trade unions not to look backwards is proof enough of their tendency to do so. However, the official festival publications speak of the contradiction at the heart of Labour's temporal attitude more clearly than this. The (presumably publicly available) Festival Programme had an assertively contemporary design and a relentless emphasis on modernity. In addition to notices about the 'Modern Art Exhibition', its commercial advertising also kept on-message, with the Co-op, for example, stressing its self-service facilities under the slogan 'Shop the *modern* way at London Co-op'.[87] The internal brochure given to party members however, told a very different story. Welcoming members to London, it assured them that 'You are among friends. Friends who share your hopes, your attitude to living, your tradition.' The inside spread of this four-page brochure was entitled 'History is past politics and politics is present history' and ran through the centuries-long 'movement of protest which flowered into our Labour Movement', beginning with the Peasants' Revolt and running up to 'the great dock strike and the pioneer match girls' strike' – all accompanied with woodcut-style drawings. It even encouraged members to make a 'pilgrimage' to the Memorial Hall where the Labour Party was founded. The only other text in the brochure was a short run-through of Labour's successes on the London County Council since 1934, but this was relegated to a secondary position overleaf.[88] The division between outward-facing, confident, progressivism and inward-looking, reassuring, nostalgia could not be more stark.

Conclusion

Since the late 1970s we have seen a convergence in temporal attitude between the parties that is more marked than a convergence in their positions on social and economic policy. This convergence can be summarised as a presentist use of historical narratives which is at odds with both socialist and conservative conceptions of the past as, respectively, radical obligation and venerated inheritance. Dating the change in the temporal positioning of contemporary British politics to the start of the first Thatcher government suggests immediately that this tendency is associated with neoliberalism, with its ambiguous juxtaposition of aggressive modernity and its attendant nostalgia, described as 'regressive modernisation' by Stuart Hall.[89] While this is a major part of the story, another important element comes from the left. As we have already noted, in the year that Thatcher came to power, Henry Drucker's seminal study of *Doctrine and Ethos in the Labour Party* described the way in which 'social democrats urge that Labour is a party of the future' in opposition to Labour's 'sense of a common past' which serves as the party's '"organisational glue"'. This was, he felt, 'in harmony with the dominant time-perspective of our age'.[90] It is now the orthodox position of Labour politics.

The modern is now regarded, in and of itself, as progressive. And this temporal notion of progress is taken to be an uncontroversial good. The cross-party consensus is that we live in a post-nation state global network and must learn to compete on that terrain; there is little hope or desire to change this situation. The past is called in to support these attitudes, not to challenge them. The need for parties to tell a story of events, actions and progress has constrained the alternative voices of both left and right who see political possibilities in worlds lost and roads not taken. This is Whig history, in Butterfield's sense, which favours the forces of progress even where it defends conservative principles and which emphasises the power of parliament even as it celebrates radical outsiders. It is absolutely history in the service of the present.

Notes

1 Hayden White, *Metahistory: The Historical Imagination in Nineteenth-century Europe* (Baltimore: The Johns Hopkins University Press, 1973), pp. 22–9.

2 Stuart White, 'Introduction: New Labour and the future of progressive politics', in Stuart White (ed.), *New Labour: The Progressive Future?* (Basingstoke: Palgrave, 2001), p. x.

3 Andrew Gamble and Tony Wright, 'Introduction: the new social democracy', in Andrew Gamble and Tony Wright (eds), *The New Social Democracy* (Oxford: The Political Quarterly Publishing Co. Ltd, 1999).

4 Michael Freeden, 'True blood or false genealogy: New Labour and British social democratic thought', in Gamble and Wright (eds), *The New Social Democracy*, p. 164.

5 Andrew Gamble, *The Conservative Nation* (London: Routledge & Kegan Paul Ltd, 1974), p. 9.

6 Quintin Hogg, *The Case for Conservatism* (Middlesex: Penguin, 1947), pp. 84–5.

7 Walter Benjamin, 'Theses on the philosophy of history', in Walter Benjamin, *Illuminations* (London: Pimlico 1999 [1955], tr. Harry Zorn), p. 252.

8 Michel-Rolph Trouillot, *Silencing the Past: Power and the Production of History* (Boston: Beacon Press, 1995), p.150.

9 Clare Griffiths, 'Remembering Tolpuddle: rural history and commemoration in the inter-war labour movement', *History Workshop Journal* 44 (1997), 161.

10 Ibid., 158, 151, 158.

11 Dave Renton, 'The historian as outsider: writing public history from within and without a group', *Journal of the North West Labour History Group*, 25 (2000/01), 52–3.

12 Peter Glazer, *Radical Nostalgia: Spanish Civil War Commemoration in America* (Rochester, NY: University of Rochester Press, 2005), p. 37.

13 Ibid., p. 220.

14 See Lowenthal's discussion of this in 'Nostalgia tells it like it wasn't', in Christpher Shaw and Malcolm Chase (eds), *The Imagined Past: History and Nostalgia* (Manchester and New York: Manchester University Press, 1989), pp. 18–32.

15 See Alastair Bonnett, *Left in the Past: Radicalism and the Politics of Nostalgia* (London: Continuum, 2010).

16 Malcolm Chase and Christopher Shaw, 'The dimensions of nostalgia', in Shaw and Chase, *The Imagined Past*, p. 2. Original emphasis.

17 E.J. Hobsbawm, 'The social functions of the past: some questions', *Past and Present*, 55 (1972), 13.

18 Barbara Taylor, 'Heroic families and utopian histories', *Historein*, 3 (2001), 59–74. Original emphasis

19 David Lowenthal, 'Nostalgia tells it like it wasn't', p. 29. Original emphasis.

20 Svetlana Boym, *The Future of Nostalgia* (New York: Basic Books, 2001), p. xviii.

21 Ibid., p. xviii.

22 For instance, a *Salisbury Review* article in the run-up to the 1997 election lamented that 'We are now at last seeing the results of a century of democracy: namely a political elite which is no more qualified to govern than those who vote for it.' Editorial, *The Salisbury Review*, 15:3 (Spring 1997), 3.

23 Enoch Powell, 'Patriotism', in Enoch Powell, *Wrestling with the Angel* (London: Sheldon Press, 1977), pp. 2–3.

24 Editorial, *The Salisbury Review*, 16:1 (Autumn 1997), 3.

25 John O'Sullivan, *Conservatism, Democracy and National Identity*, the third Keith Joseph Memorial Lecture, 16 February 1999 (London: Centre for Policy Studies, 1999), p. 6.

26 Alasdair Morrison, 'The historic basis of conservatism', *Swinton Journal*, 15:1 (Spring 1969), pp. 22–9.

27 Robert Eccleshall, 'Party ideology and national decline', in Richard English and Michael Kenny (eds), *Rethinking British Decline* (Basingstoke: Macmillan Press Ltd, 2000), p. 164.

28 Daniel Wincott, 'Thatcher: ideological or pragmatic?', *Contemporary British History* 4:2, 26–8.

29 Margaret Thatcher, *Dimensions of Conservatism*, Iain Macleod Memorial Lecture, delivered to the Greater London Young Conservatives, 4 July 1977. Available at: www.margaretthatcher.org/speeches/displaydocument.asp?docid=103411. Accessed 09.10.2009

30 Mark Jarvis, *Conservative Governments, Morality and Social Change in Affluent Britain, 1957–64* (Manchester: Manchester University Press, 2005).

31 Lawrence Black, *The Political Culture of the Left in Affluent Britain: 1951–64* (Basingstoke: Palgrave Macmillan, 2002).

32 UCL Library Services, Special Collections (hereafter UCL), Hugh Gaitskell Papers (hereafter HG), C194, Barbara Castle, Presidential Address to Labour Party Annual Conference, Saturday 28 November 1959.

33 R.H.S. Crossman MP, *Labour in the Affluent Society*, Fabian Tract 325 (London: Fabian Society, 1960), p. 24.

34 Tony Blair, speech to Labour Party Conference, 28 September 1999. Available at: http://news.bbc.co.uk/1/hi/uk_politics/460009.stm. Accessed 23.10.2009.

35 Ibid.

36 Gamble, *The Conservative Nation*.

37 Osborne, 'Progressive reform in an age of austerity'.

38 Ibid.

39 Freeden, 'True blood or false genealogy', p. 152.

40 David Steel, Parliamentary Debates, Commons, 23 March 1977, Opposition Motion, col. 1314.

41 LSE Special Collections, Liberal Party Papers (hereafter LiP), Lib Lab Pact 19/1, 'Putting over the Pact: A guide for Liberal activists', p. 4.

42 LiP, Lib Lab Pact 19/1, press release of David Steel speaking to London Liberal Party Rally, Conway Hall, Red Lion Square, Thursday 3 November 1977.

43 Compass Conference, 'A New Hope', Saturday 12 June, London. Personal observations.

44 See, for instance, David Blunkett, *Politics and Progress: Renewing Democracy and a Civil Society* (London: Demos, 2001).

45 See Communist Party of Great Britain, *Manifesto for New Times: A Communist Party Strategy for the 1990s* (London: Marxism Today, 1989).

46 Communist Party of Britain, *41st Congress Report: Branches, Districts & National Committees: Resolutions* (London: CPB, 1991).

47 Maurice Cowling, 'The present situation', in Maurice Cowling (ed.), *Conservative Essays* (London: Cassell, 1978), pp. 19–20.

48 John Casey, 'Tradition and authority', in ibid., p. 88.

49 Ibid., pp. 98, 88.

50 Fredric Jameson, 'Marxism and historicism', *New Literary History*, 11:1 (Autumn 1979), 70.

51 Ibid.

52 Ibid.; Casey, 'Tradition and authority', p. 100.

53 Ibid., pp. 82–100.

54 Herbert Butterfield, *The Whig Interpretation of History* (Harmondsworth: Penguin, 1973 [1931]).

55 See for instance *It's About Freedom*, The Report of the Liberal Democrat Working Group, Policy Paper 50 (June 2002), p. 11; Gerald F. Gaus, 'Ideological dominance through philosophical confusion: liberalism in the twentieth century', in Michael Freeden (ed.), *Reassessing Political Ideologies: The Durability of Dissent* (London and New York: Routledge, 2001), pp. 13–34.

56 J.H. Plumb, *The Death of the Past* (Basingstoke: Palgrave Macmillan, 2003 [1969]), p. 17.

57 Drucker, *Doctrine and Ethos*, p. 32.

58 Plumb, *The Death of the Past*, p. 86.

59 Bonnie G. Smith, *The Gender of History: Men, Women, and Historical Practice* (Cambridge, MA and London: Harvard University Press, 1998), p. 151.

60 Ibid., pp. 151–2.

61 Gordon Oakes, Parliamentary Debates, Commons, 29 April 1991, cols 129–30.

62 For an example of the latter see Arthur Bryant's Greenwich Naval Pageant, papers available in Liddell Hart Centre for Military Archives, Kings College London, Arthur Bryant Papers, J/6 (1–3); also Arthur Bryant, *A History of Britain and the British People, Vol. 2, Freedom's Own Island: The British Oceanic Expansion* (London: Grafton Books, 1987). Julia Stapleton's *Sir Arthur Bryant and National Life in Twentieth-Century Britain* (Oxford: Lexington Books, 2005) is an excellent guide to this idiosyncratic figure.

63 *Western Luminary*, 23 January 1837, 2. Quoted in James Vernon, *Politics and the People: A Study in English Political Culture, c.1815–1867* (Cambridge: Cambridge University Press, 1993), p. 298.

64 'Charter 88', *New Statesman and Society*, 2 December 1988, p. 10.

65 Parliamentary Debates, Commons, 1987–88, vol. 136, 7 July 1988, col. 1233.

66 Ibid.

67 J.C. Davis, *Fear, Myth and History: The Ranters and the Historians* (Cambridge: Cambridge University Press, 1986), p. 130.

68 See for instance Tristram Hunt, 'A jewel of democracy', *Guardian*, 26 October 2007.

69 Quoted on: www.levellers.org.uk/levellersdayhistory.htm. Accessed 22.05.2008.

70 Thomas Hobbes, *Leviathan*, ed. Richard Tuck (Cambridge: Cambridge University Press, 1996, pp. 225–6.

71 Parliamentary Debates, Commons, 23 November 1988, col. 158.

72 http://blogs.telegraph.co.uk/daniel_hannan/blog/2007/06/11/picking_sides. Accessed 15.04.2009.

73 Griffiths, 'Remembering Tolpuddle', 146.

74 Levellers' Day, Burford, 17 May 2008. Personal recording.

75 Ibid.

76 www.levellers.org.uk/levellersdayhistory.htm. Accessed 22.05.2008.

77 It does not even dwell on the implications of the fact that in 1979 no one in the parish objected to the WEA fixing a plaque commemorating the Levellers to the wall of Burford Church.

78 Parliamentary Debates, Commons, 28 June 2001, cols 867–8.

79 John Vincent, *The Seven Voices of Conservatism*, CPC pamphlet no. 0510/821 (London: Conservative Political Centre, February 1991), p. 14.

80 Aneurin Bevan, *In Place of Fear* (London, Melbourne and New York: Quartet Books, 1998 [1952]), p. 26.
81 Interview with Greg Rosen, Director, Labour History Group, London, 9 June 2008.
82 www.labourhistory.org.uk. Accessed 06.05. 2009.
83 See Mark Bevir, *New Labour: A Critique* (Abingdon and New York: Routledge, 2005).
84 For a more detailed discussion of the Festival of Labour and its relationship to Labour's programme of modernisation, see Black, *Redefining British Politics*, pp. 143–4, 198–201.
85 London Metropolitan Archives, London Labour Party papers (hereafter LLP), ACC 2417/G/98, Circular, 'Festival of Labour – June', 1962.
86 LLP, ACC 2417/G/97, letter from A.L. Williams to Affiliated TUs and Socialist Societies advertising 'Brighter Party Premises Competition', 4 November 1962; ACC 2417/G/99, May 1962 'Festival Fanfare!'. Original emphasis.
87 LLP, ACC 2417/G/117, Festival of Labour Programme, p. 19.
88 LLP, ACC 2417/G/105, Brochure: 'Welcome to Labour London from the London Labour Party'.
89 Hall, *The Hard Road to Renewal*, p. 2.
90 Drucker, *Doctrine and Ethos*, p. 35.

2
Structures of memory: parties and their pasts

This chapter examines the ways in which parties explicitly attempt to structure and preserve memory, through written histories, commemorations, party history groups and archives. One of the most striking aspects is the degree of similarity between the three principal parties on this point. Whilst there are differences of detail, of emphasis and of ideology, the overall picture is surprisingly homogenous. This could be viewed as a consequence of the increasing professionalisation of the political parties, which – as noted in Chapter 1 – tends to bring them together under a shared parliamentary narrative. Indeed, it is significant that the widest divergence between the mnemonic cultures of the parties occurs at local level. Moreover, memory is largely maintained by a small group of interested individuals, rather than by the parties on an institutional level.

By looking at the structures, or technologies, of memory, this chapter examines how ideological approaches to the past, explored in the previous chapter, are instituted within the parties in practice. One of the main themes here is the relation of 'history' and 'memory'. Perhaps the best-known consideration of this question is that of the historian Pierre Nora in his seven-volume exploration of the 'sites of memory' of the French state, nation and Republic. For Nora, history was memory's pale replacement. He described how *'lieux de mémoire* exist because there are no longer any *milieux de mémoire*, settings in which memory is a real part of everyday experience'.[1] Instead, he argued, living memory had been replaced by 'historicised memory', that is memory which has ceased to function naturally and has instead become a form of 'prosthetic memory'.

Nora identified three key characteristics of 'historicised memory'. First, the modern 'obsession with the archive ... in which we attempt to preserve not only all the past but all the present as well'.[2] Second, the desire to research the pasts of various groups to which we belong, from professions to ethnicities. Nora links such practices to the rise in interest in individual psychology, which he believes coincided with the decline of memory as a 'social practice'.[3] And third, 'alienated memory'. Historical knowledge has the effect of distancing us from the past – it creates a sense of discontinuity rather than reinforcing the links between past and present. This seems to be closely related to Svetlana Boym's description of reflective nostalgia, discussed in Chapter 1. Nora's category is similarly reflective and similarly characterised by an awareness of absence: 'The whole dynamic of our relationship to the past is shaped by the subtle interplay between the inaccessible and the nonexistent. If the old ideal was to resurrect the past, the new ideal is to create a representation of it.'[4]

Mainstream political parties provide a particularly interesting case study in terms of historicised memory. First, we might expect that because parties exist to fulfil a definite purpose and perpetuate habits and traditions as a matter of necessity rather than through a self-aware desire to connect with the past, memory is more likely to be 'living' rather than historicised. Second, parties are (often painfully) aware of their role in 'history' and thus have a particular interest in shaping the conditions by which written history can be created. Third, they occupy a curious position between official, top-down memory and bottom-up or 'community' memory.[5] While political actors are 'elite' voices and certainly well represented within the national archive, they are there as individuals leaving their papers to university collections and as actors in the official records of Whitehall and Westminster. Records of the parties as political institutions have only been developed relatively recently and it is significant that the first official party political archives were the Labour and Communist parties, rather than the more established, 'elite' Liberal and Conservative parties. This grew out of the bottom-up desire to document working-class and labour history, beginning in the early twentieth century with the Plebs' League and the *Book of Labour* and really taking off in the 1960s and 1970s with History Workshop, the Working Class Movement Library and the *Dictionary of Labour Biography*. The Conservative and Liberal party archives may not be part of the cultural democratisation of archives themselves, but they could be seen to have grown out of a growing awareness of the importance of archives, which that movement has created. The difference of course is that they (and the Labour Party archive now) are kept 'for the nation' rather than as a particular form of identity affirmation. These are not 'community archives' of memories and memorabilia; they are repositories of formal documents: minutes, letters, reports.

Party archives

Each of the parties has its own archive. The Labour Party's forms the core of the Labour History Archive and Study Centre (LHASC), attached to the People's History Museum (formerly the National Museum of Labour History) in Manchester. In January 1994 the Museum also acquired the papers of the disbanded Communist Party of Great Britain, which had previously been held at the Communist Party Library in Hackney. These are now also part of the LHASC as are, for instance, the papers of Militant, the Unity Theatre and Socialist Sunday Schools. Until 1988 the Labour Party archive was part of the central organisation of the party, held at its head-quarters and managed by a salaried member of staff. However, conditions in the basement storage area had become cramped and were restricting the ability of the archivist to collect further materials. The chance to move to a purpose-built archive centre, which could become the focal point of labour history more widely was gratefully seized.[6]

It is significant that neither the Labour Party nor the Communist Party archives were housed in university libraries, although discussions did take place with the LSE. They were deliberately kept as specialist collections, rather than subsumed into larger national collections; they were also initially intended primarily for the use of party members rather than the wider public or academic researchers.[7] The Labour Party archive initially had an entrance fee of £1 for non-party members; the Communist Party archive was never intended to be open to anyone beyond the party. In contrast, the former Secretary of the Conservative Archive Trust, Sheridan Westlake, is very proud that the Conservative Party archive is at the Bodleian Library with the status that brings with it. In an interview, he emphasised that this was a collection of national importance and 'the biggest and the best political archive, in terms of size, in terms of budgets, in terms of full-time staff devoted to it and as reflected as well by its location in the Bodleian'.[8]

The Conservative Party archive was only assembled as a single body in 1978, under the influence of historian Lord Blake. Previously the papers had been scattered among a range of institutions, including Conservative Central Office and Newcastle University

Library. It is unclear why the decision was made to establish a complete archive at this time, except a general sense that 'the collection was too fragmented and no one was in charge of it.'[9] The aim was 'to consolidate [the records] and get them catalogued ... to bring it all together in one place and make them available to people'.[10] The Bodleian was chosen partly because of Blake's personal connections as Provost of The Queen's College but also because 'there was a recognition that it was a collection of national interest, it wasn't just of local interest to the party ... there doesn't seem to have been any doubt that it should go to an academic library'.[11] The collection is managed by the Conservative Party Archive Trust, which became independent from the party in 1998, following the Political Parties, Elections and Referendums Act. It maintains strong links with the party through its Secretary, who is a senior member of party staff as well as the day-to-day contact with the archive.

The Liberal Democrats are a particularly interesting case in terms of the production and preservation of memory as they were formed through a merger of two parties. Each of the parties coming into the merger had its own historical narrative, institutional structure and political heritage. The Liberal Party, a shadow of its former self, had a stake in reiterating its achievements of the nineteenth and early twentieth centuries. The Social Democratic Party, in contrast, was just seven years old, but its founder members were renegades from the Labour Party and saw themselves as the heirs to Attlee and Gaitskell, rather than to Asquith and Lloyd George. This complicated situation is explored in more depth in Chapter 4, but it clearly has important implications for the structures of memory examined here. The Liberal Democrats are formed of two mnemonic communities, two historic traditions.

The Liberal Party archive was established at the London School of Economics (LSE), following the discovery of a great many records in a disused room at the National Liberal Club around the time of the 1987 election (shortly before the merger), when space was being cleared. They went to the LSE and were supplemented with further material from the party's headquarters in Cowley Street.[12] The LSE is also the official depository for material produced by the Liberal Democrat Party since 1989, although, as we will see below, deposits are infrequent and limited.

The papers of the SDP, produced during its brief life from 1981 to 1989, are housed at the Albert Sloman Library at the University of Essex. The driving force behind the acquisition of the papers was Professor Anthony King who was preparing to write a large study of the SDP with Professor Ivor Crewe, his colleague at Essex. He 'indicated to the librarian in 1987 that the SDP might be looking for a home for their archives' and, following a speculative letter from the librarian to the party's headquarters, the transfer of 'three vanloads' of material was arranged in the late spring or summer of 1988.[13] A number of further small accessions were made up until 1990 and the library has also acquired the papers of a number of individuals associated with the SDP, including Bill Rodgers and Alec McGivan, its National Organiser.

Nigel Cochrane, who manages the collection, was not at the library at this time but thought that from looking at the transfer papers, 'it appeared that the SDP were anxious to get their papers off the premises at Cowley Street as quickly as possible'. In particular, he highlighted that 'the papers were actually here in the library, in the university before ... there was a formal agreement in place. It seemed important for them to be moved quickly.' It is, however, unclear whether this was due to political reasons or more prosaic considerations such as 'boxes piling up on the floor – space ... having to clear an office'.[14] There does not seem to have been any feeling from either side that it would be appropriate to house the papers of the Liberal Party and the SDP together. In contrast to much of the political rhetoric of the time, examined in Chapter 4, the two histories were not presented as the path to a shared present and future when it came to establishing the archives.

The archivists' main concern is with the researcher; they intend to preserve records of the past and present to enable their study in the present and future. The motivations of depositors – whether organisations or individuals – are somewhat more obscure. Reasons include a general sense that 'what they were involved with was important' and that records of it should be retained,[15] a desire 'to preserve their own record, to show what they've achieved'[16] and the intention to ensure a particular perspective is 'represented in the history of the party'.[17] In this way, archives could be seen as attempts to speak directly to history. However, politicians 'can be quite selective about what they actually give' to the archive.[18] This is where history collides with myth – myths are not necessarily untrue, but they can involve a certain shaping of the evidence, a certain moulding to fit an agreeable narrative arc. As Raphael Samuel and Paul Thompson put it, 'Many, maybe most, of the facts will be true. It is the omissions and the shaping which make these stories also myth.'[19] There are occasionally significant gaps in archives. The papers relating to Margaret Thatcher's period as Secretary of State for Education when she was required to implement the previous Labour government's policy of closing down grammar schools at the same time as she was actively campaigning for their retention is one example. The 'fragmentary' nature of Industrial Department papers of the Communist Party of Great Britain in the sixties, seventies and eighties is another. As Kevin Morgan noted in his introduction to the online collection, 'it is clear that they had also learnt the necessity of discretion in the compiling of written records of discussions of any sensitivity'.[20]

However, these are fairly limited examples and the evidence suggests that for the most part, political parties are not doing anything as active as attempting to mould history. That might be the concern of individual politicians, concerned for their own reputation, but the parties as a whole seem to be largely unconcerned with the preservation of their documents. Stephen Bird, former archivist at the Labour History Archive and Study Centre (LHASC), emphasised the extent to which the Labour Party was focused on the present, on the need to win elections, run councils and act as Government or Opposition. He contrasted this with the more 'historically-inclined' Communist Party, who did not have such practical concerns.[21] Helen Roberts, then LHASC archivist, explained that the relationship between the Labour Party and its archive had deteriorated in recent years. The archive no longer has a 'direct obvious channel or link within the party'; instead they have to make contact individually with the ever-changing staff in a number of departments 'and try and get archive material out of them'.[22] Similarly, the Liberal and Liberal Democrat archivist, Sue Donnelly, explained that the archive has 'received absolutely nothing' from the Liberal Democrats 'since they were formed', with the single exception of papers from the Policy Unit. The reason for this one exception is that a transfer system was set up by Duncan Brack, editor of the *Journal of Liberal History*, when he was also Director of Policy. Without this initial contact, it is possible that no papers would have been transferred at all.[23]

The Conservative Party does maintain a more active link with its archive and ensures that a senior member of staff is responsible for transferring documents – when the research for this text was carried it out, this was the Deputy Director of the Research Department, Sheridan Westlake, and is now Adrian Harris, manager of the party's online communications. But even Westlake admitted that it was an uphill struggle to obtain documents from members of staff who are concerned about the present and future far more than about the past. When asked if he felt his selections were moulding the archive he replied, 'that's not the issue. It's quite rare that I decide not to transfer something across'; the real issue was 'how do I get hold of some of the stuff?' He was very aware that 'we're not transferring enough across'.[24] Across all the parties, this was seen to be an occupational hazard of party politics, with its forward-looking focus.

This lack of interest in the past for its own sake reinforces the impression of the presentist inclination of practical party politics. It could also be seen as the desire to 'do without archives', described by Achille Mbembe as a 'denial of debt'.[25] This judgement appears time and again in formal and informal conversations about the Labour Party's attitude to its history. There is a clear feeling that New Labour denied its debt, that it refused the obligations which might previously have been seen as an intrinsic part of Labour leadership. As noted in Chapter 1, Labour's past has become heritage, of interest to historians and useful for reinforcing identity when necessary but no longer an active presence. Neither is this attitude restricted to New Labour: all of the archivists feel that the parties 'are not always that actively interested in the history ... and in fact a lot of the time they want to distance themselves from the past', in the interests of the political present.[26]

Labour is, however, unusual in that its disregard for the past seems to be a fairly new phenomenon. It had 'always been an archival party', founded by resolution and structured around minutes, motions and memoranda. Much of this is to do with the way in which 'it was established by the grassroots ... [not] by a group of people in Parliament, so everything is done by the book'.[27] This is not archival in the sense of historicised memory – it is a world of working, breathing documents. Some of these documents are of course archived; for example, the LHASC holds all the minutes of the National Executive Committee (NEC) from its formation. But they are not created with history in mind; they are an ongoing record which the party generates as it works. Yet these records are no longer preserved in the quantities they once were. It is clear that the party is becoming less bureaucratic as it becomes more centralised; it no longer depends on policy resolutions passed up from the grassroots and debated at Conference. Indeed even the NEC no longer plays the role it once did. After describing how the NEC minutes grew in size over the decades, former archivist Stephen Bird observed that now 'they're getting smaller and smaller and smaller' because 'the policy making's done elsewhere'. He added a note of reflection: 'so how the Labour Party's going to operate in the future and where the records are going to come from, I don't know'.[28] Bird's linking of the operation of the party with its production of records is telling but no longer seems to reflect the way the party works.

Despite having much longer histories than Labour, both the Conservative and Liberal Party archives are primarily focused on the post-1945 period. While the Conservative archive is far more complete, due to the way papers were stored at Central Office, in both cases this is down to internal organisation. Although Conservative Central Office was founded in 1870, the earliest CCO document in the archive dates from 1911. The party's archivist, Jeremy McIlwaine, attributes this to the fact that 1911 was the year when the first Party Chairman was appointed. He also hinted that the party's attitude to the past has not always been as reverent as modern sensibilities expect. In particular, 'during the war there were some recycling drives' and 'the attitude of the party towards old papers' seems to have been along the lines of 'we can chuck this out, get it recycled for the war effort'. Therefore, he concluded, 'a lot of the pre-war papers went for recycling'. He attributed this attitude to the fact that 'it's primarily a political archive'.[29] While the Conservative Party archives 'are working documents' they are not 'consulted as much as they probably should be'; consultation of the documents by party workers is 'rare' and McIlwaine could only think of one example when somebody from the party had come to carry out archival research in order to learn from previous policy work done within the party. While McIlwaine regretted this neglect of the archive in contemporary Conservative politics, Sheridan Westlake, the party man, seemed less concerned. Apart from a concession to the view that 'those who forget history are condemned to repeat it', his main interest was that documents should be preserved and made available to historians and that the Archive Trust should take a role in 'promoting the study of Conservative history' within wider society.[30]

If a neglect of archives is a feature of national politics, it is even more pronounced at local level. As Jeremy McIlwaine put it:

> I think the thing is with the party and particularly constituency associations, they're volunteers, they're party activists, their primary motivation is politics, not history and so if they've got minute books back to 1885 it's not interesting to them, it's interesting to me but it's not interesting to them.[31]

Stephen Bird explained how, as Labour Party archivist, he had encouraged Constituency Labour Parties (CLPs) to preserve their own material and deposit it at their local records offices. However, this does not seem to have been a particular success. Indeed, the historian and Battersea Constituency Labour Party member, Penelope Corfield, commented that 'there's never any advice or comments about what to do with our minutes [or] our memorabilia'. She felt that the official attitude in relation to the preservation of records was 'pretty casual', and attributed it (like Stephen Bird) to the fact that the Labour Party is 'an organisation on the move, not institutionalised in quite that way'. As a historian, she admitted feeling 'a certain amount of anguish' at disposing of material and explained that, following the research for their centenary celebrations, members of the CLP were hoping to put together their own local archive, with the aim of encouraging others to research the party.[32]

Where local party activists have undertaken history activities, these often have the specific aim of recovering and/or preserving both documents and first-hand testimonies before it is too late. The author of one of the rare histories written by a Conservative Association,[33] explained that this work was undertaken to mark the rather unusual milestone of ninety-two years in the life of the organisation because 'Many of the records of the growth of the Association have already been lost or destroyed. It was felt that a summary of those that survive should be made before they too get lost or destroyed.'[34] Writers of party histories of all political persuasions commonly complain about the dearth of source material and the carelessness with which what does remain has been treated. These comments are typical:

> I found it almost impossible to find any relevant photos or election leaflets to reproduce here. Even the party faithful seemed to have the unfortunate habit of throwing out what are really priceless records of the past.[35]

> When the study began it soon became evident that the local libraries and County Archives Office were almost totally devoid of documentary material much of which must be lying stored in people's attics, or long since destroyed.[36]

John Saville made a similar plea in his introduction to the first volume of the *Dictionary of Labour Biography*, noting that he and his co-author, Joyce Bellamy, had been constantly surprised by 'how quickly quite prominent personalities can fall into obscurity'. They hoped, he said, 'in the years ahead to persuade as many of the living as possible to set down at least some of the basic facts of their lives' as 'The most grievous problem for all who work in this field is the continuous loss of original records' due to 'thoughtless destruction'.[37]

Research as memory

The interview with Penelope Corfield took in the context of a DVD history project she had co-ordinated to mark the centenary of Battersea Labour Party in 2008. This was a serious and professional undertaking, involving the skills of Corfield as researcher and script-writer, actors Prunella Scales and Timothy West as voiceover artists and many other members of the constituency in providing materials and memories, contributing to the research and adding their voices to the narration. The DVD project grew out of Battersea CLP's response to the national Labour Party's centenary celebrations of 2006. It is striking that both the Battersea and the national centenary celebrations revolved around historical research projects. Each was seen not only as an opportunity to learn more about the party's past but also to pass on that learning – and the historical sources which document it – to imagined researchers of the future. As Corfield noted, 'we have achieved something that's permanently on the record, as well as stimulating comrades to criticism'.[38]

Dianne Hayter initiated the Labour Party's 2006 celebrations through a 'sense of injustice' that the 2000 centenary of the Labour Representation Committee's foundation in 1900 had passed with very little activity within the party as a whole. It is striking that she framed this in terms of an obligation to the future as well as (or perhaps even more than) to the past: 'it was because I felt that the Labour Party hadn't done anything to lay down any future in 2000, they hadn't done any original research; they hadn't made anything of it'.[39] Much of Labour's 2006 centenary celebration focused on encouraging CLPs and trade unions to undertake their own events and research to mark the occasion. They managed to generate interest in the party's past and this served as a focus for demonstrating continuity and solidarity. They did not however, leave 'a lasting impression' on the party. The aspect of ongoing historical political education which Hayter had advocated 'soon became just a means of promoting best practice in electioneering'.[40] This is a clear case of the 'presentist' mindset.

The importance of academic history and archive materials are key here. Similarly, Hayter's decision to write her history of Labour's right wing in the 1970s and 1980s was partly inspired by a need to preserve the story before it disappeared. She said, 'I was really worried that people were dying or they were retiring, going to smaller houses and clearing out their attics. So to begin with, I just wanted to stop things being thrown away.'[41] The other motivating factor was a desire to correct the mythology which was being constructed around the birth of New Labour. This is discussed further in Chapter 4, but was compounded by the knowledge that if the story was not set straight now, while the documents and witnesses were still accessible, perhaps it never would be: the historical record would be fixed. It is telling that Dianne Hayter wrote *Fightback!* as a PhD thesis. Though she 'never thought of [her]self as an historian at all, at all, at all' and still doesn't think of herself as being 'an historian in the sense of really knowing history', she felt it was necessary to become one, 'otherwise it would have been Dianne's take on it'. In order for her book to have the authority to challenge the prevailing wisdom, she felt it needed to have an academic weight, to be 'respected' and seen as 'objective'. She also wanted to learn how to handle the source materials she was now collecting. Similarly, Penelope Corfield repeatedly emphasised her role 'as a professional historian' in scripting the Battersea centenary DVD and the faith that the other party members had placed in her 'professional expertise as a researcher'.[42]

The faith placed here in history (perhaps with a capital H) over political narrative and memory is important to our story. Hayter noted that 'had I just written it from memory it would have been so wrong'. Her research revealed the flaws in her own memory, both in comparison with the stories she gained from oral history interviews ('There was a lot I just hadn't understood. But a lot I had just misremembered.') and in terms of the rigour demanded by her supervisor ('I couldn't write "We met on a dark day" without "Was it dark? What time did the sun go down that day?" Everything had to be proved, sourced and footnoted.'). Hayter's experience in compiling *Fightback!* convinced her of the importance of saving immediate, accurate records. She now writes 'incredibly detailed notes' at NEC meetings which she regularly sends to the Labour Party archive in Manchester, with the thought that 'sometime in the future when they're opened there will be a very good verbatim report'.[43]

Ilaria Favretto has described the British parties' archives as 'an exemplary' case, in comparison with those of other countries. She particularly singles out the Labour and Conservative parties and attributes the quality of their records to the British electoral system which has discouraged party schism and encouraged parties with enough resources to care for their records. The relative scarcity of

Liberal records is therefore attributed to its more turbulent history and small size in the mid-twentieth century.[44] While there is clearly a great deal of truth in this, it fails to take account of the curious position of the Labour Party's papers, which were collected from almost the beginning of its history and carefully preserved for the future. As Favretto herself notes, Morgan Phillips, General Secretary from 1945, had a long-standing desire to found a museum and archive for the collection.[45] A three-volume history of the Labour Party, *The Book of Labour*, was written as early as 1925, on the grounds that 'The history of the Labour Movement, as the story of the workers' achievement in establishing their political and industrial organisation for the pursuit of a policy they have defined for themselves, has yet to be told in a complete and comprehensive narrative ... The want of such a work has been increasingly felt.'[46] In his introductory section, Arthur Henderson put it in these terms:

> The Labour Party is still in the making, and its history has yet to be written. Nevertheless, it is surprising that a complete, detailed, and authoritative account of its origin, its developing organisation, and its broad general aims has not been penned. Perhaps it is that most contemporaries of this already formidable and still expanding movement are only now beginning to realise the enormous importance and the permanence of the Labour Party as a vital force in our national and international life. The historian only deals in retrospect; he treats of the accomplished, seeking to record the facts and to interpret their meaning accurately for succeeding generations. The writing of history does not coincide with its making. The building up of the Labour Party belongs to history in the making that remains still to be dealt with by the historian.[47]

The Labour Party's early formation of its archive and reverence for the written record was associated with its working-class autodidact culture. It was also an awareness of the needs of this projected future historian which inspired Communist Party activists Ruth and Eddie Frow to scour the country, collecting the thousands of texts relating to the history of the labour movement and working-class radicalism which make up the Working Class Movement Library:

> We know that eventually there will be a change in our social system; that the country will by governed by those who produce the wealth; that there will be a need and a longing to know what preceded these changes. Recognising this we set out to gather a library of books and ephemera relating to the labour movement in its broadest aspects.[48]

The Frows' dedication to the creation of a labour movement archive was not a question of resources; it was a political, ideological task, an attempt to carve out a niche of history and make a mark on the memorial landscape of the country. The decline of this culture in recent decades could then be taken as a reflection on the labour movement's growing self-confidence as an object of historical study and, in the case of the Labour Party, the sense that it was functioning as a potential party of government, guaranteed a place in history by the power of its actions, not the richness of its archive. The opposite dynamic can perhaps be seen in the modern Conservative Party. McIlwaine noted that the party has recently become 'a little more interested in its archives' and is showing an interest in 'ensuring that records survive in the archive for their own sake'. He attributed this partly to a generally 'more optimistic outlook' but also to the party's 'increased reverence for its past history now that it is in government again'.[49] For a party which has suffered a severe loss of confidence in its status as a national party, as examined in Chapter 3, this could be seen as recognition that their activities are, once again, clearly of national importance and as such should be documented.

The Frows' work also contributed to a change in the form of labour history, from the *Book of Labour*'s focus on the Labour Party and its leading figures to labour movement history, rooted in the wider academic turn towards 'history from below'. The Society for the Study of Labour History was founded in 1960, as 'a critical response to top-down tendencies' in labour history. The new society aimed to correct this bias by 'recuperating the rank and file, their aspirations and activities, the texture of their lives and the content of their culture'.[50] Other groups soon followed. The North West Labour History Group, for instance, was established in 1973 to bring together 'those interested in the history of the working class and its organisations, unions, co-operative societies or political bodies'.[51] Articles in its regular journal tend to focus on social and economic themes; typical titles include 'An End to Sweating? Liverpool's Sweated Workers and Legislation 1870–1914', 'Liverpool's Women Dockers' and 'Labour Migration, Racial Foundation and Class Identity: Some Reflections on the British Case'.[52]

Labour Heritage is quite similar in its focus. Although it explicitly 'promotes the history of the Labour Party'[53] its primary focus is clearly local labour movement history, which broadens out into working-class, women's and radical history more easily than it reaches upwards to Parliamentary Labour Party history. Typical articles in the *Labour Heritage Bulletin* include an oral history of residents of two housing estates built for employees of the Great Western Railway and 'A worm's eye view of the General Strike'.[54] Labour Heritage provides a useful perspective on the relationship between labour history and Labour politics. Reports of Labour Heritage meetings reflect a great deal of unease about the New Labour project and particularly its distance from the movement's history. For instance, at the West London History Day in 2006, John McDonnell MP reportedly complained that 'too little had been done to celebrate Labour's centenary and this was because New Labour did not want to acknowledge the history of the Labour Party'. He felt that 'New Labour was not part of the Labour tradition and Labour's aims to redistribute wealth and power to working people and their families had been abandoned.'[55]

In an interview, the group's Treasurer, John Grigg, explicitly connected knowledge of Labour Party history to ideology, commenting that the tendency of the membership to elect left-wing candidates to the constituency section of the National Executive Committee indicated 'that the membership still knows the history and where the party should be. Sadly it's the leadership that have detached themselves from that.' However, when asked whether there was a link between his historical and political activities, Grigg said that the two were rather separate, with the history being just 'an interest'. In his words, 'People don't vote Labour because they know about the 1993 strike at the Firestones Tyre factory in Brentford. Living standards, and how events are shown in the media, determine today's voting habits. Even cracked paving stones are more influential than history in local elections.'[56] Grigg clearly feels that his interest in local labour (and Labour) history is rather marginal to the party and perhaps somewhat unfashionable. During our interview, he commented several times on the group's lack of expertise with modern technology and joked that they were 'old Labour' in terms of both age range and political orientation. Perhaps significantly, Labour Heritage has more of a link with the Socialist History Society, which came out of the Our History group within the CPGB, than with the parliamentary-focused Labour History Group established in 2002. This does not seem to be due to any deliberate decision; Grigg mentioned that he had tried to set up a network of all the labour history groups but that 'didn't really get off the ground'.

Party history groups

The Labour History Group, like its Conservative counterpart, is closely modelled on the Liberal Democrat History Group, something which not only aids close comparison but which also indicates in itself a convergence between the parties in their treatment of their pasts. All three are organised by volunteers outside of the official party structures, but are closely connected to the parties. They combine written history, memory and commemoration and bring together professional historians, key actors from the parties' pasts and party activists with an interest in history. Each has its own journal, in which articles from professional and amateur researchers are printed alongside reminiscences from political actors. They also hold meetings at which the views of historians are reinforced or challenged by first-hand recollection. Each of the groups was formed in response to a perceived lack – a sense that the parties' pasts were not being remembered as much as they should be and that consequently the lessons of the past were not being learned. In the case of Labour, this was a desire to challenge the labour movement focus of groups like Labour Heritage and to assert a far more institutional sense of Labour as a successful parliamentary party.

While this does not require the painstaking social history research of Saville's *Dictionary of Labour Biography* or the other labour history societies, Greg Rosen, chair of the Labour History Group, is still concerned with the role of historical research. He sees the role of the history group as bringing authenticated 'history' to party members who would otherwise be 'happy to wallow in the myths'. Rosen is explicit about the Labour History Group's role in 'bursting the balloons' of myth. Again, this is strongly connected to archival research and returning to the original texts:

> How many people can spend the time to go to the British Library, spend an hour, spend more than an hour finding where something might be, ordering it, waiting for it to come out, tracking through the dog-eared copies of the 1907 Labour Conference transcript? Not many. And why should they have to? So one of the things we've tried to do with the Labour History stuff is to make, it's a sort of people's history, to make it more accessible, to make history easier, not in any dumbing down way but literally just making it easier to get to and giving people those opportunities, which not all take up but some do.[57]

The editor of the *Journal of Liberal History*, Duncan Brack, is somewhat more optimistic, finding himself 'pleasantly surprised by how much [Liberal Democrat History Group members] seem to know about the history'.[58] The Liberal Democrat History Group places more emphasis on its members' own historical research, which Brack describes as 'contributing to ... real ... academic thought'. This was a deliberate strategy aimed to counter a perceived lack of interest in the party among academics in the 1980s and 1990s when 'hardly anyone was writing papers about the party, it was all about the Conservatives or Labour'.[59]

There is a strong pedagogic element to the party history groups and Rosen places a particular emphasis on the need to provide 'a forum where younger politicians and activists (who in some cases will be in the position to repeat the mistakes of the past) can learn from history'.[60] The directors of all three of the history groups express a desire 'to learn the lessons of history';[61] 'to learn from specific instances in the past'.[62] They have all organised meetings on particular past events with lessons for contemporary politics: in September 2009 the Liberal Democrats explored hung parliaments in the twentieth century, and particularly the problems faced by the Liberals in 1924; the Conservatives have tried to learn the lessons of the 1906 opposition; and in November 2009 the Labour History Group held a meeting to discuss whether 'Labour's history [can] offer a guide to weathering the [current economic and political] storm?'. Duncan Brack and Greg Rosen also emphasised the role of historical knowledge in contemporary political debates, both in terms of demonstrating political legitimacy ('So if we're writing a paper on social justice or equality, we will say, "Look, the Liberal Party has a great record on this."'[63]) and in order to pass on learning from the past ('There's not much point in having fantastic new ideas that aren't actually new ideas, that are just the same ideas as previously but people haven't realised it.'[64]). However, Iain Dale, director of the Conservative History Group, stressed that the pressures of party politics often don't leave room for learning from the past:

> I think politics is so in the moment that you're constantly wrestling with the problems of today and if you have learnt from the past it's fairly sub-conscious and there's nothing I could point to where I think, 'well the Conservative party made the right decision there because they learned from what happened in 1943, or something'. Politics just doesn't work like that.[65]

The Liberal Democrat History Group was also established with another particular role in mind: to assert and celebrate a Liberal identity, which had become marginalised in the mid-twentieth century. Brack described this as 'partly about morale raising' as it shows the 'lonely activist' that they are part of a 'great tradition', that the Liberals 'weren't always the third party, we were in power, we have a great record of really great legislative issues behind us, we can do it again'.[66] The Liberal Democrat History Group also plays a more explicitly bonding role than those of the other parties. It was established soon after the merger between the Liberal Party and the SDP and was partly intended to socialise the SDP members into Liberal traditions and history. Brack remembered thinking 'We have two different traditions trying to come together and we ought to try and encourage an awareness of historical tradition in the activists in the new party and ... don't pretend that everything started in March 1988, it had long historical roots.' This narrative expresses a clear sense that it was the SDP who were joining the Liberal tradition rather than vice versa. Yet, although the Liberal tradition took precedence, Brack also stressed that he was not promoting a rigid interpretation of what that tradition entailed, or what it meant in the present day:

> There was a very solid tradition and, in a sense, I didn't really care what people thought it was but I wanted to give them the forum in which people could help work out for themselves what it was and what they thought the party's traditions were.[67]

Yet this openness to challenge and to suggestions only works if members have their own interpretation of history. Otherwise, the stories the groups choose to tell (and those they don't) help shape the limits of what the party's history and its traditions are. This is perhaps particularly important for new members. The inherent tension of socialising new members into an identity based on tradition and historical lineage can be seen in another of Brack's statements: 'I wanted to ... help people understand where they came from, particularly for new members who might not be aware of the historical roots.'[68] The idea that by becoming Liberal Democrats, former SDP and Labour Party members (and those who were entirely new to party politics) could discover 'where *they* came from' is striking. It speaks volumes about party political identity and the notion of discovering one's true self in the history of the collective.

All of the party history groups stress the importance of witness seminars to their historical understanding, but these are particularly central to the Labour History Group's view of its role. While Brack emphasised the need for 'analysis' alongside the 'anecdote' of the witnesses, Rosen views these seminars as a way of getting to a truth which might otherwise remain obscured. On the one hand, this is a matter of having 'a great opportunity to ask questions of people involved ... was it a mistake? You did this at the time, do you regret it? Or, what are the lessons for now, what happened?'[69] This is an example of 'living history' in a very full sense. First, spectators are treated to 'real, live exhibits' who not only speak *of* the past, they also speak *from* it. This chimes with Mark Salber Philips' observation on the recent turn towards what he terms 'sentimental history' in that it reflects our desire to know not so much 'What happened?' as 'What did it feel like to be there?'.[70]

Secondly, and most importantly, the audience also sees 'History' itself – the work of telling, ordering, understanding and recording the past – in process. A certain narrative is begun, imposed by the title and structure of the event and by its choice of speakers, but it is open to challenge, to revision, from others who were also there or who have evidence to support their view. It may be that no agreement is reached and that dual or multiple narratives are allowed to stand. Or it may be that the process goes further. For example, at the Labour History Group meeting 'Labour and Militant – Twenty Years After Liverpool' (24 June 2003), Charlie Turnock responded to a challenge to his depiction of events from a member of Militant in the audience by producing from his briefcase his own evidence, his notes from the inquiry into Militant – his *archive*. Faced with this, his challenger not only gave way but also apparently revised his own version of events, his own history.[71] For Rosen this is emblematic of the meetings:

> the wonderful thing about Labour History meetings is that people can be enormously frank in the way that is almost a cathartic thing perhaps, people can be almost confessional. It's one of the things that keeps us organising the seminars because, if we we didn't do it, they wouldn't happen and the historical record would be missing out on some potentially quite useful evidence ... on source material.[72]

As the final stage in this process, many of the events themselves are recorded, described, archived. They become 'unique historical records', source material for future generations.[73] It has been said that journalism is the first draft of history; the Labour History Group could be seen as an attempt to write the *final* draft, to get the story straight and iron out any creases. This is history of a type that academia could not hope to recreate; it is produced through the live confrontation of participants, of narratives, of histories. Yet this is also history with the doubt left out, untouched by the uncertainties of academic scholarship. Subjective 'memory work' is used in an attempt to reach a rather empirical idea of 'fact'. Rosen speaks as though by getting the right people in the room it is possible to discover *what really happened*.

The meetings also have a nostalgic function, providing a chance for political activists to relive their pasts together. Other mnemonic communities are solely focused on personal reminiscence. In 1992/3, a group of Conservative Party workers in Finchley established a Friends of Margaret Thatcher group. The purpose of this group was that it 'kept those people that had really been around her together'. It was largely a social grouping, which visited the Thatcher Archive and organised film evenings showing footage of Thatcher speaking at constituency events. It was a place for internal reminiscence and camaraderie rather than for the transmission of memories to those who did not have first-hand contact with Thatcher. After the deaths of several key members, the group ceased meeting.[74]

In the absence of living witnesses, relatives or others with personal connections to the memory can become substitutes. Throughout Battersea Labour Party's centenary celebrations, it was frequently emphasised that one of the current members, Lily Harrison, former Lady Mayor of Battersea, had known Caroline Ganley, MP for Battersea South in 1945–51, who, in turn, had been election agent to Charlotte Despard, a founding member of the party and one of its first group of female candidates. The importance of this direct line of personal (and, crucially, female) continuity was later stressed in interviews:

> I think particularly the feminist thing is important. The Charlotte Despard, Caroline Ganley tradition. It's the fact that we have a member here, Lily Harrison, who knew Caroline Ganley and Caroline Ganley knew Charlotte Despard and that matters to me.[75]

> So, to have this connection, just through three women to one born in 1845, I think that's tremendous.[76]

Local member Joan O'Pray described how the Battersea Party's Women's Section had been strongly influenced by its research into radical women from the past. Yet whilst women such as Aphra Behn were an inspiration, it was Charlotte Despard, with her history in Battersea, who became their figurehead.[77] The legacy of Battersea's Women's Section provides an important reminder that the history of a party cannot be fixed into a single narrative. The campaigns of the 1970s and 1980s, particularly those associated with the Women's Section, did not receive as much attention in the Battersea centenary DVD as members such as O'Pray, Jeanne Rathbone and Anne

Reyersbach might have liked. Moreover, Rathbone expressed disquiet about the focus placed on John Burns; she felt that the reverence given to such 'male working-class heroes' contributed to an overly masculine style of history which 'ignore[d] the fact that women were the first subject class'.[78]

Individual figures

The connection of party memory with identifiable individual figures is clearly important. In 2007 the Liberal Democrat History Group held a 'Greatest Liberal' competition, won by J.S. Mill. By all accounts, this was a crowded and highly entertaining meeting. The other history groups repeated this format in 2008, with Margaret Thatcher and Keir Hardie the respective winners. These events captured the attention of both party activists and the media. Of course the competitive element helped, but the focus on individual figures was also important.

However, individual figures also have a slightly ambiguous position in party memory. In the Labour Party, for instance, we see a clear desire to acknowledge and honour the founders of the party. The 1925 *Book of Labour* noted that 'Personality has counted for so much in the development of the Labour Movement, that thrice the space could have been devoted to biography without doing justice to the men and women who have made the Movement.'[79] It devoted most of its third volume to biographies of leading activists and the 'pioneer' MPs, whom it treated with an almost mystical reverence:

> Nearly all the pioneers have passed on in life's march – men and women who had the faith that will remove mountains. They tilled and harrowed the soil and planted the seed. They sowed that others might reap.[80]

The celebrations for Labour's fiftieth jubilee in 1950 laid great stress on the presence of living witnesses. Advertisements invited members who had been in the party since 1900 to contact the organisers so that they could provide 'testaments' and also be there on the night. Great efforts were made to compile lists of the surviving 'pioneers'.[81] Similarly, the centrepiece of the 2006 centenary of the PLP was a collection of obituaries of the pioneers, written by the Labour MPs then representing their constituencies.[82] This speaks to the themes of place, continuity and personal connection explored elsewhere in this chapter. It also resonates with the idea of individualised memory, evoked by both Pierre Nora and Peter Mandler.

Hayter explained that the personal and geographical link was very important and that some of the MPs had become very enthusiastic and were still carrying out research three years later. Speaking at a conference fringe meeting on the project, Ian McCartney, for instance, seemed moved by the correspondences he discovered between his own life and that of his predecessor, Steven Walsh: both were short, both married women named Ann, both stood as district councillors before becoming MPs and both lost sons in tragic circumstances. He also read the eulogy from Walsh's funeral in order to 'inspire all representatives of the Labour Party to keep on working for a better future for all'.[83]

However, this emphasis on parliamentarians and other national figures, whilst a staple of the Labour History Group, does not sit easily within the social history style of 'labour movement studies'. This tension was acknowledged in the *Book of Labour*, as it noted that 'Both in the Labour Party and in the Trade Unions there are scores of men and women whose personal history is as romantic and whose services to the organised workers are as great as any dealt with within these volumes.'[84] We have already seen the personal pilgrimage undertaken by Eddie and Ruth Frow to assemble their vast Working Class Movement Library. Their desire that no aspect of working-class history should be lost can also be seen in the huge *Dictionary of Labour Biography*, begun by Joyce Bellamy and John Saville in 1972 and now under the editorship of David Howell at the University of York. Saville's introduction to the first volume foresaw the never-ending nature of this work, explaining that 'It was at first intended to produce a single large volume on the lines of *Who's Who*.'[85] However,

> It became clear as work went forward that one or two volumes would be quite insufficient to encompass the many hundreds of names for whom detailed information was being accumulated. The present editors, let it be said at once, see no end to the Dictionary, and if they themselves can count upon something approaching the biblical span of life, they estimate that eight or ten volumes might be produced under their auspices. Even then at least as many again will be needed to clear arrears down to 1914.[86]

In fact, Bellamy and Saville managed ten volumes between 1972 and 1997. Their insistence that the *Dictionary* should 'include not only the national personalities of the British labour movement but also the activists at regional and local level' made it an immense research task, led by the availability of documents.[87]

The Labour History Group has published its own *Dictionary of Labour Biography*, which is modelled more closely on the *Dictionary of Liberal Biography* rather than its Labour predecessor. The editor, Greg Rosen, described how it was partly assembled as an alternative to Bellamy and Saville's works, which were pricy, unwieldy, mostly out of print and difficult for the lay reader to access except through a university library. He wanted it to be an 'accessible' way to find out about key party figures – like Frank Pickstock, Jim Cattermole, Peggy Herbison, Frank Chapple, Jim Mortimer and Dickson Mabon – who might not attract the direct attention of biographers.[88] This is very much a working view of history, which aims to enable party members and students to understand the route by which the party arrived at the present. It is not the labour of love which demands that tribute be paid to 'everyone who made a contribution, however modest, to any organisation or movement' involved with labour history.[89] It is, rather, a guide to Labour's institutional party history, to its key figures and the factions from which they came. As we have seen, this is a very different approach to Labour's history than that taken by Labour Heritage. For instance, the Labour Heritage Women's Research Committee was established to focus on 'rescuing from obscurity the women stalwarts of the past', largely through oral histories and autobiographical writing. The emphasis was very much on lived experience, to the extent that the second issue of its *Bulletin* carried a letter complaining that 'The articles seem more like straightforward reminiscences without any direct link to the Labour Party.'[90] The editor defended the stance of the *Bulletin* on the grounds that 'Until we have a much fuller account of how Labour women have acted, thought and felt', analysis would be 'premature'.[91]

The authors of CLP histories have expressed similar difficulties in representing the lived experience of political activism in the form of a historical narrative. The chronological narrative of key events or the veneration of certain key figures does not seem to be quite adequate. This remark from the then Secretary of Colne Valley CLP eloquently summarises the problem:

> This is but a brief glimpse into the history of the Colne Valley Labour Party – perhaps more of a reference than a history. I say that because the real history, the complete history, can never be written. To do so it would be necessary to involve everyone who had ever played a part; for the story of the Labour Party is the story of its people – their ideals, their struggles and their personal beliefs that society could and should be ordered in a more egalitarian way. Such a task is clearly impossible.[92]

Some books dispense with general histories altogether, preferring to collect the anecdotes and reminiscences of local political activists and councillors. Two with intriguingly military titles are Hugh Jenkins' *Rank and File* which profiles forty members of his Putney constituency and John Cornwell's *Tomb of the Unknown Alderman*, with its amusing tales from Sheffield city councillors.[93] Jenkins declared himself 'relieved' that 'no clear picture' came out of the forty 'deliberately unstructured interviews' as it 'would depress [him] mightily if [he] thought all members of the party came out of the same pod'. Interestingly, he attributed this heterogeneity to political philosophy, declaring that 'I sometimes have this feeling about the Conservative Party – that it is uniform because it is not interested in ideology; but rather in the preservation of class privileges and rights over property.'[94] Whilst this is clearly a partisan point and contradicts the Conservative emphasis on individuals as an alternative to ideology, there is some truth in the idea that a concern with difference, with attempting to record and represent the totality of views and experiences, has been associated with Labour (or rather labour) history. For instance, Penelope Corfield was insistent that the Battersea DVD should not have a single authorial voice and, although she was responsible for the bulk of the research, certain parts were carried out by other members. Similarly, the DVD voiceover was divided between a range of party members, even though the actors Timothy West and Prunella Scales are local members and voiced the core of the narrative. While this made the process more difficult and the plans had to be somewhat scaled back, Corfield felt that it was important 'to make sure that the story is told by a number of voices ... to show the range of people in the party, the range of accents and tones'.[95] However, this may have been rather more aesthetic than substantive. Another member of Battersea CLP pointed out that the range of voices was only apparent in a literal sense – the perspective was all Corfield's.[96]

It is worth considering the extent to which a focus on individuals – whether famous or unknown – is *easier* than outlining philosophical positions and less contentious than naming factions. Conservative claims to the *entire* national past are made considerably easier by the way in which they revel in the contradictions of the legacies of a diverse range of Great Individuals, rather than adhering to a single philosophy or – worse – ideology. In a speech to the Centre for Policy Studies, Paul Johnson argued that Conservative leadership 'is not shaped primarily by ideas and certainly not by any one stream of ideas'. Instead, he cited the importance of attitudes, personal predilections and events.[97] Similarly, John Vincent insisted that

'Conservatism is, always has been, and forever should be, a place where enriching contradictions meet.' He was happy to include Whigs and Liberals in his list of the voices of Conservatism, 'for as a historical Party we know that history cannot be undone, and for two centuries the English inheritance was not expressed through a Tory governing Party. We do not argue with the history of England: instead we absorb our national past.'[98] It is striking that Vincent saw conservatism as so rooted in the national past that it should 'absorb' even those figures, events and philosophies which are antithetical to its basic ideals. If they are part of history, so they are part of conservatism. This recalls Ian Gilmour's description of the party as 'layer upon layer of structure and remains'.[99]

At the other end of the political spectrum, Jon Lawrence has highlighted the extent to which high-political divisions in the Labour Party have come to be associated with individuals (Bevan and Gaitskell; Castle, Wilson and Callaghan). He sees this as a deliberate strategy on the part of Labour's leaders to transcend the 'high-politics' narrative of 'internecine struggles' and 'to imbue their accounts of complex disagreements over policy and ideology at Westminster with a bold mythic quality' which will resonate with party activists. Thus 'Labour's myths of division have, for the most part, been intensely personal affairs.'[100]

Individuals can become a shorthand for their ideological and institutional positions. But, crucially, they are also more malleable. In his biography of Nye Bevan, John Campbell provides a compelling account of the hollowing-out of one of these iconic figures in an attempt to claim and to celebrate his legacy, whilst stripping it of everything that made it his: 'His memory was in fact adopted as a sort of mascot to disguise the abandonment, by professed left-wingers, of practically everything he had meant by socialism.'[101] The extent to which Bevan had become a cipher for the full range of Labour positions is well demonstrated by a series of letters sent to Michael Foot in November 1981 following his condemnation of Tony Benn's pronouncements on the nationalisation of North Sea Oil. The first extract is from a correspondent urging Foot to take a stand against the right wing of the party; the second wants him to move against the left:

> You know very well that the late Aneuran [sic] Bevan, and Ernie Bevan [sic] would wring their bloody necks!!![102]

> What the electorate expect from you now Mr. Foot is the *exorcism of these revolutionary elements from the Party*. Mr. Aneuran [sic] Bevan *could*

and *would* do it, and so can you, now that you have asserted yourself as Leader! It has been done before![103]

In another interesting example, at the time of the Liberal–SDP Alliance, the name of the Welsh Liberal Weekend School was changed so as to include the SDP members. Perhaps somewhat surprisingly, the name chosen was the Lloyd George Society. It is striking that the naming of a figure from one particular tradition was felt to be more appropriate than something along the lines of 'The Liberal–SDP Alliance Weekend School'. Whilst the title 'Lloyd George Society' might not explicitly exclude SDP members, it is a clear statement of the kind of history and traditions which the group wants to see continued. Yet the use of Lloyd George's name is in some ways less rigid than the specification of 'Liberal' as it allows for the more generally progressive heritage of, for instance, the People's Budget of 1906.

The position of individual figures is as ambiguous for the Liberal tradition as it is within Labour. Sue Donnelly explained that Liberal Democrats 'probably would see something like John Stuart Mill's papers as being more important for them, more iconic than the party papers which they see as being more prosaic, more about accountability, not about image so much'.[104] In his Foreword to the *Dictionary of Liberal Biography*, Ben Pimlott claimed biography as a particularly Liberal form of writing, because 'liberals have always placed particular emphasis on the uniqueness and limitless potential of the individual'. In support of his claim that 'one of the finest traditions in British biographical writing should be associated with liberalism and the Liberal Party', Pimlott cites Morley's *Life of Gladstone*, and Lytton Strachey's *Eminent Victorians* and *Queen Victoria*, which 'revolutionised biography ... by showing how it could be used to explore the human soul in all its complexity'. This tradition was taken forward in Churchill's biographical essays and, most recently, 'the distinguished biographical writings of Roy Jenkins (always a Liberal at heart), which have always used biography as the most sensitive of dialectical tools'.[105]

Pimlott's claiming of biography and its celebration of individuals as particularly Liberal is interesting as it contrasts with the findings of Brack's 1995 survey of leading Liberal Democrats, which found that the most frequent response (15%) to a question about influential political figures was along the lines of 'I don't have heroes' or 'I do not like hero-worship'.[106] In my own survey of Liberal Democrat History Group members, carried out in 2008, thirteen of eighty-five respondents said that they were not inspired by any historical figures (and of those, eight stressed that they didn't think in terms of being inspired by historical figures). To put this in perspective, 'none' was the third most frequent answer, on a par with Churchill but behind Gladstone and Lloyd George, who were named by twenty-six and twenty respondents, respectively. This was, however, an open-ended question and in total, ninety separate names were mentioned.[107]

There is, as yet, no dictionary of Conservative biography but this does not seem to be through a lack of interest in individual figures. Conservative Party archivist, Jeremy McIlwaine, explained that to party members, papers relating to Thatcher, Churchill and possibly Enoch Powell ('it depends on who you talk to') were the big attractions of their archive. He had been consistently 'amazed at the effect Thatcher has', citing conference visitors' eagerness to buy signed reproductions of the 1979 'Labour Isn't Working' election poster: 'They'd come along and they'd see this, just they look at it like it's god-like, the deference they still have.' Similarly, one of the big attractions among the archival documents is a 1950 letter written by a Central Office party agent in Dartford constituency praising a speech made by the twenty-three-year-old candidate, Margaret Roberts. In McIlwaine's words: 'That works wonders – show this to the party faithful.'[108] Andrew Riley, senior archivist of the Thatcher papers at the Churchill Archive Centre, has also received visits from party members, including the Friends of Margaret Thatcher group of party workers and activists from her former constituency of Finchley and Friern Barnet (as it was then). He is able to show them numerous personal and political items – including a carefully preserved handbag.[109]

As we saw in Chapter 1, Conservatives have tended to focus on the examples of past leaders in lieu of defining an ideology and the *Conservative History Journal* deals in biography at least as much as the other party history journals. It is, then, tempting to suggest that this is more of a marker of the Conservative Party's disregard for its institutional past. Indeed, it feels significant that in the run-up to the 1997 election defeat, as the party realised it was losing the mantle of the 'national' party, the Conservative Political Centre chose to host a series of lectures on Conservative leaders of the past.[110] This is examined in more depth in Chapter 3.

Performative memory

Place can be a particularly emotive aspect of memory. In the case of political commemoration, the link to place is often about laying claim to the site of remembrance, as much as it is about the experience of retracing steps. For instance, Levellers' Day not only involves reclaiming a part of English history for the left, but it also involves the physical claiming of a village for the day. The resonance of a procession of communist, anarchist and socialist banners through a picturesque village in Conservative-dominated Oxfordshire cannot but be felt.

The constituency basis of UK politics is an important basis for memory. In treading the streets, delivering leaflets and canvassing constituents, party activists are physically walking in the steps of their predecessors. Anne Reyersbach explained that one of the intentions of Battersea CLP's centenary history was that it could be used in campaigning; it would allow the party to demonstrate its long-standing claim to what is now a very marginal seat:

> One of the original ideas of the 2006 [research] was that we'd use it for campaigning ... we'd say to people, 'Look, you live in Sanders Court; you live in Ganley Court. Do you know why they're called that?' ... We were going to try and tell people really about how the Labour Party had made their built environment and sort of explain the place-making, to use the trendy expression, the place-making that Labour had done, I suppose. And really remind them of the legacy, with a view to saying, 'Do you really want the Tories to go on running this place when what we did was so much more important?' ... I think it's about reclaiming local history.[111]

However, Reyersbach felt that, in the end, the project had focused on history for its own sake, rather than as an active tool in the fight to retain Battersea. She therefore had 'huge philosophical difficulties' with it.[112] This is another illustration of the way in which party memory tends towards a rather general sense of heritage rather than an active political relationship with the past.

While Reyersbach felt that political continuity had been sidelined in the Battersea centenary project, some non-party campaigns have emphasised continuity with the past in order to further their campaigns. The 1981 People's March for Jobs consciously drew on the heritage of the Hunger Marches of the 1930s. Similarly, a great deal of the cultural activity surrounding the 1984/5 miners' strike drew on the legacy of earlier strikes. For instance the 7:84 agitprop theatre company staged a 1928 play about the General Strike, advertised with the slogan 'The end of a long miners' strike ... Joe Corrie's play is about 1926 ... it could be about today'.[113] In 1985 Mere Commodity Arts staged a play about the 1942 Betteshanger miners' strike. The company was made up of NUM members, support groups and miners' wives 'with some professional help', the production was sponsored by the Kent Area NUM and profits went to the Sacked and Imprisoned Miners Fund.[114] 'The Coal Board's Butchery', a short film produced by the Miners' Campaign Tape Project during the strike, also paints a picture of continuity with previous strikers.[115]

Other campaigns make a slightly more tenuous use of the past. In 2007, a delegation from Somerset's district councils and trade union UNISON joined up with members of the Sealed Knot Society in seventeenth-century dress to make their case against proposals for Somerset becoming a unitary council. The *West Somerset Post* reported that they were 'light-heartedly invoking the spirit of the "Pitchfork Rebellion" of 1685 ... [which] was, in some senses, the first battle for democratic rights in Somerset'.[116] The use of the term 'light-heartedly' militates against direct comparison between this polite campaign on local government reorganisation and the armed uprising against James II's rule. Another campaign which uses 'heritage' costumes in aid of modern causes is Climate Rush. Members of this group explicitly model themselves on the Suffragettes, dressing in Edwardian costume – complete with 'Deeds not Words' sashes – and organising stunts to coincide with the anniversaries of key actions in the suffrage campaign. Their campaign literature describes super-gluing themselves in a chain 'around the same statue as a Suffragette did 100 years ago, to remind our politicians that they need to drastically cut our CO_2 emissions'.[117] This statement invokes a sense of collective memory 'to remind' politicians to take action on an entirely different matter than that for which the original campaign was undertaken. The campaigners are trying to impose a line of continuity between events which do not straightforwardly connect.

The basic continuity of party political election campaigning is far more clear-cut. The methods, technologies and social context may differ but the essential activities remain very much the same, particularly the highs and lows of polling day.[118] Electioneering is a functional activity rather than a form of mnemonic contemplation; it is a means by which party members 'perform' their duties. Yet it also helps to orient narrative accounts of activism, both in terms of individual life stories and as a cross-generational account of collective identity and group activity. In particular, this can be seen with the

Liberal Democrats' explicit ritualisation of campaigning through songs which preserve and animate stories of significant victories and defeats in the history of the party. The Glee Club, held at the annual federal conference, is an interesting case study of perfomative memory and re-enactment. The songbooks reveal what might be termed a 'bricolage' approach to memory, a self-aware, self-parodying mixture of old and new, serious and silly, relevant and tangential. The 2008 songbook included the theme tune to *Doctor Who* on the grounds that 'Of course, all Liberals are Doctor Who fans; it goes with the territory.'[119] There is a constant renewal – or, rather, a layering – of memory, with songs frequently added and updated. This is a clear example of living memory, firmly tongue-in-cheek, irreverent yet vital.

The experience of singing is important across all three political parties, with 'Jerusalem' as the one constant, able to appeal to patriots, reformers and socialists alike. Singing has been seen by some commentators as an important embodied experience, which does not only reference political ancestors but enables the singers to re-experience the passions of their forbears. In his study of the commemorative activities of a Spanish Civil War veterans' association, Peter Glazer is clear that the performances they put on are not just 'mimetic representations' but instead exert a transformative power over the audience: 'While singing or listening to this march, this martial anthem – a practised rhythmic artefact of bodily cama-raderie and militance – audiences may take in and perform some lingering physical trace of what it meant to go to Spain in the 1930s.'[120] This is reminiscent of Paul Connerton's argument that 'Commemorative ceremonies prove to be commemorative (only) in so far as they are performative' and that 'performative memory is bodily'.[121] Connerton believes that it is through commemorative bodily performances that the narrative of social memory is transmit-ted. This narrative is 'more than a story told – it [is] *a cult enacted*'.[122] Connerton rejects the common view that there is a 'real' meaning behind ritual and stresses instead the intrinsic value of re-enactment 'as a special kind of actualisation' which can cause the reappearance of 'that which has disappeared'.[123]

David I. Kertzer has proposed that collective ritual serves to mask the internal contradictions of ideology: 'Consensus comes through collective action, not only because the different participants have different beliefs, but also because each of the participants has a formless mass of conflicting beliefs.'[124] Crucially, Kertzer believes that 'Solidarity is produced by people acting together, not by people thinking together.'[125] It is clear that political songs can take on radically different meanings, not only for singers/listeners of different political persuasions but also in terms of generation and historical mindset. An interview conducted with Jeanne and Dave Rathbone in Battersea is instructive here. Jeanne had been involved with the centenary celebrations of both 2006 and 2008 and had carried out her own research into local history, particularly the life of Charlotte Despard, with whom she strongly identifies. Jeanne is passionate about political heritage and about the 'resonance' of songs, places and figures across generations. Her husband, Dave, is also a Labour Party activist and core member of the Battersea Labour Party choir, which sings socialist songs at party functions, including the national party's annual conference. However it became clear during the interview that they did not approach the songs in exactly the same way. The first sign of disagreement came when Dave said that the 'March of the Women' (brought up by Jeanne) was 'not really a socialist song' but 'got incorporated' into the repertoire. This upset Jeanne, a committed feminist, who responded that anti-war songs might not be strictly socialist either but 'They're all about ... caring and the movement and our history.' It later transpired that Dave was more concerned with the experience of singing itself, rather than the content of the song, and despite being a humanist sings religious music in a choral society on the grounds that 'you don't have to sign a thing saying that you believe in it to be moved by Mozart's Requiem'. Only when really pressed did Dave admit to any level of connection with the historical element of the songs, and even then somewhat unconvincingly:

> I think it is quite intriguing to go to Conference because it's always been sung there, even though people didn't always know the words of the 'Red Flag' ... Yeah, there is a historical sense of it all running through there, yeah, I agree. I like singing anyway, just go along and have a good sing.

He did not, however, respond to Jeanne's prompting about the joy of 'reclaiming' Holst's music for 'I Vow to Thee My Country' through a new set of lyrics written by Billy Bragg, saying only that it had been good fun singing the song. Dave's perspective reminds us that performative memory is not always what it seems. Great play has been made of the continuance of singing the 'Red Flag' at Labour Party conferences, despite Blair's supposed discomfort.[126] At the 2006 centenary conference Ann Clwyd remarked (perhaps slightly playfully) that the photograph of the PLP in the House of Commons had been a 'very moving occasion for all of us' which had 'ended with everybody – including the Prime Minister – singing the Red Flag!'[127] But it is difficult to penetrate the many layers of meaning which come into play here. For many party members, such as Jeanne Rathbone, the 'Red Flag' remains a powerful statement of political commitment and also carries important historical overtones. Others may take the politics but leave the history, and others still might see it as a playful piece of nostalgia, emptied of real political meaning. Overarching all these different positions remains the simple, emotive aspect of communal singing, a joyful experience through which solidarity can be experienced as an immediate physical sensation (even if that doesn't always translate into an ongoing political commitment).[128]

It is also possible to perform political division. The 2004 *Liberator Songbook* includes a variation of the old parody 'The Pink Flag', with the opening lines 'The people's flag is slightly pink / It's not as red as most folks think / We must not let the people know / What socialists thought long ago.'[129] It also included 'Bandiera Rossa', the original 'Red Flag' and the 'Internationale', all under the heading 'Red Scum Songs' with the comment 'On the principle that even a broken clock is right twice a day, occasionally the socialists have produced a good song ... or had a good song written about them.'[130] There is an aspect here of playacting party division, while alluding to a certain crossover of radical sentiment, if not of policy platforms, between the liberal and socialist traditions. The more serious songs are drawn from the liberal tradition, with 'The Land' as centrepiece, but the SDP also gets a look in with light-hearted songs such as 'If You Were the Only Shirl' affectionately satirising the relationship between Shirley Williams and Roy Jenkins.[131] It is, however, noticeable that most of the songs relating to the period of the alliance and merger are written firmly from the Liberal point of view. These are typical:

> Eternal David, for the fight
> With others thou bidd'st us unite.
> With prophets odd; with doctrine strange
> For these we must our seats exchange.
> O hear us when we cried to thee:
> Why must we love the SDP?[132]

> They could have been Liberals;
> They could have stayed put;
> They could have backed Healey;

They could have fought Foot;
They could have had
One new idea in their head,
But decided to pinch all
The Liberals' instead.[133]

On the first day of merger
The soggies gave to me
Well, not much actually[134]
[To be sung to the tune of 'Twelve Days of Christmas',
with further verses including the lines 'Absolutely zilch',
'Sweet F.A.', 'A very small amount', 'Bugger all' etc.]

The continued presence of these songs in the Liberal Democrat songbook twelve years after the merger does not seem to indicate a continued animosity between Liberals and Social Democrats; rather they seem to be nostalgically performing long-past divisions. That said, it seems that even when the division was still meaningful and passions were running high, the songs provided something of an outlet or safety valve for those feelings. The songbook notes that 'only hours after massively endorsing merger at the Blackpool Special Liberal Assembly, delegates crowded in to the Liberal Revue at the Tower Ballroom to sing [Twelve Days of Merger] with great enthusiasm'.[135] It is worth noting that at the 2011 conference, this song was adapted to 'Twelve Days of Coalition'.

A similar kind of playacting was also in evidence in the Battersea centenary project. The DVD was entitled 'Red Battersea' and at the party screening laughter and cheers greeted its title screen with the image of Battersea Power Station silhouetted against a red sky. Throughout the DVD, the emphasis was on radicalism with something of a knowing playfulness. For instance, the statement that Battersea was expelled from the Labour Party for its support of communist mayor Saklatvala, was again greeted with laughter and cheers. At the other extreme, whilst the DVD revelled in listing the contribution the constituency had made to the Labour Party's history at national level and was themed around the structure of 'lost leaders', Tony Blair's (admittedly brief) involvement with the constituency was treated in a rather tongue in cheek manner and received with mocking rather than proud laughter. The narrative was of a rebellious, left of centre party, not afraid to be at odds with the national leadership, yet the atmosphere was knowing and jocular, self-aware rather than self-righteous.[136]

To party members nostalgia is often more appealing than history.

When Jeremy McIlwaine took an exhibition stand to the Conservative Party conference, he found that people were 'really pleased to hear that there was an official party archive but they weren't really interested in the history'. In fact, 'all they wanted was memorabilia – they wanted the postcards, mugs, they weren't interested in the history of the party ... if we didn't have what they were looking for, they wanted to know which other stands had memorabilia'.[137] McIlwaine also noted that the more recent memorabilia sold much better than that relating to earlier periods. This could be a reflection of the personal popularity and success of Margaret Thatcher as opposed to Stanley Baldwin but he also felt it had something to do with historical distance – the older material was 'ancient history'; it did not speak to living memory.[138] He also noted that in the only visit so far from a Conservative Association to the party archive, it was papers relating to the constituency itself which caused the greatest stir – even above the Bodleian's star acquisitions:

> We showed them some material from the archive but we also showed them some of the treasures from the Bodleian ... a couple of people looked at that but most of them were more interested in the files from the 1940s and 50s about their constituency. Some of them didn't even look at the Anglo Saxon Chronicle ... they had more of a buzz looking at Conservative files from the 1950s.[139]

Conclusions

Despite the very great differences between the traditions of the three main parties and their differing philosophical approaches to the ideas of inheritance, history and preservation, what is perhaps most striking is the degree of convergence between their structures of memory, particularly at national level. Each has a professionally staffed archive, used mainly by academic researchers rather than by the party itself, each finds itself more concerned with the demands of day-to-day politics than with its duty either to the past or to posterity, and each has a history group, run by volunteers and organised around witness seminars, with a mixture of academic analysis and personal testimony. There are of course differences between the history groups, with the Liberal Democrats' being far more established than either of the other two and Labour's run in parallel to older, more specific history groups. Yet their basic formats and purposes are very similar indeed, as is their bias towards events within living memory. The emphasis on 'great lives' is also a common thread across the three parties. This seems to indicate that –

at least nationally, although important local differences should be acknowledged – it is a shared memory of an entwined history which sustains them. When it comes to history, even political divisions can often have the flavour of play-acting (as with the *Liberator Songbook*'s inclusion of 'Red Scum Songs'). The closeness of the three history groups is shown by the interactions of the three directors. In the acknowledgments to the *Dictionary of Labour Biography*, Greg Rosen thanked the publisher, Iain Dale, and also Duncan Brack for their help.[140] Iain Dale in turn explained that he was keen to put on a joint event with the Liberal Democrat History Group, especially as Duncan Brack was a friend; he also noted that John Schwartz (who established the Labour History Group with Greg Rosen) designs the *Conservative History Journal* as a favour. In Dale's words: 'It's all very incestuous these history group things.'[141]

As this example indicates, the political memory of all three parties is perpetuated by a relatively small number of individuals, who tend to share a concern both for the preserving of contemporary documents and participant observations, and for recovering and remembering the stories of the past – usually with an intention of 'learning from history'. Duncan Brack was instrumental in transferring Liberal Democrat papers to the archives and in setting up and running the Liberal Democrat History Group; Iain Dale runs the Conservative History Group and has published histories of all three parties through Politicos; Greg Rosen is chair of the Labour History Group and was on the 2006 Centenary Committee; Dianne Hayter organised the centenary celebrations, wrote her own history of a particular time in Labour's history, is on the editorial board of the *Labour History Journal* and has previously been involved with Labour Heritage; Stephen Bird was Labour Party archivist and is a key figure in Labour Heritage, as is the former Labour Party librarian, Irene Wagner; Graham Lippiatt is a central member of both the Liberal Democrat History Group and the Lloyd George Society. There is also a great crossover between party memoirists, diarists, biographers and historians, with Roy Jenkins, Michael Foot, Tony Benn and Winston Churchill being only the most obvious examples. It is significant that William Hague acknowledges Jenkins' 'valuable advice' and encouragement in writing his biography of Pitt the Younger: an interest in political history seems to override party political divisions.[142]

From the preservation of archives to the staging of anniversary celebrations, party political memory seems to be highly dependent on the instigations (and exertions!) of individuals with a particular interest in history. It may be that they are later able to encourage others to join them and even to gain institutional support, but without their initial interest, these activities would not take place. Archives are an unusual case in that they are managed by professional archivists within institutional and often academic structures. Yet these archivists feel that they spend a large proportion of their time chasing for records and trying to maintain a relationship with parties more concerned with their present than their pasts. In terms of writing party histories or organising commemorative events, the impetus seems to come from individual party members with a personal interest in history. This could be seen as institutional history recovered and preserved through individual memory work, rather than 'institutional memory' in any formal sense. This remark, from the author of a history of Lowestoft CLP, speaks of this lack of structured memory:

> This history is the result of an unguarded remark I once made about the lack of local political history. On complaining about this to a party member I was told that if I wanted more information I should have to get it myself.[143]

The sudden decision in 1972 to undertake a study of Richmond and Barnes Conservative Association's 92-year history seems to suggest the action of a particular individual (or perhaps a group of individuals). Similarly, the Parliamentary Labour Party's centenary celebrations were the result of the efforts of a small group of committed individuals, led by Dianne Hayter. She found that the first time she raised the idea of celebrating the 2006 centenary of the Parliamentary Labour Party at an NEC meeting 'no one was particularly interested'. This was not surprising, given the similar lack of interest within the party in marking the 2000 centenary of the Labour Representation Committee. However, once she had assembled a group to work on the project 'quite quickly people got quite interested in it' and 'one or two people became really enthusiastic'. Hayter felt this enthusiasm may have been due to the fact that the project was organised around the stories of individual MPs, which made it easy for people to catch on to.

Once they begin, mnemonic activities acquire something of a self-perpetuating momentum. There will always be another anniversary to mark, another compilation to produce. Indeed, sometimes anniversaries come so thick and fast that it is difficult to keep up with them. In 2009 the Liberal Democrat History Group marked the centenary of the People's Budget, the bicentenary of Gladstone's birth and 150 years since John Stuart Mill's *On Liberty*. As a result, the commemoration of the founding of the party in 1859 will be celebrated 152 years later in 2011. Despite that, the group easily managed to raise more than the required amount for a blue plaque to mark the site of the founding in an appeal at the end of 2009.

There are two key conclusions we can draw from this. First, that for the majority of party activists and, particularly, those involved with parties at national level, these formal structures of memory may be something of a peripheral interest. Party history group events are very well attended and biographies, memoirs and diaries keenly consumed but for the most part, memory is left in the hands of those who care enough to maintain it. The lack of activity around the Labour Party's 2000 centenary is a case in point; without an enthusiastic advocate, it passed with very little attention. Second, the political parties produce and preserve a very particular type of parliamentary history which resonates far more within the circle of political actors than it does outside, in the nation more widely. This was not true in the early decades, perhaps even the first half century, of the Labour Party, when their history and their mnemonic references were allied much more closely with the struggles and experiences of the working classes. Taken together with the Conservatives' recent attempts to emphasise their institutional past, this seems to indicate the temporal convergence posited as a key theme in party political approaches to their pasts.

Notes

1 Pierre Nora, 'General introduction: between memory and history', in Nora (ed.), *Realms of Memory*, p. 1.
2 Ibid., p. 8.
3 Ibid., pp. 10–11.
4 Ibid., p. 12.
5 For a full discussion of the nature and history of 'community archives' see Andrew Flinn, 'Community histories, community archives: some opportunities and challenges', *Journal of the Society of Archivists*, 28:2 (October 2007), 151–76.
6 Interview with Stephen Bird, former Labour Party Archivist, founder of Labour Heritage, Manchester, 6 November 2008.
7 Ibid.
8 Interview with Sheridan Westlake, then Secretary to the Conservative Archive Trust, London, 28 November 2008.
9 Ibid.
10 Interview with Jeremy McIlwaine, Conservative Party Archivist, Oxford, 16 December 2008.

11 Ibid.
12 Interview with Sue Donnelly, Liberal Party Archivist, London School of Economics, London, 17 December 2008.
13 Interview with Nigel Cochrane, SDP Archivist, Albert Sloman Library, Colchester, 5 December 2008.
14 Ibid.
15 Interview with Helen Roberts, then Archivist, Labour History Archive and Study Centre, Manchester, 15 August 2008.
16 Jeremy McIlwaine interview.
17 Helen Roberts interview.
18 Ibid.
19 Raphael Samuel and Paul Thompson, 'Introduction', in Raphael Samuel and Paul Thompson (eds), *The Myths We Live By* (London and New York: Routledge, 1990), p. 9.
20 Kevin Morgan, *An Introduction: Communist Party of Great Britain*. Available at: www.communistpartyarchive.org.uk/9781851171354.php#IND. Accessed 22.09.2009.
21 Stephen Bird interview.
22 Helen Roberts interview.
23 Sue Donnelly interview.
24 Sheridan Westlake interview.
25 Achille Mbembe, 'The power of the archive and its limits', in Carolyn Hamilton *et al.* (eds), *Refiguring the Archive* (Cape Town: David Philip Publishers, 2002; Dordrecht: Kluwer Academic Publishers, 2002), pp. 19–26.
26 Sue Donnelly interview.
27 Stephen Bird interview.
28 Ibid.
29 Jeremy McIlwaine interview.
30 Sheridan Westlake interview.
31 Jeremy McIlwaine interview.
32 Interview with Penelope J. Corfield, Battersea Constituency Labour Party, London, 24 July 2008.
33 At local level, Constituency Labour Parties (CLPs) have been far more likely to produce written histories and publications celebrating anniversaries than either of the other two parties; local Liberal parties have occasionally published such histories but Conservative Associations and clubs only rarely. However, Conservative Associations are much more likely to produce yearbooks than either of the other two parties. As of 16 June 2009, the British Library catalogue shows 108 records for Conservative Association yearbooks, from Acton to Wycombe but only two for Constituency Labour Parties (Ipswich and Leeds) and none at all for either Liberals or Liberal Democrats. This suggests a different attitude towards past and future, a different positioning of themselves on the temporal axis: a tendency to focus on the present as the history of the future, rather than on the past as an institutional legacy. It would also seem to tie in with the Conservative Party's less developed sense of itself as an institution with a partisan history.
34 W.S. Carroll, *92 Years: A Chronicle of the Richmond and Barnes Conservative*

Association, 1880–1972 (Surrey: Thameside Property Trust, 1972), p. i.

35 Don Mathew, *From Two Boys and a Dog to Political Power: The Labour Party in the Lowestoft constituency 1918–1945* (Lowestoft: Lowestoft Constituency Labour Party, 1979), p. 3.

36 Muriel Burton, *100 Years of Liberalism: General Elections in Mid & North Oxfordshire* (Mid-Oxon Liberal Association, June 1977), p. i.

37 John Saville, 'Introduction', in Joyce M. Bellamy and John Saville (eds), *Dictionary of Labour Biography* vol. I (London and Basingstoke: The Macmillan Press, 1972), p. xi.

38 Penelope Corfield, email correspondence, 14.02.2011.

39 Interview with Dianne Hayter, Chair of the 1906 Centenary Group, 22 May 2009.

40 Dianne Hayter, 'Practioners: the PLP 1906–2006', *Parliamentary Affairs*, 60:1 (2007), 162, 161.

41 Dianne Hayter interview.

42 Penelope Corfield interview.

43 Dianne Hayter interview.

44 Ilaria Favretto, 'British political parties' archives: an exemplary case', *Journal of the Society of Archivists*, 18:2 (1997), 212.

45 Ibid., 206.

46 Herbert Tracey (ed.), *The Book of the Labour Party: Its History, Growth, Policy and Leaders* (London: Caxton Publishing Company, 1925), p. ix.

47 Rt Hon Arthur Henderson MP, 'Introductory: Labour as it is to-day', in ibid., p. 10.

48 Edmund and Ruth Frow, 'Origins of the Working Class Movement Library: travels with a caravan', *History Workshop Journal*, 2. Reprinted in Michael Herbert and Eric Taplin (eds), *Born with a Book in his Hand: A Tribute to Edmund Frow, 1906–1997* (Salford: North West Labour History Group, 1998), p. 29.

49 Jeremy McIlwaine, email correspondence, 18.02.2011.

50 John McIlroy, 'The Society for the Study of Labour History, 1956–1985: its origins and its heyday', in John McIlroy *et al.* (eds), *Making History: Organizations of Labour Historians in Britain Since 1960: Labour History Review Fiftieth Anniversary Supplement*, April 2010, p. 22.

51 North West Labour History Group, www.workershistory.org/about_us .html. Accessed 20.11.2009.

52 Janet A.C. Golding, 'An end to sweating? Liverpool's sweated workers and legislation 1870–1914', *Journal of the North West Labour History Group*, 21 (1996/97), 3–29; Jo Stanley, 'Liverpool's women dockers', ibid., 25 (2000/2001), 2–14; Laura Tabili, 'Labour migration, racial foundation and class identity. Some reflections on the British case', ibid., 20 (1995/96), 16–35.

53 Labour Heritage, www.labourheritage.com/. Accessed 20.11.2009.

54 Veronica Kelly, 'Little Moscow and Moscow Row', *Labour Heritage Bulletin* (Autumn 2008), 1–5; Dr Peter Kingsford, 'A worm's eye view of the General Strike', *Labour Heritage Bulletin* (Spring 2007), 12–13.

55 Report on West London Labour History Day – '1906 and all that', *Labour*

Heritage Bulletin (Winter 2006), 6–7.

56 Interview with John Grigg, Treasurer, Labour Heritage, London, 20 July 2010.

57 Interview with Greg Rosen, Director, Labour History Group, London, 9 June 2008.

58 Interview with Duncan Brack, Editor, *Journal of Liberal History*, London, 24 June 2008.

59 Ibid.

60 Greg Rosen interview.

61 Interview with Iain Dale, Director, Conservative History Group, London, 24 October 2008.

62 Duncan Brack interview.

63 Ibid.

64 Greg Rosen interview.

65 Iain Dale interview.

66 Duncan Brack interview.

67 Ibid.

68 Ibid.

69 Greg Rosen interview.

70 Mark Salber Philips, 'On the advantage and disadvantage of sentimental history for life', *History Workshop Journal*, 65 (2008), 56.

71 Greg Rosen interview.

72 Ibid.

73 Ibid.

74 Interview with Tessa and Derek Phillips, Finchley Conservative Association, London, 12 March 2009.

75 Interview with Anne Reyersbach, Battersea Constituency Labour Party, London, 29 May 2008.

76 Interview with Jeanne Rathbone, Battersea Constituency Labour Party, London, 4 June 2008.

77 Interview with Joan O'Pray, Battersea Constituency Labour Party, London, 4 June 2008.

78 Jeanne Rathbone interview.

79 Tracey (ed.), *The Book of the Labour Party*, p. x.

80 Henderson, 'Introductory', in ibid., p. 9.

81 Various letters to and from Morgan Phillips, October 1948–December 1949, Labour Party Papers, LHASC: LP/GS, 1945–64, Box 22.

82 Alan Haworth and Dianne Hayter (eds), *Men Who Made Labour* (Abingdon: Routledge, 2006).

83 Minutes of 1906 Centenary Fringe Meeting, Labour Party Conference, Blackpool, 28 September 2005.

84 Editor's Preface, Tracey (ed.), *Book of Labour*, p. x.

85 Saville, 'Introduction', in Bellamy and Saville (eds), *Dictionary of Labour Biography*, p. ix.

86 Ibid., p. x.

87 Ibid., p. xiii.

88 Greg Rosen interview.

89 Saville, 'Introduction', in Bellamy and Saville (eds), *Dictionary of Labour*

Biography, p. ix.

90 Letter from Freda Maxwell in *Labour Heritage Women's Research Committee Bulletin* 2 (London: The Labour Party, Labour Heritage, Spring 1987), p. 17.

91 Christine Collette, 'Editorial', in ibid., p. 2.

92 Molly Walton, Foreword to *Colne Valley Labour Party, 1891–1991: Souvenir Centenary History* (Colne Valley Constituency Labour Party, July 1991), p. i.

93 Hugh Jenkins (ed.), *Rank and File* (London: Croom Helm, 1980); John Cornwell (ed.), *Tomb of the Unknown Alderman and Other Tales from the Town Hall* (Sheffield: J.C. Cornwell, 2006).

94 Jenkins, *Rank and File*, p. 168.

95 Penelope Corfield interview.

96 Anne Reyersbach, email correspondence, 15.02.2010.

97 Paul Johnson, *The Spring Address: What is a Conservative?* (London: Centre for Policy Studies, May 1996), p. 12.

98 John Vincent, *The Seven Voices of Conservatism*, CPC Pamphlet No. 0510/821 (London: Conservative Political Centre, February 1991), p. 14.

99 Ian Gilmour, *Inside Right: A Study of Conservatism* (London: Hutchinson, 1977), p. 144.

100 Lawrence, 'Labour: the myths it has lived by', pp. 357, 359.

101 John Campbell, *Nye Bevan: A Biography* (London: Hodder and Stoughton, 1994 [first published as *Nye Bevan and the Mirage of British Socialism*, Weidenfeld & Nicolson, 1987]), p. 373.

102 LHASC, Michael Foot Papers (hereafter MF), MF/L/4, 14 November 1981, 119.

103 Ibid., 14 November 1981, 59. Original emphasis.

104 Sue Donnelly interview.

105 Professor Ben Pimlott, 'Foreword', in Duncan Brack (ed.), *Dictionary of Liberal Biography* (London: Politico's, 1998), pp. x–xi.

106 Duncan Brack, 'What influences Liberal Democrats?', in *Liberal Democrat History Group Newsletter*, no. 8 (September 1995), p. 3.

107 Survey of Liberal Democrat History Group members, September–October 2008. I am grateful for the assistance of the LDHG committee, and particularly Duncan Brack, for their help in sending out the survey and to all the members who took the time to complete and return it.

108 Jeremy McIlwaine interview.

109 Interview with Andrew Riley, Thatcher Papers Senior Archivist, Churchill Archives Centre, Cambridge, 27 November 2008.

110 Alistair B. Cooke (ed.), *The Conservative Party: Seven Historical Studies, 1860s to the 1990s*, CPC Pamphlet no. 914 (London: Conservative Political Centre, 1997).

111 Anne Reyersbach interview.

112 Anne Reyersbach, email correspondence.

113 Bishopsgate Institute, London, Raphael Samuel Archive, 121, theatre programme: 7:84 Theatre Company Scotland, *In Time of Strife* by Joe Corrie.

114 LHASC, LPGS Collection (uncatalogued) Arts for Labour (inc. Red Wedge 1988), theatre programme: Mere Commodity Arts, *In the National Interest*, 1985.

115 *The Coal Board's Butchery*, Miners' Campaign Tape Project / NUM, 1984.

116 'Modern-day "pitchfork rebellion" goes to Westminster to save West Somerset', West Somerset Post, 15 March 2007. Available at: http://criernews.blogspot.com/2007_03_01_archive.html. Accessed 21.02.2011.

117 See www.climaterush.co.uk/index.html. Accessed 19.06.2009. Also a campaign leaflet entitled 'Climate Rush', distributed June 2009.

118 For a detailed study of changing practices in electioneering, see Jon Lawrence, *Electing our Masters: The Hustings in British Politics from Hogarth to Blair* (Oxford: Oxford University Press, 2009).

119 *Liberator Songbook*, nineteenth edition (London: Liberator, 2008), p. 42.

120 Glazer, *Radical Nostalgia*, pp. 35, 211.

121 Paul Connerton, *How Societies Remember* (Cambridge: Cambridge University Press, 1989), p. 71.

122 Ibid., p. 43. Original emphasis.

123 Ibid., pp. 68–9.

124 D.I. Kertzer, *Ritual, Politics and Power* (New Haven: Yale University Press, 1988), p. 68.

125 Ibid., p. 76.

126 See for example: www.independent.co.uk/news/labour-to-keep-the-red-flag-flying-1364875.html; http://news.bbc.co.uk/1/hi/uk_politics/462871.stm. Accessed 19.06.2009.

127 Ann Clywd speaking at the Labour Party Centenary Conference, Blackpool, 12 February 2006.

128 The place of the Red Flag in the debate over Clause IV in 1994/5 will be discussed further in Chapter 4.

129 *Liberator Songbook*, fifteenth edition (London: Liberator, 2004), p. 30.

130 Ibid., p. 27.

131 Ibid., p. 13.

132 Ibid., p. 11.

133 Ibid., p. 14.

134 Ibid., p. 21.

135 Ibid., p. 21.

136 Screening of *Red Battersea: One Hundred Years of Labour*, Clapham Picture House, 14 December 2008. Personal observations.

137 Jeremy McIlwaine interview.

138 Ibid.

139 Ibid.

140 Greg Rosen (ed.), *Dictionary of Labour Biography* (London: Politico's, 2001), p. xviii.

141 Iain Dale interview.

142 William Hague, *William Pitt the Younger* (London: HarperCollins, 2004) p. xvii.

143 Mathew, *From Two Boys and a Dog to Political Power*, p. 3.

3

Against the tide of history: conservatism in the 1980s and 1990s

Having looked at the formal and informal structures of memory within political parties, the rest of this book turns its attention towards the use of historical narratives as signifiers of party political identity and as rhetorical tools. In order to make comparisons across the parties, it will look at a number of moments of political change, when identities were called into question and imagined futures collapsed. Later chapters will focus on the breakaway of the SDP from the Labour Party in 1981, Blair's revision of Clause IV in 1994/5 and the dissolution of the Communist Party of Great Britain between 1988 and 1992. This chapter examines the Conservative Party's reaction to its electoral defeat in 1997 as part of a longer-term loss of confidence regarding its place in the dominant narrative of British history.

As we saw in Chapter 1, a great deal of conservative thought rests upon the notion of adapting to historical change and flowing with the tide of history. Resounding electoral defeats are therefore, arguably, more problematic for Conservatives than for members of other parties; without the sense of being in touch with the nation, they have very little to fall back on. This chapter therefore examines the process by which the defeat of 1997 was rationalised, absorbed and set into a historical framework. However, this process unavoidably came up against the unresolved legacy of Margaret Thatcher's leadership. The question of how to historicise this period was made more complicated by Thatcher's ambiguous relationship to the Conservative Party's past and her attempts to mobilise a very particular view of British history.

Facing defeat

Whilst the Conservative defeat in 1997 was not unexpected, its scale was devastating. As the new party leader, William Hague, emphasised, it could not be brushed aside. Even as the party prepared itself to move ahead and 'to put behind us the shock and dismay' of the defeat, it was important that they 'must never forget how bad it was, or fail to understand why it happened'.[1] Pamphlets and speeches of 1997 certainly did not shrink from the facts. They listed again and again the depressing roll call: the smallest number of MPs since 1906 (48 fewer even than 1945); the total loss of parliamentary representation in Scotland and Wales and most of the large English cities. But they did not stop there. Hague in particular refused to let the party excuse itself on the grounds of electoral cycles and voters who simply thought it was 'time for a change'. He insisted that the party had 'been in serious decline for years ... not just suffering from a cyclical downturn at the end of a difficult period'. In fact, Hague felt that the party had not only been declining for most of his own lifetime, but it had 'gone on declining even during some of the Party's great electoral victories of recent years'. It had a declining and ageing membership and suffered from poor organisation.[2]

Under the shock of defeat, a campaign to reorganise the party was launched, making it, for the first time in its history, a single party with a constitution, central membership database and model rules for constituency associations. The old system was criticised on the grounds that it 'was not designed to be what it is today, but rather has grown up through history' and had become 'a serious barrier to modernisation' due to its 'disparate' nature.[3] This was a far cry from the conservative commitment to the contingent nature of inheritance and the virtues of organic development. While it was recognised that 'no constitution [should be] cast in stone. It should be a living framework which can be amended and developed as time progresses', the answer to this was a 'constitutional college' system requiring the support of both the National Convention and the parliamentary party for any changes that were proposed.[4] A consultation exercise at all levels of the party showed overwhelming – if lacklustre – acceptance of the changes.[5] The long-cherished independence of Conservative Associations in the country was sacrificed in the desperation of the times, much as Tony Blair's reforms of the Labour Party would be accepted in 1994/5.[6] However, John Charmley, then Chairman of the Mid Norfolk Conservative Association, counsels that this lack of public opposition should not be taken to indicate support for the changes. He estimates that the 67% of members who did not return their ballot papers were 'more or less uniformly hostile' to the changes and that 'there was a real dislike of the new notion of joining the Conservative Party', so much so that the leadership 'introduced the concept of "founder member" to keep the old guard happy'. Charmley attributes the lack of public opposition to 'the "shell-shock" post 1997' and the desire 'not to rock the boat – as though it was still afloat!'[7]

It is unsurprising that the party turned in on itself at this moment. The need to regroup was strong and led to a renewed emphasis on the institutional past of the party – comparable to that in the early years of the twentieth century when Keith Feiling, in particular, sought to explore the Conservative and Tory inheritance in the face of the threat of mass democracy and the rise of Labour.[8] In late 1996 and early 1997 the Conservative Political Centre organised a series of lectures on past Conservative leaders delivered by historians, chosen, it insisted, because they were 'experts in their field and not because the CPC was attempting to foster a particular interpretation of the Party's history'.[9] However, Alistair Cooke's introduction to the published collection of those lectures makes clear that it was also a political project, designed to bring the scrutiny of academic analysis to bear on the party's myths, and particularly the myth of Disraeli, which had been debunked by Richard Shannon's analysis and should in turn be re-examined by the party:

> Tories, then, need to be reminded that there is much more to their history than they have been generally encouraged to suppose. Their excessive preoccupation with Disraeli and a few other heroes (and heroines) needs to be checked. That is what this volume seeks to do above all. A keener and more profound appreciation of the Party's history has never been more necessary than it is today – at the start of a new era in its affairs.[10]

The particular significance of the legacy of Disraeli and 'one nation' Conservatism will be discussed in more detail below. Conservatives also attempted to learn lessons from the histories of other parties, with Kenneth Clarke, in particular, declaring that defending the pound would be 'Bennery' and risked marginalising the party in the way that Labour had marginalised itself in 1983.[11] This set the Conservatives' predicament within a recognisable historical narrative.

We have been here before

One of the most frequent responses to the defeat was to seek consolation and inspiration in the past. The Conservative Party had been in this position before – in 1906, if not quite in 1945 – and having fought back before it could fight back again. In Martin L. Davies' terms, this was history understood as 'the same old thing', comprehensible and manageable because familiar.[12] One letter to the *Daily Telegraph* reinforced this point, telling readers 'I have in my possession an *In Memoriam* card printed by my grandfather, a Conservative printer, in Wantage 91 years ago. It reads: "In mournful memory of the Conservative majority ... which died of mendacity and somnolence, January 17 1906, aged 21 years. – *Lo, we look for a joyful resurrection*".'[13] Leadership candidate Peter Lilley emphasised the need to rebuild the party from the grassroots and reminded his colleagues that after the 'crushing defeat in 1945, Rab Butler's renewal of Tory policy thinking paved the way for our return within six years'.[14] His successful competitor, William Hague, made the same point: 'We learned lessons too from our defeat in 1945. The reforms introduced by Lord Woolton and Rab Butler reinvigorated the Party ... It is our duty to do now, at the turn of the twenty-first-century, what Disraeli, Woolton and Butler did then.'[15] The parallels with previous defeats point to a similar sense of not being on the side of history – a recurring fear for conservatives. John Ramsden reminded his party that each time it had been defeated 'not only its foes but many of its friends too have written it off as a curious survivor from the distant past, an anthropological exhibit of great interest no doubt to historians and political scientists, but one whose importance lay entirely in the past. Time, it was all too often felt, did not lie on our side.'[16] However, each time the party had renewed itself and come back stronger, despite protests (as in 1997) that each defeat was different and would be final.

As conservative historian John Charmley argued, Conservatives could 'take counsel and comfort from the past'. In fact, he thought, the manner in which progressive parties failed to fulfil the hopes invested in them and consequently fell apart 'almost amounts to a pattern.'[17] However, his optimism that a 'Peel-like figure' such as 'a certain ex-Chancellor with shabby suede shoes' could lead the party back to victory was questioned by Michael Keith Smith. He suggested that 'in no way was the leadership of Sir Robert Peel a recipe for "happy ever after"' and concluded that 'History indeed carries many messages for the Tories, but not necessarily the ones they wish to hear.' In fact, 'history offers the defeated and broken Conservative Party no consolation whatsoever'.[18] *Telegraph* journalist Robert Hardman saw something rather desperate in the party's evocation of past defeats. On election night he observed that 'The broader remnants of the Tory spin-machine gamely attempted to invoke 1945 as they rallied round John Major. "He's like Churchill. They voted against him but they were very grateful for what he had achieved," said one.'[19]

Like Churchill in 1945, the party seemed to have lost what had seemed a natural ability to speak to the nation's soul. Instead, as Theresa May would tell the 2002 party conference, they had become known as 'the nasty party'.[20] In a rather telling speech, David Willetts discussed the ease of the Conservatives' Britishness:

> Quite simply, the Conservative Party has been, and has seen itself to be, the national party; the British party; the one nation party. Critics are quick to dismiss what they see as a Conservative attempt to hijack the language of patriotism for party purposes. But this makes us sound far too calculating. Conservatives were never detached from Middle England but straining to work out what it felt; we are in it, and of it. Underneath the criticisms from the Left there is a deep, if anxious, respect for the Conservatives' role as the national party.[21]

As the changing tenses in Willetts' speech indicate, this position was now far from secure. The purpose of the speech was to analyse the means by which 'large swathes of the nation had turned against us.' When canvassing, Conservatives found that many people (teachers, health workers, single parents) 'took it for granted that just by describing who they were, they could not be voting Conservative'. Willetts raised this discussion above the level of electoral politics and framed it as a psychological trauma for the party:

> The worst possible thing for Conservatives, worse even than intellectual decay, is for us to feel strangers in our own land; to come to feel that we are some 'sect', possessing a special political insight hidden from the vast majority of people. But we confront a Labour Party more determined than ever before to align themselves with central aspects of our national identity.[22]

It was this latter point which proved particularly galling. While the Labour Party of 1945 could still be opposed as an ideological party, intent on 'dosing the country with copious draughts of Socialist legislation',[23] by 1997, such attacks were not credible. The Labour victory of 1997 was won on the neoliberal terrain created by the Thatcher government by a party which had demonstrated an easy affinity with the national mood. Yet in contrast to his earlier denial of a 'calculating' attempt 'to hijack the language of patriotism for party purposes', not only did Willetts claim Labour's new-found connection with the national soul to be the product of calculation, but he also seemed to advocate a similarly deliberate strategy on the part of Conservatives to regain the support they had lost. They must find 'real, substantial things to say about England or Great Britain which strike a chord with most people and which tie in with our principles and policies'.[24] No longer a simple matter of being 'in' and 'of' Middle England, the Conservatives now felt the urgent need to develop a strategy in order to reclaim their role as 'the national party'. Peter Lilley noted that 'Churchill always advised Conservatives to "trust the people"', adding 'That is harder to do when the people have lost faith in us – and in such a dramatic manner.'[25]

Other voices also sought to reaffirm the party's national status. Despite the electoral defeat, Viscount Cranbourne assured an audience at Politeia in 1999 that 'The Conservative Party stands for the nation. That is what it is for. The day it ceases to stand for the nation it will have ceased to be.'[26] As late as 2004, the then party leader Michael Howard introduced an illustrated history of the Conservative Party with the words, 'While recognising the substantial contributions that other political parties have made to the development of Britain, Conservatives are deeply aware of the extent to which their history is also the history of their country.'[27] Moreover, much of the official rhetoric around the need to reform and renew the Conservative Party framed this as a duty *to the country*. For instance, the *Blueprint for Change* consultation paper assured members that it was necessary 'to rebuild the Party to ensure it is equipped to provide our nation with leadership and good government in the new millennium'.[28] A letter from Lord Parkinson (Chairman of the Party), Robin Hodgson CBE (Chairman of the National Union) and Sir Archie Hamilton MP (Chairman of the 1922 Committee) which accompanied the paper stated: 'We owe it to the country to recreate the great fighting force that the Conservative Party used to be.'[29] In William Hague's words, 'The Conservative Party ... belongs to the nation – past, present and future. We are merely its trustees for the time being. And like all trustees, our duty is to ensure that we hand our Party over to our successors in a better state than we found it.'[30]

Defending the record

Seeking solace in the renewal of 1951 was, however, problematic given that so much of the past eighteen years had been predicated on the argument that the path taken by the party in the post-war years was wrong – wrong for the party and, above all, wrong for the country. As Willetts put it, 'Some Conservatives may be reluctant to learn from this period out of a guilty feeling that somehow all we did then was offer the electorate a paler shade of pink.'[31] The party certainly wasn't ready to jettison its more recent past. Amidst all the public admissions of defeat and seemingly deep commitments to change, Conservatives also sought to salvage the party's record, to make sure that the achievements of the Thatcher and Major years were not forgotten. Even Michael Portillo – the poster boy of the *mea culpa* campaign – was determined to 'be clear about our successes and achievements':

> The Labour Party is determined to create the myth that our 18 years represented a period of misery and failure. So let me deal briefly with what really happened.
>
> The Conservative Government took a country that was on the brink of being ungovernable and restored the authority of government and the ability of management to manage.[32]

Conservative Central Office was similarly robust in declaring that 'under Margaret Thatcher and John Major, Conservative governments reversed years of national decline. Britain is a better place because of those Conservative governments.'[33] And William Hague celebrated the way in which the party 'achieved what we were told was impossible: we reversed the ratchet of socialism and restored our sense of national pride'.[34]

There were two possible responses to the problematic and contradictory legacies of the 1951 and 1979 victories: to emphasise the radicalism of the post-war years or the conservatism of Thatcher. David Willetts is a good example of the first strategy. He argued that it was 'simply bad history ... to imagine that we should dismiss the Party's entire political experience from 1945 to 1975 as the triumph of the wets'. He reminded his readers that 'The Party did, after all, give up some of its precious wartime paper ration in 1945 so that more copies of Hayek's *Road to Serfdom* could be published.'[35] Michael Portillo took the opposite approach, pointing out that the party under Thatcher 'never argued that free markets were everything. We increased sharply spending on social security ... and on health and education. ... we were anything but *laissez-faire*.'[36] The party 'never departed from a one-nation approach, but rather updated it for their times'. Moreover, he argued, even if this was the perception, John Major was very different from Thatcher, and could in 'no sense ... be mistaken for a "two-nation" politician'.[37]

The 'one nation' legacy

Portillo's concern with this matter was part of a much longer debate about the 'one nation' legacy under Thatcherism. Reba N. Soffer makes the point that 'Even after Thatcherism adopted a policy that in practice created "Two Nations", the ideology expressed by the conservative historians continued to echo, with accommodation to new times, in the rhetoric of the faithful.'[38] Conservatives like Ian Gilmour and Peter Walker saw themselves, rather self-consciously, as following the tradition of Disraeli, in opposition to the Gladstonian approach of Thatcher. Indeed, they discovered that such historical narratives provided cover for contemporary disagreements, allowing them to invoke nineteenth-century paternalist values in support of the victims of monetarism. Raphael Samuel described this approach as 'cognitive dissonance', a deliberate strategy whereby praise of Disraeli and 'one nation' conservatism was used as a camouflaged critique of Thatcher by Tory wets.[39]

However, the opposite strategy was used by T.E. Utley, who tried to enlist Disraeli to the side of the Thatcherites, opposed to 'the crusading, moralizing, universalistic sentiments of Gladstone' (and, the implication runs, the current wets) reminding the party that 'Disraeli regarded these sentiments as a load of cant'. He went on to argue that Disraeli, 'if he were to come among us today, would look elsewhere than in the division between the rich and the poor for the forces which are sapping our national unity and strength'. Instead he would look at defence and especially the threat from the USSR, at immigration, the threat to the Union and at public order. He went on:

> Mrs Thatcher's government is engaged (I do not blush to say it) in a great campaign for national regeneration ... So it falls to the Tory Party to mount an evangelizing campaign. For those of us in the Burkeian and Saliburyian traditions this is not an easy task; we are not accustomed to defending our beliefs, we just believe them. Nevertheless, the task has to be performed and, a hundred years on, it can still be performed under the motto 'One Nation'.[40]

In fact, by this account it seems to be the Thatcherites who were 'crusading' and 'moralizing'. As Utley acknowledged, this was a major shift in outlook from the organicism of much of conservative thought. Conservative historian Paul Johnson, speaking in 1996, also tried to reshape the legacy of Disraeli, claiming that 'He was not the first One-Nation Tory' and was not trying to turn the nation into 'a homogenous economic whole'. This was, Johnson argued, an 'illusion' based on *Sybil*. Instead, he argued that Disraeli discovered 'something quite different: that gaps between the classes, though profound, could be bridged by appeals to conservative emotions and needs in all of them, and hence that Conservatives, if they learnt how to make such appeals, had nothing to fear from democracy'.[41] In the dog days of the Major administration, this could be read as an appeal for fewer hopes of a 'classless society' and more stirring evocations of patriotism and traditional values, in Margaret Thatcher's style. As E.H.H. Green reminds us, despite the wets' appropriation of the 'one nation' legacy in opposition to Thatcherism, the One Nation Group of the 1950s included Enoch Powell, Angus Maude and Keith Joseph. He felt that Thatcher was justified in her claim to be defending the One Nation legacy of 'all [her] predecessors, yes ... Disraeli; yes, Harold Macmillan' through the extension of home ownership and share ownership.[42]

Without attempting to adjudicate between these claims, it is clear that the degree of speculation devoted to the question of Thatcher's political inheritance, both at the time and since, is in itself significant. She was characterised by turns as an adherent of 'traditional Conservatism',[43] 'a Conservative revolutionary',[44] a 'nineteenth-century Liberal'[45] following 'the liberalism of Mr Gladstone'[46] and 'not a Liberal'.[47] This concern with placing Thatcher within a historical narrative suggests a deep uneasiness not only over *which* narrative she belonged within but also over her unwillingness to be part of an organically unfolding narrative at all. As she declared in 1977: 'We see nothing as inevitable. Men can still shape history.'[48] In 1990 Daniel Wincott suggested that her desire to enact change had resulted in a 'hyperactive' style of government, more usually associated with left-wing politics.[49] We might take this further and suggest that it resulted in a shift in temporal outlook, from passive conservatism to active presentism.

This shift cannot be attributed to Thatcher alone. Beginning in 1968, the *Swinton Journal* ran a series of articles debating the future of conservatism and the paths it could follow: Disraelian or Peelite, organic or radical, conciliatory or ideological. This was the background to 'Selsdon Man' and Heath's 'U-turn', as well as the context of Margaret Thatcher's election as party leader. The root of the debate was whether Conservatives should continue to *conserve* or whether they should, instead, *confront*. This was, in essence, a debate about the historical process. As Michael Harrington put it: if Conservatives were not to 'take a determinist view of history' and accept that 'socialism is historically inevitable', then it was necessary for them to intervene, to stop being 'political "corks on the water"' and to start creating their own historical narrative. Whilst this felt 'unconservative', they had no choice. And it was to the Conservative past that they could turn for inspiration.[50] Harrington and John O'Sullivan both argued that it was time to abandon paternalist conciliatory conservatism and return to a sceptical liberal conservatism, founded on the principles of Burke, Smith and Peel.[51]

Whigs *and* Tories?

In an idiosyncratic argument, Robin Harris explicitly declared 'modern' (i.e. Thatcherite) Conservatism as the heir to *both* the Tory and the Whig legacies. Emphasising the contingent nature of history, Harris argued that 'the process of living with – sometimes resisting and sometimes compromising with – Liberalism for almost a century' had left a lasting impact on conservatism and meant that 'the modern Conservative Party is heir to a substantial part of the Liberal legacy'. The legacy of opposing liberalism was credited with the Conservatives' acceptance of free-market economics, development of urban and working-class support, identity as the 'patriotic party' and commitment to the Union.[52] Harris suggested that 'Within Conservatism, there had always existed two contrasting strains, one paternalist and interventionist, the other non-interventionist and "libertarian"' but that neither dominated the party until it was forced to confront 'the over-extension of State power' brought about by socialism. Then Margaret Thatcher and Keith Joseph took

> the implications of the fight against socialism, which had long since been the Conservative party's primary purpose, to their logical conclusion by developing an unashamedly free market, capitalist Conservative set of beliefs. [...] So from the basis of a Conservative disposition, from the attitudes of Toryism, from the ambiguous relationship between Conservatives and Liberalism and from the Conservative Party's decisive struggle with Socialism, today's Conservative beliefs and policies have evolved.[53]

Harris's account is striking in its attempt to claim the legacies of both conservatism and liberalism as the *natural* birthright of modern conservatism, rather than as a political innovation. It is a clear example of the Conservative rhetoric of continuity, of absorption and of an ability to embrace the entirety of British history in a single political party. It also stresses the contingent nature of political identity. This melding occurred through a combination of particular circumstances, rather than through a coherent ideological or philosophical mission. This is a quintessentially Tory argument.

Another side of the new right was marked by its rejection of this approach and specifically of liberal values. Paul Johnson located Thatcher's Conservative radicalism in the way she 'decisively repudiated the Peelite maxim that it was the task of Conservative administrations to accept, build on, and operate efficiently the reforms of their opponents'. This was, Johnson felt, 'something not even Salisbury dared to carry out' and 'marks the most important change in the character of Conservatism since the Party was first christened by Peel in 1834'. On this basis, Thatcher alone of twentieth-century party leaders was seen to be straightforwardly Conservative, with no traces of whiggism; prepared to expose and defeat the delusions of the post-war consensus. Nigel Lawson cast Thatcher as the successor to Peel and Churchill in reversing the party's mistaken embrace of social democratic 'delusions' after the war. In her hands 'The old consensus is in the process of being re-established' and 'what we are witnessing is the reversion to an older tradition in the light of the failure of what might be termed the new enlightenment'. Lawson explained that the significance of this reversion to Tory tradition was 'not in the sense of some kind of appeal to ancestor-worship or to the legitimacy of scriptural authority'; rather it was because – in the now-familiar model – 'these traditions are, even today, more deeply rooted in the hearts and minds of ordinary people than in the conventional wisdom of the recent past'.[54] Maurice Cowling traced the roots of these delusions to J.S. Mill's liberalism, the insidious influence of which he believed had infected the country and was responsible for the attitudes which led to appeasement as well as to the development of the welfare state. In particular, he focused on the language of liberalism, feeling that it had become ubiquitous to the point where 'To use liberal language has been taken to be *intelligent*: to reject it evidence of *stupidity*.'[55]

Thatcher herself took a different approach. She presented the post-war consensus as straightforwardly socialist and therefore best defeated by a *return* to liberalism 'in the old-fashioned sense ... the liberalism of Mr Gladstone not of the latter day collectivists'. And in seeking to re-establish that old-fashioned liberalism, she insisted that far from being radical modernisers, she and Keith Joseph were 'acting as conservatives, with a small "c"'.[56] Even if this protestation of conservatism is accepted at face value, it still depends on a *radical* restoration of older values; an attempt to reverse the course of recent history.

In 1986, John Biffen MP warned the party of the dangers of unrestrained radicalism as with the efforts of 'Tory Maoists' to undertake a 'Perpetual Revolution'. Instead, Conservatives should remember that 'The pursuit of Tory radicalism can be most successful when it marries the desire for major change with the matching Conservative instinct for continuity.' This was, he felt, 'the triumph of Conservatism since 1979'.[57]

> The Tory radical success since 1979 has not deprived the Conservatives of initiative: they have [*sic*] given the Party something to conserve. Since 1945 there has not been a happier moment within the Conservative party for the twin partnership of both radical reform and also the spirit of continuity.[58]

Biffen's sense of finally having 'something to conserve' is key to understanding the position of the Conservative Party in the 1980s. It speaks of the extent to which Conservative confidence in both the state of the nation and its own status as the national party had collapsed in the post-war years. This is the background against which Thatcher's radicalism makes sense. It is only possible to preach continuity and stability when one is relatively happy with the direction of political developments and also when one has the social and cultural authority to speak for the national interest. Nigel Lawson explained that in the nineteenth century 'Conservatives could afford to disavow theory and affect a disdain for abstract ideas and general principles, for the simple reason that the theories, ideas and principles on which Conservatism rests were the unchallenged common currency of British politics.' Since the rise of social democracy, however, 'Conservatives have a need ... to fight the battle of ideas.'[59] It may be objected that Conservatism has always been in competition with a progressive tradition. However, Soffer makes a convincing case that despite their 'considerable differences' the Conservatives could at least accept the Liberals as 'historically English' in contrast with the 'unacceptable' 'alien import' of socialism which 'could not be accommodated within a conservative idea of an English/British nation'.[60]

Even before the 2010 coalition, the relationship between the Liberal and Conservative parties has occasionally been close. In the years immediately following the 1945 election the Conservative Party discussed forming an alliance with the Liberals in order to present a 'United Front' against socialism. The 1946 Conservative Party Conference voted against uniting formally or changing the name of the party, settling for an appeal to 'attract into the Party all those who oppose the Socialist policy of the Government'.[61] From 1947, Conservatives and National Liberals joined together to form joint associations in many constituencies[62] and at the 1951 election the Conservatives gained from the votes of former Liberals, leading the re-elected Churchill to offer Liberal leader Clement Davies a ministerial post, which he refused.[63] This was, of course, the time when Margaret Thatcher became active in party politics. Indeed, at her adoption meeting as the prospective parliamentary candidate for Dartford in February 1949, her father made a speech explaining that 'by tradition his family were Liberal, but the Conservative Party stood for very much the same things as the Liberal Party did in his young days'.[64] Similarly, Thatcher's later Chancellor, Geoffrey Howe, explained that at university in the late 1940s he felt '*because* rather than in spite of his Liberal upbringing, "that the post-war Conservative party should inherit the Liberal mantle".'[65] This shared history has been rather obscured by the dominant narrative of the 'progressive consensus' between Labour and Liberals, explored in Chapter 4. We might have expected this shared Liberal–Conservative history to have been used to legitimate the 2010 coalition. Instead the coalition partners preferred to present their relationship as entirely novel, unexpected and counter-intuitive.

A crisis of history?

It was not only the Conservative Party's institutional and ideological past which was under negotiation post-1997; the national past and national *history* was also up for debate. David Willetts laid part of the blame for the change in national mood on a 'serious academic shift in writing about British history'. The originators of this shift were the Communist Party Historians' Group and particularly Eric Hobsbawm, E.P. Thompson and Christopher Hill, of whom he noted that 'their Marxism seems to have come before their history'.[66] He went on to attack the next wave of progressive historians whose work contained a 'residual influence of the Marxist analysis' in its insistence on the 'false consciousness' thesis. The culprits here were

Hobsbawm and Ranger's *The Invention of Tradition*, Benedict Anderson's *Imagined Communities* and – especially – Linda Colley's *Britons*. Willetts took particular exception to Colley's subtitle: 'Forging the Nation': 'What is being attempted is to show that the conventional national identities – and particularly those of British men and women – are somehow artificial, invented or forged.'[67] While Willetts accepted Colley's central thesis that national identity and patriotism are intensified by war, he found that 'the rhetoric of "invention" and "forging" was absurd'.[68] More than that, it was politically motivated and damaging, spreading 'uncertainty and unease which creates the conditions for Blair's attempts to create a dominant new progressive electoral coalition, focusing on a European and constitutional agenda'. He drew an analogy with 'what the progressives did' to traditional views of family: 'What was once seen as an unproblematic and fundamentally right way of living – a married couple with their children – has come to be just one of a variety of lifestyle choices.'[69]

Willetts insisted on a 'common sense', straightforward narrative of British history, in the face of seemingly ideologically driven, theoretical conceptions of the national past. This was an argument for an inspirational, identity-affirming past in the face of damaging, critical history; it hoped to keep the dominant interpretation of the past intact, rather than pour doubt upon it. This insistence depended upon Willetts' faith that the existing cohesive, triumphant, national story was true, rather than – as the 'invention of tradition' thesis suggested – based on a myth which has suited the ruling class and is not borne out by the historical evidence. Yet Willetts was not entirely opposed to counter-intuitive, revisionist history. He emphasised the way in which Alan Macfarlane 'painstakingly assembles the evidence' for his thesis of an individualist market-oriented peasantry, thus implicitly recognising his status as a serious historian, in a way he does not allow for Colley.[70] The difference was that Macfarlane's argument fed into Willetts' existing historical framework, rather than undermining it. It was also useful for Conservatives in the political present, allowing them to 'tie [their] belief in the free market economy to [their] interpretation of Britain's economic history'.[71]

Whilst Willetts' argument was rather an unusual contribution to the 1997 debate, his concerns had long roots and can be traced to another landslide election defeat in 1945. As Paul Addison and Angus Calder have shown, the idea of a 'people's war', developed by public figures such as J.B. Priestley, took root and seemed to

express the experience and solidarity of wartime.[72] This was reinforced by the beginnings of a re-slanting of the national narrative;
most strikingly the Army Bureau for Current Affairs tried to create a
'citizen army', along the lines of the New Model Army and also
promoted discussion of the Putney Debates amongst the troops.[73]
This was very much at odds with the Churchillian grand narrative of
glorious and aristocratic battles. After the war, the Conservative
reaction to this initiative was venomous, condemning it as a left-
wing conspiracy.[74]

The Right Angle, the journal of the Association of Conservative and
Unionist Teachers, was established in 1948. All four issues of its first
volume were dominated by an intense fear of 'the threatened tide of
communism as it is likely to affect your schools and your profession'.[75] The first Editorial asserted that although political bias had
previously been 'almost non-existent' in the teaching profession,
'times change'. The rhetoric was military and confrontational: 'the
man who carried a sword was vanquished by the man who fought
with a gun. The sacred cause of Education has been pushed into the
front line of the political battle; we cannot fight our opponents with
obsolete weapons.'[76] In places an apocalyptic tone was reached.
Hugh Linstead MP urged teachers to recognise and contribute to 'the
urgent need for Great Britain to ... take over firmly the moral leadership of Europe' at a time when 'the civilisation of Europe as we
have known it is at an end and a new civilisation is waiting to be
born'.[77] Other articles encouraged teachers to 'Know Your Enemy'.[78]
The impression was given of a long-term orchestrated communist
campaign 'infiltrating into the educational movement' because 'it
has for a long time realised the immense value of a trained intelli-
gentsia to forward its activities'.[79] The suggestion was that
Conservative teachers needed to set aside their 'scruples' and begin
to promote their own political 'faith'. Again, there was a note of
defensiveness, a sense of Conservatives being excluded from their
traditional sphere:

> So it is high time for the Conservative in the teaching service to assert
> *his* faith; it is a duty he owes to his country and particularly to the
> parents of his pupils. One thing will perhaps astonish him; he will note
> that many of his neighbours will be surprised to learn that he is both a
> teacher and a Conservative.[80]

One way in which the Conservative Party set out to promote its
values was in the re-formation of the Young Britons organisation, 'To
teach patriotism, love of Empire, good citizenship and the basic prin-

ciples of the Conservative faith to its members.'[81] This was an explicit attempt 'to counteract the blasphemous and seditious doctrine of the Communists', particularly in relation to the Woodcraft Folk, presented in this literature as a communist youth movement but actually linked more closely to the co-operative movement.[82] One parent wrote to *The Right Angle* to respond to suggestions that the Young Britons was itself exercising a political influence on children. His or her argument was that this would be true 'Had British tradition prevailed unchallenged in this country'. However, in the face of the 'threat of a foreign creed' parents and teachers had a duty to equip children 'with a certain degree of knowledge which will render their tender minds more capable of resistance'. The main fear was the 'acutely uncomfortable doubts and questionings' which an 'indoctrinated Socialist child' might be able to rouse in his or her playfellows. The 'faith' necessary to resist these doubts and to enable the next generation 'to preserve the British tradition and way of life' was to be based on a particular reading of British history.[83] This was truly a vision of the past as inspiration, as reassurance, as a political resource:

> Faith in such historical things as religion or the Empire requires a certain knowledge of the past. To look at the achievements of past generations in fair perspective does not demand unquestioning and fanatical allegiance to their ideas. What it does is to make us aware of the eternal spiritual values.
>
> Men and women in the past were as frail as we are, but when they were true to great ideals they achieved great things. That knowledge is the fount of faith, and that is the knowledge which our children need to protect them from the undermining cynicism of Marx.[84]

The suspicion that teaching in general (and history teaching in particular) had been hijacked by a left-leaning educational establishment continued throughout the later twentieth century. In 1975 Dr Rhodes Boyson MP claimed that 'There are Rank and File International Socialist cells planted in many London schools'.[85] Even without such fears of direct communist influence, it seemed that the left had captured not only the lecture halls but also the history classroom. Rather than a high-politics, grand narrative tale of kings, queens and diplomacy, children were being taught a social history of 'ordinary people', trade, struggle and oppression. Divisions in history teaching widened in the late sixties and early seventies with the growth of 'New History' and the Schools History Project. This not only challenged the touchstones of the national historical narrative, but also sought to change the nature of history teaching itself by emphasising its capacity to develop skills of critical analysis. This was anathema to many on the right. In Geoffrey Partington's characterisation, this period saw a shift from what he terms a 'mild socialist consensus' in which 'Peterloo was likely to be better known than Waterloo' to a 'relativistic neo-Marxism' which displayed a 'deep hostility to the notion of ever establishing any objective facts' and was consequently based on '*a priori* ideological conviction'.[86] In the late 1970s, the Conservative opposition launched an Education Campaign focusing on parental rights and influence (1976), standards (1977) and values (1978), with the latter being considered 'the most important of the three' as it dealt with the fundamental purpose of education, which was, it considered, 'to ensure that every child leaves school with a sense of values', adding that it was 'the duty of schools to transmit to new generations the essence of what constitutes our civilisation and culture'.[87] This was a very specific view of the purpose of teaching – and of history teaching in particular.

A National Curriculum for History

Despite the Thatcher government's rejection of the post-war consensus and radical rewriting of Britain's political trajectory, it seemed that, ten years in, the party had not managed to regain control of education. The fear of left-wing influence in schools remained high. A pamphlet produced by the 'No Turning Back' Group of Conservative MPs in July 1986 is typical. It lamented that children 'might not be able to read and write, but they do really well at "social awareness". History and modern languages might be in decline, but real gains have been made in such vital subjects as "peace studies" and "anti-racism".' They felt that schools were in the grip of a 'kind of extremism' whereby 'a vicious and corrupt ideology' was imposed upon schoolchildren. The blame for this situation was laid on an educational system subject to 'complete domination by the producers ... be they teachers, educational academics, local authority administrators or ministerial civil servants'.[88] The idea of a nationally controlled curriculum began to seem very attractive. It would place power in the hands of central government rather than 'experts' or 'politicized' Local Education Authorities, with their 'standing ability to corrupt the minds and souls of the young'.[89]

Whether in faux-naiveté or genuine innocence, Margaret Thatcher remarked in her memoirs: 'Though not an historian myself, I had a very clear – and I naïvely imagined uncontroversial – idea of what history was. History is what happened in the past.'[90] That others did not see it in quite such simple terms should not have been surprising. The debate over the National Curriculum for History is the most explicit argument about the national past in recent politics; it attracted intense interest from professionals, politicians, press and the public. Thousands of newspaper columns followed its progress, debates were held at Ruskin College and a series of pressure groups emerged to fight their corners. It was not just about using the past, or laying claim to a particular interpretation of it; it was about defining and fixing the whole concept of history itself. Anthony Freeman highlighted what was at stake: 'There is a distinct likelihood, of course, that what the government of the day doesn't license, either as a subject or what a subject consists of, becomes "un-knowledge".'[91] Yet this risk seemed worth taking, even to the libertarian right. A sense of crisis was evoked, sanctioning extreme measures. A pamphlet produced by the Hillgate Group sympathised with the view that 'A national curriculum is alien to the British educational tradition, which has always based itself in consensus rather than in central command.' But, they emphasised, a national curriculum was 'unfortunately' essential because of the current education establish-ment which, 'prey to ideology and self-interest, is no longer in touch with the public'. A government-controlled national curriculum, on the other hand, would 'win the approval of most people who know the difference between fact and opinion, knowledge and ignorance, culture and barbarism. It is therefore more likely to renew the under-lying consensus than to destroy it.'[92] This appeal to the common sense of 'most people' was a key feature of the arguments put forward by the Campaign for Real Education pressure group. The idea that a 'simple', 'uncontroversial', 'common sense' version of history was under attack could be read as the death throes of an epis-temological hegemony. It seemed 'uncontroversial' only because it had not been questioned so effectively before.

One of the driving forces of the Campaign for Real Education was Stewart Deuchar. He particularly played on this appeal to the common sense of ordinary people, describing himself as a 'small farmer' who gained a history degree in 1939 and had once 'taught history in a private school for two years'. His credentials for his sustained and forthright contributions to the debate were based on his 'concern' about 'what is going on in our schools'.[93] Deuchar's language conveyed a sense of crisis, of division, almost of civil war: 'The LEAs and the governing bodies of the schools are already packed with "activists" or "wets"', 'there is a gulf of distrust and incomprehension between [them] and the public.' Deuchar counselled his supporters to 'keep a steady nerve, and keep your powder dry … The System [is] on the defensive' but 'Already they are mounting a counter-attack.' He took a with-us-or-against-us approach, regretting the 'unedifying' fact that the Historical Association had 'identified itself with The System'.[94] 'The System' was a common target, predictably for its emphasis on multi-culturalism ('which because it engages our post-colonial guilt-feelings, threatens to destroy altogether the basis of our national culture'[95]) and women's history ('Should the books lie and say that these men were in fact women[?]'[96]). Deuchar complained that many in the 'intellectual establishment … have adopted a stance which is neutral or hostile towards our western civilisation. They are happy to enjoy all the perks of living in a free society, without feeling under any obligation to raise so much as a murmur in its defence.' This was, Deuchar felt, a 'deplorable' situation.[97]

Grand narrative history?

However, right-of-centre opinion on the purpose of history teaching was by no means unified. While the grassroots organisation run by Deuchar appealed for a history of national pride, this was not shared by some new right thinkers and conservative historians. In February 1991, the Centre for Policy Studies took issue with the political narrative as set out in the National Curriculum Council's Proposed Draft Order for History. With its themes of suffrage and the widening franchise, the decline of the Liberal Party and rise of Labour, the Celtic Fringe, welfare state, Britain and Europe, the European Community and NATO, the CPS felt that it was 'determined by a Whiggish history'.[98] Sheila Lawlor objected to the Draft Order's statement that:

> Through their history lessons pupils will learn that change is inherent in any democratic society and that democracy, like freedom, has to be won, is vulnerable, not perfectable, is valuable beyond price and needs to be maintained and defended.

She responded:

> Is this to suggest that 'democracy' is the best form of government – or that the democratic world today is a *better* place than, for example, the world and governments it replaced? This is a pretty contestable generalisation. [99]

Lawlor also complained about the range of historical sources suggested by the History Working Group and asked why a schoolboy should 'be confused with "myth" and "music" rather than being taught the historical truth?'[100] Yet it is precisely such methods of cultural transmission which underpin a great many Conservative appeals to the national past. In 2005 the right-wing think tank Civitas republished H.E. Marshall's 1905 *Our Island Story*. This was a clear political statement, designed to reignite the debate over history teaching and revelling in the *Guardian*'s criticisms, which, it suggested, showed that the left 'wish bitterly to resist' the possibility of schoolchildren acquiring 'a national identity'.[101] Yet, while it is a perfect example of narrative history, designed to inculcate 'a sense of national identity', *Our Island Story* can hardly be described as objective, fact-based history. H.E. Marshall described her own work as a 'story book', containing episodes 'which wise people say are only fairly-tales'.[102] Indeed, her tale begins with the story of Albion, the son of Neptune, being led to the island by a mermaid. Its 'brave mixture of truth and myth' was described as 'cutting edge' and 'impeccably postmodern' by the *Economist*.[103] Marshall asserted that these fictions 'are part of Our Island Story, and ought not to be forgotten, any more than those stories about which there is no doubt'.[104] *Our Island Story* was not seen as objective fact-based history even by its author; what it offered was a chronological, engaging narrative. Perhaps this wasn't a debate about truth and fact at all; it was about the importance of stories in transmitting a usable, inspirational national past.

This was not a left–right issue and identity-affirming history is not restricted to tales of national or imperial glory. During a parliamentary debate on the National Curriculum, Labour MP Peter Archer argued that local social history could be a source of inspiration and 'self-respect' for working-class communities, previously 'ashamed' of their identities.[105] Archer's argument was firmly based in the 'dig where you stand' philosophy of history pioneered by Raphael Samuel at Ruskin College. It was predicated on the importance of history and community to developing a sense of self. Whether the referent is class consciousness, local pride, national glory or apparently neutral evolution, the principle is the same: our understanding of the present must be based upon a knowledge of the past. As Rhodri Hayward has shown, this is a culturally specific understanding of the human condition, which grew out of the concurrent professionalisation of history and of Freudian psychoanalysis. An inability to give a coherent, chronological account of the past has thereby become a marker of disorientation and – at the extreme – insanity.[106] The alternate view advocated historical study as a means of learning not about the past *for its own sake* but in order to think critically about the information we are receiving; to be able to judge and value a range of evidence. This was – perhaps in caricatured form – the position attributed to both the Schools History Project and to the Interim Report of the History Working Group, as seen in Deuchar's and Freeman's critiques, above.

The hinge of the argument over the National Curriculum became the four Attainment Targets and the things which they required – or rather did not require – of students. The right-wing pressure groups (and Thatcher herself) leapt on the fact that 'historical knowledge' was not included in the targets. Stewart Deuchar protested that 'The nihilists will use every possibility to make History completely meaningless. Many of them hanker for a "content-free" syllabus.'[107] Eventually, the argument was resolved by a calculated fudge by the Secretary of State John MacGregor, who (apparently at the direct insistence of Thatcher) asked the History Working Group to include the words 'historical knowledge' in the first Attainment Target without changing the actual assessment criteria. That this had become such a totemic issue reveals a deep and political division over the nature of history itself. We have already noted Thatcher's view that 'History is what happened in the past.'[108] One author of a pamphlet thought that the use of the plural 'interpretations of history' in the second Attainment Target was 'subversive because it must tend to the view that there is no truth to which we can aspire'.[109] The fear was that national history – indeed national *identity* – would be lost in a sea of doubt and relativism. We might see this as nostalgia for a time when history was history: it was political, patriotic and chronological. It was what the public understood to be history – before it had been corrupted by left-leaning historians and post-Marxist theory.

However, this nostalgia was not universally embraced, particularly at the more intellectual end of the Conservative Party. Indeed, Maurice Cowling felt that liberalism was far more of a danger to students than Marxism. He singled out Julius Gould's *The Attack on Higher Education* for particular criticism. He felt that its attacks on 'illiberal groupings' (i.e. Marxists) in higher education were misplaced; instead he commented that 'It is a matter rather for gloom and regret that anyone as clever as he is should consecrate the unthought-out pluralism in which we live.' Therefore, he felt that Marxists 'perform a valuable, destructive function in disclosing the gulf that divides the doctrinaire liberal from nearly the whole of the rest of the human race'. The divide over education was, then, 'part of a faction fight' based on 'liberal jealousy at the advances made by Marxists from the very point in the late 1960s at which university expansion was expected to confirm the stranglehold of liberal thinking on higher education.'[110]

As we have seen, the typical approach of conservative historians is one of opposition to teleological Whig narratives of progress and 'freedom gradually broadening down'. Instead, they prefer to see history as a patternless accumulation of accidents of personality, circumstance and chance. Their emphasis on scepticism and rooting out 'humbug'[111] places them rather closer to Linda Colley and Benedict Anderson's attempts to deconstruct national identity than to Margaret Thatcher's unproblematic story of romantic Englishness. It was not just the particular narrative of whiggism which the conservative historians set out to counter; they resisted grand historical narratives and teleological explanations altogether, seeing history as an essentially random combination of social and political circumstance and individual agency. Yet Thatcher's view of history remained determinedly celebratory, whiggish and presentist. That this did not accord with the view of history advocated by historians like Maurice Cowling and John Charmley seemed rather less important than perhaps it should.

Thatcherism and pastness

Conservative historians' suspicion of grand narratives did not preclude a commitment to a conservative sense of inheritance, continuity and tradition. As we saw in Chapter 1, John Casey's contribution to Cowling's *Conservative Essays* bemoaned the attempts of Conservatives to justify their attachment to the nation's historic institutions on the basis of rational, *liberal*, judgements, such as the House of Lords' ability to scrutinise legislation. In contrast, 'A conservative attitude will be in some manner directed towards institutions and pieties as things in themselves, as ends.' Yet this was not an argument for 'a merely aesthetic, or nostalgic or whimsical attachment'; rather a 'political being' must view customs and institutions 'as having a claim upon him, as deserving allegiance, as having authority'. He argued that, 'Any attempt to "depoliticise" such loyalties (as Tories now wistfully aim at depoliticising their attachment to a certain form of education) makes them unintelligible.' Indeed, 'It is precisely the attempt to depoliticise conservative attitudes that has made the conservative position intellectually unavailable.'[112] This is a clear rejection of Whig teleology. The British state has not been developed as a result of rational judgements; we do not owe allegiance because of its structural attributes. Rather it comes to us through the accidents of history and our allegiance should be unconditional, based on the power of tradition and heritage.

Margaret Thatcher certainly made gestures towards this spiritual sense of heritage. The year before becoming Prime Minister, she spoke at a Conservative rally held at Blenheim Palace. The choice of location was significant. She quoted Churchill's evocation of Blenheim's past: 'Blenheim is heir to all the memories of Woodstock. Here kings – Saxon, Norman, Plantagenet – have held their courts and they loom in vague majesty out of the past.' She continued:

> It was here that Winston Churchill was born, a man of destiny whose courage and inspiration are immortal. It was here that the shades of those who marched with Marlborough and who served with Churchill, gathered to remind us – and I use the words of one of Marlborough's officers after the battle of Blenheim – without vanity – 'I think we did our part'. But Blenheim is not a memorial for one man alone. It is the tribute of a nation to what Winston described as weary, faithful soldiers who by their sacrifice and devotion made Britain the foremost power in Europe, and subsequently the world. Their names may now be forgotten. But this is their memorial too.[113]

It was this mystical past of kings and armies, national honour and personal sacrifice from which Thatcher hoped the party could draw inspiration to rebuild Britain. She spoke of the way that, 'today we gather together here to renew confidence in our people, and to express our faith in our future'. There is a powerful sense here of the past as eternally present in the 'shades' of fallen armies, to which one can return in order to refresh the present and gain the strength to face the future. This is similar to Enoch Powell's 'old sense of the symbolic, numinous kingship' discussed in Chapter 1.[114] However, Cowling was sceptical about the depth of Thatcher's connection to the past. He felt that she had 'only a low-level, Neville Chamberlain-type conception of the spiritual glue which is one of the Conservative Party's special needs'.[115] It is clear that her sense of the past was shaped by the needs of the present – the essence of Whig history in Butterfield's analysis. The idea of looking back in order to go forwards is a constant theme in Thatcher's rhetoric. In this speech, it comes through a reference to Burke, who 'said that people will not look forward to posterity who never look back to their ancestors'. Thatcher's approach has also been well summarised by Tim Bell of Saatchi and Saatchi:

> We made a party political broadcast in 1978, which was called Going Backwards and Forwards. And the idea was that as a result of the way the country had been governed for the previous years, Britain had gone backwards in its achievements, whereas in the past it had gone forwards. And if we could bring the past into the future, into the present, then we could go forwards ourselves ... And the argument was that if we could bring the glory of the past into the present and gain the economic strength that the past had had, then we had a chance of regaining the glories of the past in the present day.[116]

Thatcher's sense of the past was rooted in the needs of the present day. Her speech accepting the leadership of the Conservative Party played on conservative notions of the need to renew the 'heritage which our forefathers bequeathed us', yet she described the consequence of the failure to do this not as a loss of the past but, significantly, a loss of the *future*: 'We have lost our vision for the future, and we know that where there is no vision the people will surely perish.' This present rootlessness was set against the 'great' moments of the past, when such a vision had been firm: the founding of the Commonwealth, Elizabethan exploration and the development of parliamentary democracy.[117]

This presentist use of the past was seen very clearly in the Thatcher governments' approaches to the preservation of 'the national heritage'. This issue had been rising up the political agenda since the post-war years with Hugh Dalton's attempts to secure public ownership of country estates through his Land Fund. More than a confrontation between the ideals of private and public ownership of the country's resources, it became a symbol of the decline of 'the spacious way of life'.[118] In the mid-1970s this issue acquired the appearance of a national crisis. In the autumn of 1974 the Victoria & Albert Museum ran an exhibition entitled 'The Destruction of the Country House, 1875–1975'.[119] The pressure group SAVE Britain's Heritage was established in 1975, accompanied by a string of publications with alarmist titles: *The Rape of Britain, Heritage in Danger, The Sack of Bath*.[120] This was presented as a clash between Wilsonian, *progressive*, modernisation and conservative care for tradition and established ways of life. The Thatcher government came in on a promise to 'bring forward proposals to safeguard our national heritage of historic buildings and artistic treasures'[121] yet, as many commentators have noted, its actions in this area were ambiguous to say the least.[122] Patrick Cormack had lamented in 1976 that even if these buildings were conserved, it was too late to do anything more 'than ensure the preservation of pockets of traditional England – quaint museum-like reminders of what the countryside used to be'.[123] This is exactly what Thatcher seemed to set out to do: a 1981 consultation paper suggested that 'The presentation of monuments to the public' should be 'a significant commercial operation'.[124] At the same time, the needs of economic expansion were prioritised over those of conservation: the 'Certificate of Immunity from Listing' was introduced in 1980, for the benefit of developers, and in numerous instances Conservative Secretaries of State judged in favour of commerce rather than heritage.[125]

'Victorian values'

Another of Thatcher's most explicit and controversial engagements with pastness was her invocation of 'Victorian values': thrift, self-help, responsibility and philanthropy. As her critics were quick to point out, this was a way of disguising innovation behind the rhetoric of tradition.[126] However, the phrase was not (seemingly[127]) chosen by Thatcher. It was first used by Brian Walden during an interview with Thatcher for *Weekend World*. In response to her description of the self-reliance she hoped to inculcate in the British populace Walden suggested, 'those values don't so much have a future resonance, there's nothing terribly new about them. They have a resonance of our past ... you've really outlined an approval of what I would call Victorian values.'[128] She seized upon this, agreeing wholeheartedly with Walden and immediately incorporating the phrase into her political rhetoric. This opened her up to attack by both social historians and political opponents, much of which focused around the darker side of Victorian – or rather 'Dickensian' – life. Hansard shows that the phrase 'Victorian values' was most often used by Thatcher's questioners, who accused her of 'trying to turn our universities into Victorian finishing schools for an exclusive, tiny, elitist minority',[129] asked 'which she most fancie[d] reintroducing – the absence of a National Health Service, the absence of old-age pensions, the workhouse, or a long series of colonial wars?'[130] and demanded to know whether she 'believe[d] that mass unemployment and all the misery, poverty and insecurity that accompanies it [were] part of the Victorian values that she admire[d] so much?'[131] While this was a robust line of attack, it was based on a misconstruction of Thatcher's historical attitude. She was not advocating these values *because* they were inherited from the past; rather she set out the values she admired and then enthusiastically embraced a 'heritage' description of them. This shows a presentist rather than conservative attitude towards time.

But there is more to it that this; the controversy over 'Victorian values' stems from a greater debate concerning the interpretation of the Industrial Revolution. Thatcher felt that the story of successful, entrepreneurial progress had to be rescued from the social historians' accounts of oppression, poverty and class conflict. In 1979 Thatcher provided the Foreword to a Centre for Policy Studies pamphlet entitled *History, Capitalism and Freedom*. It set out to correct 'foolish misconceptions' about history, chief of which was Marx's reading of the nineteenth century.[132] A key line of argument in defence of 'Victorian values' was to stress the philanthropic side of Victorian society, the self-help, mutual help, friendly societies and churches which 'created a private network of welfare which the state has undermined'.[133] The implication was that the poor were, despite the arguments of the left, better provided for by Victorian philanthropy than they now were by the welfare state. This has clear resonances of conservative pessimism with regard to historical development: the present is not necessarily an improvement on the past; innovation does not necessarily mean progress. Yet Thatcher was by no means a restorationist; her sights were clearly set on the future.

Again, this carried her into disputes over what had now become known as the 'heritage industry'. Robert Hewison felt that the new emphasis on industrial heritage, particularly through open-air museums, such as Ironbridge Gorge and Beamish, was intended to serve 'both as a mask for the revolution of the present and as a compensation for it'. Both 'Victorian values' and the discovery of a sanitised industrial 'heritage' were a means of reinventing the past 'so that the conflicts of the industrial revolution were consolingly reintegrated into the picturesque and pastoral narrative that became the consumer's vision of the national story'. In this pre-packaged, presentist vision of the past, 'Cotton mills and coal mines were painted into a picture-book history as decorative artefacts ... The machinery still stood but its brutal *raison d'être* was at best dimly recalled in the act of fantasising "the way we were".'[134]

Forward or back?

As we have seen, 'pastness' is a valuable political commodity, which can be used to confer authority on present actions. Anthony P. Cohen uses Thatcher's invocation of 'Victorian values' to demonstrate the political salience of appealing to this general sense of pastness. It is the very vagueness, the malleability of a term such as 'Victorian values' which is able to evoke 'a way of life, of complex characters, or a large fabric of values and attitudes'. Therefore, these 'simple "historical" labels are made to describe complex and often ideological messages', such as monetarism.[135]

Thatcher managed to conjure up a symbolic past which resonated with the public imagination, perhaps due to the way in which it coincided with 'Young Fogeyism', the TV adaptation of *Brideshead Revisited* and the boom in Laura Ashley soft furnishings.[136] Using a heritage sheen to soften radical modernisation seemed appropriate in the 1980s. However, as David Willetts noted, the national mood in 1997 was above all for change, for novelty, for modernity. Blair's declared intention to make Britain a 'young country' again chimed with the national mood, perhaps best summed up by Ikea's 1996 'Chuck out your chintz' advertising campaign. This 'modernity' was itself self-consciously echoing the styles of thirty years earlier: the pop art, pop music and pop fashions of the 1960s. Nevertheless, heritage frills were out; sleek 'modernity' was in.

Given this national mood, it is perhaps not surprising that there were very few attempts to return to a 'true' pre-Thatcherite conservatism in the wake of 1997. The extent of the defeat obviously necessitated a painful post-mortem of its causes but this was not without an element of self-awareness or irony: the first post-election issue of the *Spectator* was labelled 'Special Recriminations Issue'.[137] In addition to the ever-thorny question of the party's European policy, the main debate seemed to be the extent to which Major was guilty of betraying Thatcher's legacy – whether he had 'fatally ... discarded the notion that Conservatism should be based on an argument with the post-war consensus'[138] or whether 'the principles on which Mrs Thatcher refounded the Tory party were never lost sight of, merely pursued with less vigour'.[139]

The most high-profile argument for a pre-Thatcherite Conservatism was that made by Peter Lilley, failed leadership candidate, at the Carlton Club on 20 April 1999. He argued that the root of the Conservatives' unpopularity lay in their 'supposedly hostile attitude to the Welfare State and particularly to Health and Education'. Lilley sought to demonstrate that this was a misapprehension; in fact, Conservatives 'have had to run the welfare state and in practice they have assiduously preserved, expanded, and improved it. To coin a phrase – it has been safe in our hands.'

Moreover, 'Conservative governments have very consistently increased spending on both health and education more rapidly than have Labour governments.' But the problem was not merely 'decades of Labour black propaganda', it was also the Conservatives' own rhetoric, focused as it had been on dismantling the post-war consensus.[140] This was a clear attack on Thatcher's legacy. While Lilley was delivering this Butler Memorial Lecture, William Hague, the party's leader, was making his own speech at the dinner held to celebrate the twentieth anniversary of Thatcher's election as Prime Minister. Unsurprisingly, his line was rather different. In the presence of Thatcher herself, Hague delivered a rather sickly paean to the former leader, based around the idea that 'Margaret, you took on the foolish ideas that had captured our governing classes and that had brought a once great nation to its knees. You had the courage and the vision to set the British people free.' While Hague referred briefly to Lilley's speech and accepted his argument that 'it is a great mistake to think that all Conservatives have to offer is solutions based on free markets', there was no mistaking the difference of their visions.[141]

Hague's call for the party to renew and to change was based upon an evocation of Thatcher's own modernising tendencies and a warning not to rest on the laurels of her past glories or to sink into nostalgia for the recent past. In 1997 he assured the party that 'We will never stop being proud of that record.' However, the party's role now was 'not simply to justify the past, or to defend the world as we left it. We must ... acknowledge that the world moves on, and to move in step with the hope and optimism and forward-looking confidence which will accompany the arrival of a new millennium.'[142] In 1999 he noted that under Thatcher the party 'changed Britain. It would be a tragedy if the one institution in Britain that didn't change was the Conservative Party.'[143] It seems appropriate to end with Thatcher's own response to the defeat, as told by Michael Portillo to the Centre for Policy Studies at the first party conference following the election:

> On the Friday morning, the day after the general election, even before Tony Blair had arrived in Downing Street, I received a telephone call of condolence from Lady Thatcher. But it was condolence delivered in her inimitable style. It was a call to arms and to renewal. She reminded me how after the defeat in 1974, the party had to rebuild, and in particular begin again its work on ideas and policy ... But that process cannot be based on nostalgia for old ways of thought. An idea whose time has come can quickly become an idea whose time has gone ...

Even the enduring principles upon which a party should be founded must be given contemporary forms of expression.[144]

Notes

1 The Rt Hon William Hague MP, *A Fresh Future for the Conservative Party* (London: Conservative Central Office, July 1997), p. 2.
2 Ibid., p. 5.
3 Conservative Central Office, *Our Party: Blueprint for Change: A Consultation Paper for Reform of the Conservative Party* (London: CCO, 1997), p. 2.
4 Ibid., p. 9.
5 Ibid., p. 8. However only 33% of party members returned their ballot papers. See Tim Bale, *The Conservative Party: From Thatcher to Cameron* (Cambridge and Malden, MA: Polity, 2010), p. 74.
6 Although Bale shows that a 'fierce commitment to local autonomy' survived in practice: Bale, *The Conservative Party*, p. 77.
7 John Charmley, email correspondence, 13.02.2011.
8 See Keith Feiling, *A History of the Tory Party 1640–1714* (Oxford: Clarendon Press, 1924) and *What is Conservatism?* (London: Faber & Faber, 1930). Discussed in Reba N. Soffer, *History, Historians, and Conservatism in Britain and America: The Great War to Thatcher and Reagan* (Oxford: Oxford University Press, 2009), pp. 86–94.
9 Alistair B. Cooke (ed.), *The Conservative Party: Seven Historical Studies, 1860s to the 1990s*, CPC Pamphlet no. 914 (London: Conservative Political Centre, 1997), p. 7.
10 Ibid., p. 11.
11 Bruce Anderson, 'New leader, new voting?', *Spectator*, 17 May 1997, p. 9.
12 Davies, *Historics*, p. 4.
13 Jeremy Goer, *Daily Telegraph*, Thursday 8 May, 1997, p. 15. Original emphasis.
14 Peter Lilley, 'Reunite, rebuild and renew', *Daily Telegraph*, Tuesday 6 May, p. 20.
15 Hague, *A Fresh Future*, p. 8.
16 John Ramsden, *Britain is a Conservative Country that Occasionally Votes Labour: Conservative Success in Post-war Britain*, Swinton Lecture, 4 July 1997, Churchill College, Cambridge. CPC Pamphlet no. 916 (London: Conservative Political Centre, 1997), p. 5.
17 John Charmley, 'The consolation of Tory history', *Sunday Telegraph*, 4 May 1997, p. 27.
18 Michael Keith Smith, *Sunday Telegraph*, 11 May 1997, p. 34.
19 Robert Hardman, 'Within an hour, they knew the day was lost', *Daily Telegraph*, Friday 2 May 1997, p. 3.
20 Theresa May, speaking at Conservative Party Conference, Bournemouth, Tuesday 7 October 2002. See Michael White and Anne Perkins, '"Nasty party" warning to Tories', *Guardian*, 8 October 2002. Available at: *www.guardian.co.uk/politics/2002/oct/08/uk.conservatives2002*. Accessed 16.02.2011.

21 David Willetts MP, *Who Do We Think We Are?* Speech to Centre for Policy Studies meeting at Conservative Party Conference, 8 October 1998 (London: Centre for Policy Studies, 1998), p. 2.

22 Ibid., pp. 2–3.

23 Quintin Hogg, *The Case for Conservatism* (Middlesex: Penguin, 1947), p. 314.

24 Ibid., p. 9.

25 Lilley, 'Reunite, rebuild and renew', p. 20.

26 Robert Cranbourne, *Allegiance: The Nation State, Parliament and Prosperity*, Politeia Address Series No. 7 (London: Politeia, 1999), p. 1.

27 Michael Howard, 'Foreword', in Anthony Seldon and Peter Snowdon, *The Conservative Party: An Illustrated History* (Stroud: Sutton Publishing, 2004), p. vii.

28 CCO, *Our Party: Blueprint for Change*, p. 2.

29 Ibid., p. i (unnumbered).

30 Hague, *A Fresh Future*, p. 16.

31 David Willetts MP with Richard Forsdyke, *After the Landslide: Learning the Lessons from 1906 and 1945* (London: Centre for Policy Studies, September 1999), p. 5.

32 Michael Portillo, *The Ghost of Toryism Past: The Spirit of Conservatism Future*, CPS meeting at Party Conference, 9 October 1997 (London: Centre for Policy Studies, 1997), p. 4.

33 CCO, *Our Party: Blueprint for Change*, p. 1

34 Hague, *A Fresh Future*, p. 4.

35 Willetts, *After the Landslide*, p. 5.

36 Portillo, *Ghost of Toryism Past*, p. 10.

37 Ibid., pp. 10–11.

38 Soffer, *History, Historians, and Conservatism in Britain and America*, p. 296.

39 Raphael Samuel, 'Mrs Thatcher and Victorian values', in Samuel, *Island Stories*, p. 342.

40 T.E. Utley, CBE, *One Nation: 100 Years On*, 14 October 1981, lecture to CPC at Blackpool, CPC pamphlet no. 511–521–680 (London: Conservative Political Centre, 1981), p. 18.

41 Johnson, *The Spring Address*, p. 7.

42 Margaret Thatcher, interviewed by Sir Robin Day, BBC1, 8 June 1987. Quoted in E.H.H. Green, *Thatcher* (London: Hodder Arnold, 2006), pp. 41–2.

43 Margaret Thatcher interviewed by BBC Radio 3, 17 February 1985. Quoted in ibid., p. 31.

44 Margaret Thatcher, Seoul, 3 September 1992. Quoted in ibid., p. 32.

45 J. Nott, *Guardian*, 13 September 1982. Quoted in ibid., p. 31.

46 The Rt Hon The Baroness Thatcher LG OM FRS, *Liberty and Limited Government*, the Keith Joseph Memorial Lecture, Thursday 11 January. 1996 at SBC Warburg, Swiss Bank House, London (London: Centre for Policy Studies, 1996), p. 5. Original emphasis.

47 Margaret Thatcher, interviewed by BBC1, 28 September 1977. Quoted in Green, *Thatcher*, p. 31.

48 Thatcher, *Dimensions of Conservatism*.

49 Daniel Wincott, 'Thatcher: ideological or pragmatic?', *Contemporary British History*, 4:2, November 1990, 26–8.

50 Michael Harrington, 'A conservative ideology?', *Swinton Journal*, 19:2 (Summer 1973), 31.
51 Ibid., 29; John O'Sullivan, 'The direction of conservatism', *Swinton Journal*, 16:4 (Spring 1970), 30–1.
52 Robin Harris, *The Conservative Community: The Roots of Thatcherism – And its Future*, CPS Winter Address, St Stephen's Constitutional Club, 7 December 1989 (London: Centre for Policy Studies, 1989), p. 13.
53 Ibid., pp. 14–15.
54 Nigel Lawson MP, *The New Conservatism*, a talk given to the Bow Group, 4 August 1980 (London: Centre for Policy Studies, 1980), pp. 2–3.
55 Maurice Cowling, *Mill and Liberalism* (Cambridge: Cambridge University Press), 1990, p. 1. Original emphases.
56 Thatcher, *Liberty and Limited Government*, p. 5. Original emphasis.
57 The Rt Hon John Biffen MP, *Forward from Conviction*, the second Disraeli Lecture, St Stephen's Constitutional Club, 14 October 1986, CPC no. 0510–764 (London: Conservative Political Centre, 1986), p. 9.
58 Ibid., p. 12.
59 Lawson, *The New Conservatism*, p. 17.
60 Soffer, *History, Historians, and Conservatism in Britain and America*, pp. 298–9.
61 National Union of Conservative and Unionist Associations, Conference Minutes, 1946, 67th Annual Conference, Blackpool, 3–5 October 1946, Thursday 3 October, p. 4.
62 F.W.S. Craig, *British Parliamentary Election Results, 1950–1970* (Chichester: Political Reference Publications, 1971), p. xvii.
63 Green, *Thatcher*, p. 33.
64 Alf Roberts, 28 February 1949. Quoted in ibid., p. 33.
65 Geoffrey Howe, *Conflicts of Loyalty* (Basingstoke: Palgrave Macmillan, 1989), p. 18. Quoted in ibid., p. 4. Original emphasis.
66 Willetts, *Who Do We Think We Are?*, p. 4.
67 Ibid., p. 5.
68 Ibid., p. 7.
69 Ibid., p. 6.
70 Ibid., p. 11.
71 Ibid.
72 Paul Addison, *The Road to 1945: British Politics and the Second World War* (London: Pimlico, 1994); Angus Calder, *The People's War: Britain 1939–1945* (London: Pimlico, 1992).
73 Samuel, *Theatres of Memory*, p. 208.
74 Calder, *The People's War*, p. 251.
75 Address Given by the Rt Hon R.A. Butler to the Annual Conference of the Conservative Teachers' Association, Caxton Hall, Westminster, 13 March, 1948, *The Right Angle: Journal of the Conservative and Unionist Teachers' Association*, 1:1 (June 1948), 9.
76 Basil M. Bazley, 'Editorial', in ibid., 4. Original emphasis.
77 Hugh Linsted MP, 'Education and politics', Extracts from an address given at a meeting of the London Teachers' Association, *The Right Angle*, 2:3 (Summer 1950), 5.

78 Alan Woodward, 'Know your enemy', *The Right Angle*, 1:3 (Spring 1949), 15–16.
79 Humphrey Berkeley, 'Activities in teachers' training colleges', *The Right Angle*, 1:4 (Summer 1949), 10.
80 Bazley, 'Editorial', 5. Original emphasis.
81 Conservative and Unionist Central Office, *The Young Britons Organisation*, Organisation Series, No. 11 (London: Conservative and Unionist Central Office, May 1949), p. 15.
82 Ibid., p.1; for correspondence relating to the Woodcraft Folk, see Bodleian Library, Oxford (hereafter BLO), Conservative Party Archive (hereafter CPA), CCO 60/4/13, Vice-Chairman – Women, General Correspondence, 1975.
83 A Parent, 'Supple young minds', *The Right Angle*, 2:3 (Summer 1950), 6–7.
84 Ibid.
85 Dr Rhodes Boyson, MP, 'How red *are* our schools?', *Daily Telegraph*, 16 October 1975.
86 Geoffrey Partington, 'History: re-written to ideological , in Dennis O'Keefe (ed.), *The Wayward Curriculum* (Exeter: Social Affairs Unit, 1986), pp. 64, 70.
87 BLO, CPA, CRD 4/5/49, Conservative Opposition Speeches 1974–May 1979, E2 News release: 63/78, statement by Mr. Norman St John-Stevas MP, Opposition Spokesman on Education Science and the Arts, at the launch of the Conservative Education Campaign, 'Values '78'.
88 'No Turning Back' Group of Conservative MPs, *Save Our Schools* (London: Conservative Political Centre, July 1986), pp. 6–11.
89 Ibid., p. 18.
90 Margaret Thatcher, *The Downing Street Years* (London: HarperCollins, 1995), p. 595.
91 Anthony Freeman, 'Which history?', in Nick Seaton (ed.), *Conference 1990: Which History? Whose Values? What Culture? Illiteracy, Inspectors and Primary School Matters*, no. 5 (York: Campaign for Real Education, March 1990), p. 4.
92 Hillgate Group, *The Reform of British Education: From Principles to Practice* (London: Claridge Ld, 1987), pp. 10–11.
93 Stewart Deuchar, *The New History: A Critique* (York: Campaign for Real Education, 1989), p. 1.
94 Stewart Deuchar 'The interim report of the History Working Group', in Stewart Deuchar (ed.) *What is Wrong With Our Schools?* (York: Campaign for Real Education, 1987), p.86.
95 Hillgate Group, *The Reform of British Education*, p. 4.
96 Sheila Lawlor, *The National Curriculum, CPS Response to Proposed Draft Order for History* (London: CPS, February 1991), p. 41.
97 Stewart Deuchar, 'Introduction', in Deuchar (ed.), *What is Wrong With Our Schools?*, p. 6.
98 Lawlor, *The National Curriculum*, p. 34.
99 Ibid., p. 42. Original emphasis.
100 Lawlor, *National Curriculum*, p. 20.
101 www.civitas.org.uk/blog/british_history/. Accessed 15.04.2009.
102 H.E. Marshall, *Our Island Story* (London, 2007 [1905]), p. xxii.
103 Ibid., quotation on back cover.

104 Ibid., p. xxii.

105 Parliamentary Debates, Commons, 29 April 1991, col. 135.

106 Rhodri Hayward, *Resisting History: Religious Transcendence and the Invention of the Unconscious* (Manchester: Manchester University Press; New York: Palgrave, 2007).

107 Deuchar, 'The interim report', p. 85.

108 Thatcher, *The Downing Street Years*, p. 595.

109 Freeman, 'Which history?', pp. 5–6.

110 Maurice Cowling, 'The present situation', in Cowling (ed.), *Conservative Essays*, p. 8.

111 John Charmley, 'A Conservative historian speaks…', *Conservative History Journal*, 5 (Autumn 2005), 3.

112 Casey, 'Tradition and authority', p. 85.

113 Margaret Thatcher, Speech to Conservative rally at Blenheim Palace, Woodstock, Oxfordshire, 16 July 1977. Available at: www.margaretthatcher .org/speeches/displaydocument.asp?docid=103420. Accessed 09.10.2009.

114 Powell, 'Patriotism', pp. 2–3.

115 Cowling, 'Preface to second edition', in Cowling, *Mill and Liberalism*, p. xlii.

116 Tim Bell interviewed for Adam Curtis (dir.), *The Living Dead, 3: The Attic*, BBC: 1995

117 Margaret Thatcher, speech accepting the Conservative leadership, Grosvenor Square, 20 February 1975. Available at: www.margaret-thatcher.org/speeches/displaydocument.asp?docid=102629. Accessed 04.01.2010.

118 David Eccles, Parliamentary Debates, House of Commons, 1952–53, 6 February 1953, col. 2209.

119 Robert Hewison, *Culture and Consensus: England, Art and Politics Since 1940*, revised edn (London: Methuen, 1997), p. 193.

120 Colin Amery and Dan Cruikshank, *The Rape of Britain* (London: Elek, 1975); Patrick Cormack, *Heritage in Danger* (London: New English Library, 1976); Adam Fergusson, *The Sack of Bath: A Record and an Indictment* (Salisbury: Compton Russell, 1973).

121 Queen's Speech, 15 May 1979, Parliamentary Debates, Commons, vol. 967, cols 47–51. Available at: hansard.millbanksystems.com/commons /1979/may/15/queens-speech. Accessed 17.01.2010

122 In addition to Hewison, *Culture and Consensus* and *The Heritage Industry* see, for instance, Peter J. Larkham and Heather Barrett, 'Conservation of the built environment under the Conservatives', in Philip Allmendinger and Huw Thomas (eds), *Urban Planning and the New Right* (London: Routledge, 1998), pp. 53–86.

123 Cormack, *Heritage in Danger*, p. 27.

124 *Organisation of Ancient Monuments and Historic Buildings in England* (London: Department of the Environment, 1981). Quoted in John Delafons, *Politics and Preservation: A Policy History of the Built Heritage 1992–1996* (London: E & F.N. Spon, 1997), p. 136.

125 See Larkham and Barrett, 'Conservation of the built environment', pp. 56–63.

126 See Samuel, 'Mrs Thatcher and Victorian values'.

127 Raphael Samuel hints that this might have been a set-up: ibid., p. 333.

128 Brian Walden interview with Margaret Thatcher for London Weekend Television Weekend World, 16 January 1983. Available at: www.margaretthatcher.org/speeches/displaydocument.asp?docid=105087. Accessed 09.10.2009.

129 Mr Canavan, House of Commons PMQs, 3 May 1983, Hansard [42/15–20], col. 19.

130 Mr Dobson, House of Commons PMQs, 17 February 1983, Hansard [37/463–68], col. 464.

131 Mr Winnick, House of Commons PMQs, 19 April 1983, Hansard [41/158–62], col. 160.

132 Hugh Thomas, *History, Capitalism and Freedom* (London: Centre for Policy Studies, 1979).

133 Charles Moore, *How to be British*, Centre for Policy Studies annual lecture, Blackpool, 12 October 1995 (London: Centre for Policy Studies, 1995), pp. 12–13.

134 Hewison, *Culture and Consensus*, p. 265.

135 Anthony P. Cohen, *The Symbolic Construction of Community* (London and New York: Routledge, 2004), pp. 101–2.

136 See Samuel, *Theatres of Memory*.

137 *Spectator*, 9 May 1997.

138 Janet Daly, 'They simply had no ideas', *Daily Telegraph*, 6 May 1997, p. 20.

139 Tessa Keswick, letter to *Daily Telegraph*, 10 May 1997, p. 19.

140 Peter Lilley, Butler Memorial Lecture, 20 April 1999, Carlton Club, London. Available at: www.peterlilley.co.uk/text/article.aspx?id=12&ref=859. Accessed 26.11.2009.

141 William Hague, speaking at the dinner to celebrate the twentieth anniversary of Thatcher's election as Prime Minister, 20 April 1999. Available at: www.guardian.co.uk/politics/1999/apr/20/conservatives1. Accessed 26.11.2009.

142 Hague, *A Fresh Future*, p. 4.

143 Hague, speaking on 20 April 1999.

144 Portillo, *Ghost of Toryism Past*, p. 1.

4

Negotiations with Labour's past: the SDP and New Labour

This chapter examines the way in which narratives of Labour's past functioned in the foundational discourse of both the Social Democratic Party (SDP) and New Labour. While both episodes are associated primarily with their emphasis on novelty and on breaking with the past, it is shown that both were also framed as the reclamation of 'true' history in opposition to politicised myth and nostalgia.

Blair used the traditional view of Labour as a party in thrall to its past in order to dismiss his opponents as nostalgic and sentimental. Yet he also invoked the narrative of an historic 'progressive alignment' between social democracy and new liberalism as a means of presenting himself as the guardian of an older and therefore seemingly more authentic tradition within Labour's history. This could be seen as a discursive triple whammy, allowing New Labour's architects to reject the past, to unsettle its narrative structure *and* to claim its authority all at the same time. As we will see, this narrative of a 'progressive alignment' had already been used by the SDP, especially during its merger with the Liberal Party. For the SDP's founders, this was a crucial way of maintaining a sense of personal and political continuity, of demonstrating that they remained loyal to the spirit and traditions of the party they had abandoned.

There are significant similarities between both New Labour and the SDP and earlier, Gaitskellite, revisionism. Labour's history inevitably shaped the debates over its future – and was frequently drawn upon by the opponents of the revision of Clause IV – but Gaitskell and his supporters argued only that Labour should not be bound by its past. They did not try to rework the party's history, to present an alternative narrative by which their actions appeared more authentically Labour. Instead, they argued that if Labour was anything, it was the party of change, of progress, of radicalism. Even Crosland, who 'had a firm sense of tradition, distinguishing him from other revisionists',[1] made little effort to justify his own arguments in terms of Labour's past. His analysis of the various strands of Labour history in *The Future of Socialism* did not lead him to claim any in particular as either more authentic than the others, or as his own ideological ancestry. Instead, he used their very diversity to conclude that 'nothing is more traditional in the history of socialist thought than the violent rejection of past doctrines'.[2]

New Labour

The making of New Labour has received a great deal of critical attention, much of which has inevitably focused on the way in which it placed itself in relation to past and future, its inheritances and its iconoclasm.[3] Nick Randall is right to note that students of New Labour have been particularly interested in 'questions of temporality' because 'New Labour so boldly advanced a claim to disrupt historical continuity'.[4] But it is not only academics who have contributed to this analysis. Many of the key figures associated with New Labour have also had their say. The New Labour project was not just about 'making history' in terms of its practical actions; the writing up of that history seems to have been just as important. As early as 1995 Peter Mandelson and Roger Liddle were preparing a key text designed 'to enable everyone to understand better why Labour changed and what it has changed into'.[5] This was followed in 1999 by Philip Gould's analysis of *The Unfinished Revolution: How the Modernisers Saved the Labour Party*, which motivated Dianne Hayter to begin a PhD in order to counteract the emerging consensus that the modernisation process began with the appointment of Gould and Mandelson in 1983. The result of this study was published in 2005 under the title *Fightback! Labour's Traditional Right in the 1970s and 1980s* and made the case for a much longer process of modernisation, strongly tied to the trade unions.

The present work makes no attempt to adjudicate between these accounts, still less to provide an analysis of New Labour's philosophy or experience in office. These tasks have all been undertaken admirably by others. Rather, it aims to examine the discourse of change-making; the negotiation between past, present and future. In particular, it focuses on the debates which took place in 1994/5 over the decision to change Clause IV, part iv of the party's constitution as this was one of the most striking attempts to confront the party's relationship with its own past. An association with the past cuts both ways: it can invest its holders with the authority of tradition or tie them to seemingly obsolete modes of thinking; conversely, modernisers can present themselves as vigorous and forward-looking or be damned as unthinking, free floating, rootless nobodies.

In a narrative encouraged by the rhetoric of its architects, the modernisation of the party appears to be a rejection of Labour's past, made possible through Blair's ignorance of its core traditions and ideological background. This is a compelling narrative: a straightforward rejection of Labour's history – an attempt to speak *to* the future rather than *from* the past. But it is not the full story. Although Blair has usually been characterised (particularly by his own party) as peculiarly ahistorical, displaying both ignorance and antipathy towards Labour's past, as Oliver Daddow has demonstrated, a content analysis of his speeches reveals him to have been 'obsessed with history', frequently drawing upon historical lessons, parallels and models.[6] During the debates over Clause IV – one of the most explicit attempts to break with the past – Blair and his team used nostalgia as a rhetorical tool in order to neutralise the demands of the party's left wing for a socialist programme in the present and for the future. At the same time, they tried to control the party's history, in the guise of both heirs and critical historians, 'correcting' myths and laying down a new story for the future. This drew on the account of David Marquand (who had been a founder member of the SDP) of the damaging historical division between social democrats and new Liberals and pledged to recover an older, liberal, co-operative socialism dating back before Webb's drafting of the party's constitution. Blair's revisionism was therefore *historical* revisionism.

Again, though, this account should not be taken at face value. As Michael Freeden argued in 1999, Blair's supposed rediscovery of the New Liberal tradition was nothing of the sort; in fact 'the work of assimilating some of the most advanced ideas of liberalism had already been accomplished by central social-democrats *within* the Labour movement'.[7] Moreover, he argued, New Labour's reinterpretation of core social values – civic responsibility, community, individual choice – marks a significant deviation from that progressive tradition and bears traces of an 'older and more capitalist' liberalism and even paternalist conservatism. It is not, however, the validity of New Labour's claim to this particular past that interests us here; rather, it is the value of history itself as a rhetorical, political tool.

Unlike New Labour, the founders of the SDP tried to break away from the established Labour narrative and start a new chapter in

British social democracy without – initially – breaking away from the socialist story and leaving themselves open to charges of inauthenticity, rootlessness or betrayal. This was a whole new party, a literal break, and they did not aim to carry the majority of the Labour Party with them. This was not so much refashioning as carving out a distinct legacy, by which they could demonstrate that they had stayed true to their roots while the Labour Party had moved around them. At the same time, however, novelty, difference and modernity were key to the SDP's appeal. Later they needed to find a way to integrate their own history and the history they had carried with them into their new identity as Liberal Democrats. This of course required explicit negotiations with the traditions and inheritance of liberalism. The 'progressive alliance' narrative was therefore of critical importance.

With New Labour, 'modernisation' was a case of being of their time, *appropriate* to the contemporary political and social context. It could be seen as an extension of Croslandite revisionism and also the later *Marxism Today* debates around the need to acknowledge the cultural changes associated with Thatcherism and to tailor their politics to modern Britain, rather than an imagined 'traditional' working class.[8] The slogan 'New Labour New Britain' seemed to present an exciting, but essentially orderly progression from outdated past to a contemporary present and towards an improved (if not radical) future.[9] As Bevir has shown, New Labour presented its modernisation as the *only* possible response to the circumstances in which it found itself.[10] The SDP was different. The progression between past and present here was not orderly, timely; it was ruptured. The future was unknown. Both Bill Rodgers and Roy Jenkins described feeling that 'the times were out of joint' in the late 1970s.[11] This temporal attitude can be seen in the phrase most associated with the SDP: 'breaking the mould'. There is a clear sense here that the natural political order, the party system and the relationship of the present to the past and future had been unsettled. The SDP were breaking out of the prescribed party narrative: making their own present; making their own politics. As we will see, SDP rhetoric showed a tension between the possibility of making this novelty an intrinsic part of their identity and of denying it in order to demonstrate their essential continuity with Labour's ideals and policies.

Mid-century revisionism

The common political background to both the SDP and New Labour was the revisionism of the 1950s and early 1960s. Gaitskell's own attempt to revise Clause IV was most clearly a response to the 1959 General Election defeat and the subsequent fear that Labour was seen as an 'old', outdated party, out of touch with an increasingly affluent electorate. The party's analyses of its defeat illustrate the confusion and bewilderment the leadership felt. Urgent questions were asked: 'Who are Liberal voters? ... Are the new liberals young people, and if so, from which section of the community do they come? ... Is it true, for instance, that more women voted Tory and if so, why?'[12]

The 1959/60 debate over Clause IV was rather different from that of 1994/5. In the first place, as Michael Kenny and Martin J. Smith have noted, the leadership remained committed to increasing public ownership as a matter of policy.[13] Their worry was that a pledge to achieve full 'common ownership of the means of production, distribution and exchange' was off-putting to voters and over-stated the party's intentions, not that public ownership was itself an old-fashioned policy. Although the party's opinion poll analysis placed nationalisation ninth in a list of the ten most important issues for Labour and claimed that 'Few voters of any party think that this is an important issue', the accompanying report focused on this issue, placing it third in a list of five key causes of the defeat, behind prosperity and the fear that they would not be able to pay for their programme. They asserted 'The general unpopularity of *nationalisation*' and concluded that it was not nationalisation *per se* but 'the fear of "back door nationalisation"' stoked by Tory propaganda which had been particularly damaging, particularly in relation to 'the 500 companies'. Yet again, this ended in a flurry of questions rather than answers:

> Why is nationalisation unpopular? Is it because of misunderstanding, by our failure to present our policies clearly; is it due to a dissatisfaction with certain nationalised industries, or is it a general fear created largely by Conservative propaganda?

A handwritten note in the margin of this document in Gaitskell's archive asked simply 'Do what?'[14]

This is closely connected to the second point, which is that the shape of the 'modern' state remained rather unformed. As we saw in Chapter 1, it was thus possible for the opponents of change – notably

Barbara Castle and Richard Crossman – to argue that public ownership *was* the future, *was* the 'modern' option. The achievements of the Attlee government were only fifteen years old and had not yet faced any sustained attack. Moreover, the USSR continued to provide an alternative vision of 'modernity'. The debate between Crosland and Crossman took place not over the need for Britain (and Labour) to modernise but over the form that modernisation should take.

A key element of the debate was over the need for Labour to be 'radical', to avoid 'conservatism'. While the revisionists threw this accusation at their opponents, the response came back that in fact it was the socialist left who remained committed to changing society, to real radicalism. In response to Gaitskell's suggestion that the left 'would be performing a useful function if they would only produce a stream of new, forward-looking, imaginative, practical ideas', *Tribune* produced a list of ten ideas 'originally propounded in recent years by the Left-wing of the party and later adopted or considered by the party officially'. This list included the boycott of South Africa, the right to buy council houses and the subsidising of railways and could, its authors assured readers, 'be vastly extended'. It was however, enough 'to destroy the fiction so sedulously cultivated by the "new thinkers" of the Right-wing, that they provide the modern, forward-looking element in the party while the Left has been rooted in the past'. In fact, the argument ran, it was the right who were unable to produce new ideas, bound as they were to 'accepting established orthodoxies and appeasing established ideas'.[15] This pattern of argument was repeated, as we will see below, in the 1994/5 debates. The modernisers were quick to accuse their opponents of conservatism; in reply the Tribunite left maintained that only their commitment to socialist principles allowed any possibility of radical change, whether in the present or future. Again we will see the attempt to reduce the left's position to one of nostalgia, sentiment, symbolism; again came the insistence on the active and political content of their principles.

Gaitskell's response to this stalemate was self-aware and sophisticated. Realising that it might not be possible to 'get the straight replacement' of the original Clause IV, he proposed 'embalming' it within the constitution as an historical artefact. It would be book-ended by statements which set it in historical context and made clear that it had now been superseded by the new Party Objects. This would, he hoped, 'satisfy … the more reasonable of the fundamentalists' but also make it 'unmistakeably clear (*this is essential*) that the new Statement is in fact a definitive one so that the Tories can no longer go on misrepresenting us on the basis of the original declaration'.[16] This 'embalming' arguably paved the way for Blair's final removal of the original clause from the party's constitution. By 1994, the argument was no longer over the proposed scale of public ownership but rather over the leadership's confident declaration that 'nobody believes in Clause IV'. Although, as we will see below, this was not quite true, it had certainly established itself as party orthodoxy.

The search for origins

The approach of each of the 'new' parties to the inheritance of mid-century revisionism was very different. The Gang of Four were much closer (chronologically and in some cases personally) to Crosland and Gaitskell. The rhetoric of the SDP made these roots very clear indeed. For instance, Rodgers argued that the SDP 'emerged as the culmination of a long process of shifting allegiances' beginning 'in the debate about the future of the democratic left in Britain' resulting from Labour's 1959 election defeat.[17] He claimed that the Labour Party 'failed to learn the lesson' of that defeat, resulting in the 1979 defeat, the breakaway of the SDP and, ultimately, the '1983 debacle'.[18] Rodgers also claimed to be acting through loyalty to Labour leaders of the past, in the face of others' treachery:

> From Keir Hardie to Jim Callaghan, our Party has believed in a practical humanitarian socialism ... It has owed its inspiration to British radicals, trade unionists, cooperators, non-conformists and Christian socialists – not to Marx or Lenin ... If our Party should abandon or betray those principles, it would be a tragedy.[19]

Rodgers' argument could be seen as an inversion of the traditional Labour myth that leaders betray their party.[20] In this case, the party was depicted as betraying all its leaders, past and present. The idea of legacies squandered and ancestors ignored comes through very strongly in SDP rhetoric. David Owen argued that their position was closer to the vision of the Labour Party held by the pioneers, who though 'themselves trade unionists, deliberately decided not to create a Trade Union Party but to establish a constitution for the Labour Party that made it a national party'.[21] By this rhetorical strategy, breaking away from the Labour Party became in itself an act of loyalty – an attempt to uphold the legacy of the past and bear the standard into the future.

Unsurprisingly, the SDP's opponents did not accept this narrative. They were frequently accused of ingratitude to the party which had supported and nurtured them. Their actions were presented as opportunistic, self-interested and petty. Roy Hattersley has said that although the members of the Gang of Four each had their own reasons for breaking with Labour, all of them also 'undoubtedly believed that the new party offered them the prospect of power' and that most of the MPs who left with them did so 'because they believed that they would do better in the new party and dressed up self-interest to look like principle'.[22] If the SDP was to succeed in overcoming these accusations, it was of vital importance that its founders were able to present themselves as loyal, consistent, and self-sacrificing. This they did with unrelenting energy, turning the accusation back on their opponents, as this advice to canvassers shows:

> do not be defensive. Go over to the attack. The real traitors are those who have abandoned principle and stayed in the Labour Party. SDP MPs did not leave the Labour Party: it left them. The Labour Party of 1983 is very different from the Labour Party of Clem Attlee, Ernest Bevin and Hugh Gaitskell.[23]

Ancestors

The SDP's attempts to claim the legacy of Labour's past was not limited to any particular strand within the party. Rodgers, in particular, made a clear attempt to claim the legacy of both Gaitskell and Bevan. This was not a matter of denying their political differences; rather it was a case of placing both of them (and himself) firmly within the tradition of a legitimate, parliamentary Labour tradition, which excluded the hard left and entryists. This position was echoed by some at the grassroots, who assured them that, 'Bevan would, like you have believed that the present Labour Party has betrayed the ideals of social democracy for which he fought so hard.'[24]

Bill Rodgers' 1977 inaugural speech to the Campaign for Labour Victory is a strong example of this strategy. He first testified to his and his audience's party loyalty but then questioned what it was that they were being loyal to, bringing into doubt the very identity of the party:

> The plain fact is that there are many people deeply disturbed by present tendencies. They would support the party of Callaghan as they supported the party of Attlee thirty years ago. But is it the party of

> Callaghan, they ask? Whose voice is the voice to which they should listen?[25]

Rodgers went on to distinguish between the far left activists who 'care little for our values and nothing for the survival of our party, as we have known it' and 'The real activists ... our local councillors, our fund raisers and bazaar organizers, our shop stewards and convenors, our community leaders.'[26] Finally, he defined the boundaries of the Labour Party as he saw it. By including the 'legitimate left' of the Tribune Group, he shifted his rhetorical position from the right of the party and attempted to speak for its entirety:

> The Labour party is the party of Bevan as well as Gaitskell. For Bevan was a staunch democrat, opposed to a monolithic society and with no time for tyranny. The heirs of Bevan – the legitimate left – have their role to play in saving the party. I hope that they will not neglect it.[27]

Rodgers had made a similar point in an earlier speech, in 1975, asking 'the heirs of Bevan amongst MPs [to] support the heirs of Gaitskell' in the face of the threat from a 'small number of activists' outside the 'broad framework' of the party who practise 'new style politics'.[28] Both of these speeches were made in the mid–late 1970s, when Rodgers and others still hoped that the party might not split. His argument that the Labour Party now was not the party it had been was later echoed by Bob Mclennan in his 1981 resignation speech to his CLP, in which he declared, 'I am not leaving the Labour Party; the Labour Party which I joined and which I have been proud to belong during 15 years of public life has left me and many others like me.'[29]

Emotional statements of personal commitment and continuity were by no means restricted to the party's elites. One letter sent to the *Leeds Weekly Citizen*, the *Yorkshire Post*, the *Evening Post* and the *Observer* began with a moving account of personal hardship and political service stretching back to 1926 and concluded, 'I write this letter in tears, with memories so deep that they are inexpressible. It is with bitter regret and anguish of mind that I cut myself off from the Party that has been my life for so long, remembering my dead comrades.' The author was, however, grateful that these comrades 'have not lived to see today's betrayal of all that we worked for and struggled for – democracy. No more; no less.' She urged those who felt the same to join the SDP and signed off with the words, 'I have the honour to sign myself, Social Democrat.'[30] Another long-term Labour member and former councillor wrote to offer his support, declaring that he 'left the Labour Party in January 1981 and joined the S.D.P. on day 1 of the launch'. Again he made a statement of personal continuity with the words, 'I am and always have been a loyal and committed social democrat.'[31]

It is clear that such demonstrations of continuity were important for many of the SDP's founders on a personal as well as political level, but not all members of the Gang of Four went about this in the same way. Rodgers went to great efforts to write to old friends and colleagues, assuring them that he remained the same person and would continue to hold the same views.[32] In contrast, Roy Jenkins emphasised his liberal roots and later explained that 'As Asquith's sympathetic biographer' he 'had long been well-disposed towards most liberals'.[33] He has since claimed that he had 'always been a liberal with a small "l"'.[34] David Owen was open about the 'tremendous emotional overtones' of Labour Party membership but also felt that 'To be a social democrat was a new release, a link with my Labour past but also a springboard for the future.'[35]

Innovation or inheritance?

Owen's statement attempted to bridge the inherent contradiction between the SDP's desire to present themselves as the inheritors of the Labour tradition and their claim to be 'breaking the mould' and bringing about a fundamental 'realignment' of British politics. SDP support came overwhelmingly from people who had not previously been a member of any political party. In 1984 65% of SDP members were so-called 'political virgins', compared to 22% who had come to the new party from Labour and less than 3% from each of the Conservative and Liberal parties.[36] These members stressed that 'The great attraction of the S.D.P. is that it is a NEW Party' and insisted that it should transcend the old politics of Labour by being 'free from ancient class riddled political dogma ... neither blemished or tarred with a discredited past'.[37]

Much as they stressed their loyalty to the socialist tradition, the Gang of Four knew that their main appeal was their novelty. The party might have roots in the past but it was located firmly in the present: a world of computers, credit cards and helicopters, all of which it utilised sooner and more effectively than the existing parties. The party went to great lengths to appear 'fresh', even holding a 'rolling conference' on a train rather than fall into the old pattern of seaside hotels and conference centres. The tone of much of this was almost apocalyptic, as with a letter to David Owen which read: 'Sir, I have been non-aligned all my adult life hoping against hope for the birth of a truly social democratic party. The hour has come ...'[38] Bill Rodgers has also described the birth of the new party in a similar tone, as something long-awaited which eclipsed previous (Labour) history:

> The response to the Limehouse Declaration was immediate and over-whelming. *It was as if a vast crowd of men and women had been assembled in silence to wait for the leadership we now offered.* It was a period of exhil-aration and hope quite unlike anything I had known before, even the announcement of Labour's 1945 victory which, as a schoolboy, I had witnessed from the steps of St George's Hall, Liverpool, or my first entry into government as a minister in 1964.[39]

The SDP occupied a self-constructed 'historic' present, located on the solid ground between receding past and uncertain future. The party's reluctance to commit to a manifesto or definite programme of future action only reinforced this effect.

SDP: mark II?

New Labour clearly did not represent so much of a break with the past. It was not a case of leaving the Labour Party, with all the connotations of betrayal that went along with that. This perhaps made it easier for Blair, in particular, to flaunt his apparent lack of connection to the party, his image of political rootlessness. New Labour's attitude to the party's ancestors was certainly more cautious than the SDP's. Although Blair stood himself in Gaitskell's footsteps the moment he announced his intention to revise Clause IV, this legacy was not always explicitly claimed. Indeed, Philip Gould noted that 'The language used by Gaitskell in public and others in private is *uncannily similar* to that used by Tony Blair and other modernisers a generation later' as if this was pure coincidence.[40] By depicting this as an 'uncanny', unwitting case of history repeating itself, Gould managed to present Blair both as Gaitskell's heir and as his own man. He also made the modernising of the Labour Party seem somehow inevitable; a task which would recur generation by generation until it was completed. As Gould was well aware, Gaitskell's legacy was ambiguous. Although it placed Blair firmly within a Labour tradition, it also carried its own narrative structure: that of failure and compro-mise. In an open letter to *Tribune*, half of Labour's MEPs called for the leadership to follow Gaitskell's example in accepting a compromise, by which a new statement of aims and values would stand side by side with the existing Clause IV, as with the New and Old Testaments.[41]

In igniting memories of Gaitskell's revisionism, Blair also had to be careful to avoid being burned by the SDP's flame. As Steven Fielding has argued, the SDP's example meant that 'highlighting New Labour's revisionist debt was much more hazardous than paying compliments to New Liberalism'.[42] To be seen as heirs to the 'splitters' would have meant immediate death for the incipient project of New Labour. Yet the ghost of the SDP did haunt Blair. Not only did some opponents portray him as a betrayer in the mould of the Gang of Four, but they also suggested that without the particular mission enshrined in Clause IV, Labour had become indistinguishable from the (now defunct) SDP:

> I used to be a member of the Labour Party, now it appears I belong to something called New Labour. If the leadership are really concerned to find a new name that reflects their swing to the right, how about 'Old SDP'?[43]

> When the gang of four split from the Labour Party they demanded one member, one vote, the abolition of Clause IV and the reduction of trade union power and influence within the Labour movement. Does any of this sound familiar comrades?[44]

Blair tried to counter these accusations, with the quip that, 'When you can think of no decent reason why something is wrong, you resort to saying there is to be an SDP Mark Two in the hope that everyone gets out strings of garlic and crucifixes.'[45] One particular controversy involved the Tribune Group of MPs' invitation to David Marquand to speak at their conference on the rewriting of Clause IV. The newspaper felt compelled to remind them that 'Marquand was a driving force behind the SDP which set out to destroy the Labour Party and was an early advocate of an alliance with the Liberals' and to state quite forcefully that 'Marquand, who is not a member of the Labour Party, has no business to be pontificating on our constitution'.[46]

The progressive dilemma

Tribune was right to highlight David Marquand as a key link between the SDP and New Labour. His concept of the 'progressive dilemma' was central to both of the parties' historical positioning. Marquand's thesis was first set out in a 1979 article 'Inquest on a Movement: Labour's Defeat and its Consequences' (described as the SDP's 'founding text'[47]) and was then expanded after the demise of the SDP in his seminal 1991 work, The Progressive Dilemma.[48] Its influence can be clearly seen in David Owen's condemnation of Labour's decision to follow 'the path of Fabian paternalism … pursuing nationalization and Clause Four state socialism' and his argument that it was now necessary to recover the 'radical democratic libertarian trend of decentralized socialism' of Robert Owen, William Morris and G.D.H. Cole.[49] This strategy of recovering the party's 'true' traditions was re-used in the later 1990s. Philip Gould was explicit about the importance of Marquand's thesis to New Labour's key thinkers[50] and, as we will see below, the influence of the 'progressive alliance' narrative can be clearly traced throughout the party's subsequent history. The power of academic history in shaping the way in which political actors think of themselves and therefore the ways in which they go about 'making history' has rarely been better illustrated.

Tony Blair used his Fabian Society lecture on the fiftieth anniversary of 1945, to make clear that his narrative of British democratic socialism included 'Lloyd George, Beveridge and Keynes and not just Attlee, Bevan or Crosland'.[51] Drawing heavily on Marquand's work, Blair 'liberates' the concept of socialism (or 'social-ism' as he preferred), from the question of ownership and 'economic dogma'. Instead he talked about an 'ethical socialism', which was 'based on a moral assertion that individuals are interdependent, that they owe duties to one another as well as themselves'. Although Blair made sure to say 'That, fundamentally, was Attlee's kind of socialism, and it is also mine', it is clear that he was really drawing on the heritage of liberalism and the co-operative movement.[52] This was presented as a return to the real roots of the party: 'in the rewriting of Clause IV … far from escaping our traditions, we recaptured them'.[53] Much use was made of the words '*re*-establishing', '*re*-foundation' and '*regain*' (my emphasis).

However, while this was framed in the context of Marquand's work, an extraordinary twenty-two page letter from Blair to Michael Foot, which predates *The Progressive Dilemma* by nearly a decade, reveals that Blair had already found inspiration in the radical liberal tradition, via Foot's book *Debts of Honour*:

> Like many middle-class people, I came to socialism through Marxism … For me, at university, left-wing politics was Marx and the liberal tradition was either scorned or analysed only in terms of its influence on Marx. It is absolutely plain when I read D[ebts] of H[onour] that there is a treasure trove of ideas that I never imagined existed. We need to recover the searching radicalism of these people and the breadth of vision they had.[54]

While Blair himself acknowledged that the earnest letter from the ambitious young candidate to the party leader could be seen to be 'impertinency or sycophancy', the very earnestness suggests that *Debts of Honour* really did make an impression on the young Blair (he signs off 'I expect that I will re-consider sending this on re-reading it'). More than that, it shows that he was well aware of the radical liberal tradition as an alternative past during this key period in his, and his party's, development. That this inspiration should have come from Blair's encounter with Foot's work was perhaps an irony that he was not prepared to own publicly in later years. For while Foot himself was heavily steeped in the west country traditions of radical liberalism, his period in charge of the party was so closely associated with the party's leftward turn that this other legacy could not, at that point, be extricated.

Incidentally, the letter also puts paid to any suggestion that Blair was ahistorical and unaware of Labour Party history. He emphasised that he 'actually did trouble to read Marx first-hand', demonstrated an easy familiarity with the purges and 'witch hunts' of the 1950s and quoted at length from a copy of Attlee's 1937 *The Labour Party in Perspective*, which he was 'lucky enough to find'. This was not a man with no interest in the past of his party.

At the same time as Blair and his allies were attempting to establish this alternative tradition within the party, they were also attempting to undermine and unsettle the established narrative of the Labour Party's early history. At the 1994 Annual Conference, Larry Witty attempted to give members 'a short lesson in history' and disabuse them of their image of Sidney Webb as principled idealist. In a terrifically backhanded speech, he paid tribute to Webb's 'pragmatism and subtlety' in 'fixing' a conference that was 'a bit of a shambles' and which included everyone from 'supporters of the Bolshevik Revolution' to 'people whom we should see today as well to the right of the party'. In asking delegates to 'understand the reality of your history', Witty also tried to draw a direct geneaological line from Webb and Henderson down to Blair and Prescott. He pointed out that 'Tony and John will need similar drafting skills over the course of the next few months' and also highlighted 'the commitment that the front bench and the party leadership are making to the future of socialism'.[55]

Rewriting Clause IV

As Blair and his advisers well knew, the debate over the revision of Clause IV had huge symbolic value. It was presented as a battle for the history, identity and soul of the party. As Hugo Young wrote in the *Guardian*, 'Ancient household gods will be invited to make their presence felt. The poltergeists of the past may rattle the furniture.'[56] In the event, the debate was by no means as tempestuous as expected. The revision passed remarkably smoothly at a Special Conference convened on 29 April 1995. The 6,500 responses to the party's consultation exercise were also overwhelmingly in favour of change. This is remarkable, especially as it would seem logical to assume that those who were particularly opposed to the leadership's plans would be the most keen to make their views known. Very few respondents were not prepared to agree 'that the current Clause IV does not set out Labour's actual values in a clear and concise manner'. Even among those who refused to 'agree', responses were rather equivocal. For instance, one said that he would prefer to retain the old Clause IV, with a new statement of values; another felt that although 'perhaps [there is] nothing wrong [with] Clause IV if you are to argue for it's [*sic*] principles', he was aware that he was in a minority and 'so to make the best of an unsure exercise' had completed the questionnaire anyway.[57]

It is clear that Blair did not get the battle he had bargained on. Partly this may have been because the leadership heavily promoted the postal balloting of all members, rather than relying on the votes of constituency activists. The thinking was that those who were less heavily steeped in the party's internal culture would have less of a personal investment in its totemic symbols, such as Clause IV. There is some evidence that this policy paid off. At the Special Conference, a delegate from Bristol South said:

> I have been elected to come here and vote for this new resolution, but I'm actually speaking against it, because all the ones that do work in the party – the CLP – voted against change, but when it went out to the postal vote we had an overwhelming majority for the new clause. Yet none of those people participate in the Labour Party. They pay their subs, but they don't do anything in the party whatsoever. (Applause).[58]

However, this is not the entire explanation. After sixteen years in opposition, the party was desperate to believe that Blair had the solution to their electoral woes. One respondent said, 'We have been in opposition for too long. We can only win the next General Election under Tony Blair, so if he wants to change Clause IV, he has my TOTAL support on this and any other topic.'[59] Another answered each question with one of the following statements: 'Full support for T. Blair', 'Support the line of T. Blair fully' and 'I support fully the line taken by the N.E.C. under the leadership of T. Blair.'[60]

As is well known from the work of Whiteley and Seyd, many new members were attracted to the party because of its attempts to change. They found that post-1994 recruits were 'significantly more likely to be modernizers' and 'more trusting of the party leadership' than people who had joined the party before 1994. This was in spite of being more likely to be working class (one in six as against one in eight) and slightly less likely to be graduates that the pre-1994 cohort.[61] This is borne out by the membership surveys. For instance one respondent said, 'I became a member 18 months ago – due to the changes by John Smith; Tony Blair; John Prescott. Keep this up and caring people will want to join.' Much older members were also keen to follow Blair's lead. One woman who said 'I have [been] a socialist from the day I was born, 2nd June 1912. Have fought all my life for socialism', responded to a question on Labour's economic policy with the words, 'I trust Tony Blair as our leader.'[62] The blandness of these responses speaks not of radical hopes for the future but rather a grim determination to seize political control in the present. The focus was on the immediate task of winning an election; the future would be dealt with in time.

Defending Clause IV

Yet not everyone was so easily satisfied. A vocal minority opposed Blair's plans all the way. Were they, as the leadership claimed, sentimentally holding onto old certainties or did they have other, more vital, objections? The focal point for the opposition to the rewriting of Clause IV was the Defend Clause 4 Campaign, organised by the Campaign Group of MPs, who in the course of the campaign changed their name to the Socialist Group. This grouping was led by Tony Benn MP, who emphasised the need to 'make clear to the movement and to the public that socialist ideas are still to be found within the party [in the hope that this] might discourage members of the party from resigning as some have suggested they might if Clause 4 is deleted'.[63] Numerous individual members of the party also made their opposition to the proposed change known in the letters pages of the *Guardian* and *Tribune* and by speaking at local, regional and national party meetings.

Several reports of apparently overwhelmingly pro-change conferences include references to wider disquiet. For instance, a report of the Scottish Conference's acceptance of the change also notes that George Galloway received the biggest cheer of the afternoon for the words, 'Don't sell the banner; think before you throw it in the dustbin of history.'[64] Similarly, the Labour Women's Conference voted 81.59% in favour of change, yet the *Guardian* noted that 'Clare Short, party spokeswoman on women, conceded that Mr Blair had probably suffered his worst heckling when he spoke about his clause to the conference on Saturday.'[65] Amidst a string of articles claiming that the constituencies were overwhelmingly in favour of change, a *Guardian* report on a mass meeting in Hartlepool reveals that, 'As in most of Labour's Clause 4 meetings interventions from the 450–strong audience were heavily in favour of keeping the old form of words, with activists coming ... from as far away as Southwark in London.'[66]

While this does not mean that opposition to the change was widespread, it does show that it was deeply felt. It is generally acknowledged that the reason for this strength of feeling was because the change seemed to require a painful break with the past. It was said at the time that the debate was 'as much an argument about finding a proper relationship with the past as knowing what is right for the future'.[67] An advert placed in *Tribune* by the Manufacturing, Science and Finance Union's Yorkshire and Humberside Regional Council, is a particularly neat illustration of the sense that the change violated a direct ideological line of descent between past and future. It was presented as a 'Lost and Found' classified advert and read: 'LOST – CLAUSE 4. If found please return to the Labour Party c/o Keir Hardie, Sidney Webb, Clem Attlee, Nye Bevan and all future generations of the working class.'[68]

Living socialism

Yet, despite received opinion, the most striking thing about the opponents of change is that they were not simply tied to the past. They clearly viewed Clause IV as a living statement, with real implications for policy in the present and in the future. It was held to be a succinct definition of an essential principle, as important for securing social justice and democracy in the late twentieth century as on the day it was written. As Alice Mahon MP put it in an article for *Tribune*, if Clause IV 'wasn't relevant to today's political agenda, then we would be right to abandon it. The truth is it is entirely relevant.'[69]

Numerous letter writers to both the *Guardian* and *Tribune* cited the relevance (indeed the necessity) of common ownership in tackling pressing contemporary issues, from the dominance of multinationals and the democratic deficit in the World Trade Organization to social deprivation and pension provision. As one put it, 'If Clause Four is so unrealistic as a means of organising an economy – what of the free market system?' He went on to say that 'In a few decades our unwillingness to find ways to democratise economic processes will just look plain stupid.'[70]

Perhaps the most graphic illustration of the belief in Clause IV as a statement of contemporary policy was the debate over Composite Motion No. 57, which took place at the party conference in 1994, soon after Blair's speech announcing the proposed change. The motion was brought by Glasgow Maryhill CLP through spokesman Jim Mearns and called for the NEC 'to draw up a socialist economic, industrial and social strategy'.[71] It was a cry to act upon the principles of Clause IV and – crucially – it was tabled before anyone outside the inner circle had any suspicion that Blair was to set out to reform it. Composite 57 was not inspired by Blair's direct attack on Clause IV but by a concern 'that the electoral strategy currently being pursued by the shadow cabinet places little emphasis on this constitutional aim'.[72] It was a continuation of a theme raised by motions in previous years, particularly Composite 62 in 1993, which made clear that Clause IV should be more than a symbol of socialist commitment; it should form the basis of practical policy proposals:

This Conference reaffirms its belief in an *adherence* to paragraph 4 of Clause 4 of the party's constitution as printed on every Labour Party membership card … Furthermore, Conference believes it to be essential that the present wording remains unchanged and rejects any attempt to alter what is the fundamental basis of Labour Party *policy* … and the only *practical* way of attaining a more equitable and egalitarian society.[73]

Although the tabling of Composite 57 cannot be said to owe anything to nostalgia invoked by the threat of change, after Blair's speech it became inevitable that the debate would in effect become a response to Blair's announcement that Clause IV was now under review. As Patrick Wintour put it, 'Mr Mearns had expected to move his motion to a half-full hall with little or no media attention. Only on Wednesday did it become clear that he was to be the Boy David to take on the Goliath of the party machine.'[74] Despite this, as Michael White noted, and in contrast to conference debates of the 1970s and early

1980s, 'Virtually no personal attacks were made on the leadership. Few fingers were wagged in an accusing manner. There was no rhetoric of betrayal.'[75] This is surprising and suggests either that the party had moved on further than anticipated by the leadership, or that the issue was simply too important to reduce to crude political theatre. Equally, it is striking that the debate in 1994 was far less nostalgic than that in 1993, which had invoked the ghosts of Tawney, Attlee, Robert Tressell, Ian Mikardo and the founding fathers of the party.[76]

Far from being a 'usual suspect', Jim Mearns was a last-minute stand-in. His local MP, Maria Fyfe, assured the *Guardian* that 'Jim is not a Trot. He is a mainstream member of the Labour Party.'[77] Mearns told the hall, 'I am sick of being told by political commentators that socialism is irrelevant, dead or dying ... socialism is very much alive and well and striding forward with victory in sight.'[78] His use of Blairite phrasing, 'Let's be tough on capitalism and tough on the causes of capitalism', had the effect of insisting that his calls for socialism in practice were just as serious, just as pragmatic and just as contemporary as Blair's policy proposals. In an article subsequently published in *Tribune*, Mearns reaffirmed that, 'It is important that the party fights the issues of the day in the language of the day but *always* in a socialist framework, a framework delineated by Clause Four.' He also asked:

> Why should workers not obtain the full fruits of their industry? How can this be achieved without the common ownership of the means of production, distribution and exchange which are the engines of any economy? Is it so wrong to strive for the best obtainable system of popular administration of each industry and service?[79]

Yet despite this clear call for an active commitment to the principles of Clause IV in the present day, the modernising wing of the party was able to present the debate as essentially one of sentiment versus pragmatism. Immediately after the debate, Blair said that 'no one had seriously got up to defend Clause Four, merely to criticise his tactics'.[80] Alastair Campbell's diary records a more vivid exchange. In response to a warning that 'to some people this is like going into church and taking down the cross', Blair reportedly responded, 'Oh for heaven's sake ... people believe in God, and they believe in Christ. Name me a single person who actually believes in what Clause 4 says.'[81] Over the following months, the claim that 'nobody believes in Clause Four'[82] was repeated time and again:

> A vocal campaign to keep Clause Four has been set up, which argues ... though outdated and not necessarily what we would write now [it]

has a symbolic appeal and that to change it would cause more trouble than it is worth.[83]

Labour is not going to nationalise the means of production, distribution and exchange and we should be honest enough to say that. Few believe that Clause Four is relevant today but we hang onto it as unchallenged and unchallengeable dogma.[84]

Forwards or back?

Ironically, the most fervent opponents of the change of wording would probably have agreed with Blair that, 'The idea that we cannot touch a 77–year-old constitution is farcical. We are not a preservation society guarding the ideological crown jewels. We are a dynamic living movement which seeks to change this country for the better.'[85] Where they differed was over their vision of socialism *as* a 'dynamic living movement'. Despite the modernisers' claim that their opponents remained in thrall to an obsolete form of words, there seems to have been a willingness to discuss revising the constitution, even among the left wing of the party and from the trade unions:

We are in a period of change. Anything agreed in 1918 we should be able to review in 1994. We look forward to the consultation.[86]

I was taken by surprise, but it is not an unreasonable point to say that in 1994 the constitution needs redrawing. There was no indication that this was the end of socialism.[87]

Yes – needs re-writing *but* without scrapping the principles which define socialism.[88]

The caveat of course lies in that final sentence: the retention of socialism. It seems that many party members saw the debate on Clause IV as an opportunity to commit themselves anew to socialist principles, within the context of the late twentieth century. As one CLP delegate, speaking on Composite 57 said, 'I welcome the debate we are going to have in the coming 12 months, because I am so confident in my socialism; I feel it in my bones, it is the centre of my being. It is everything I am.'[89] *Tribune* immediately launched a conference to discuss their hopes for the new Clause IV, noting that, 'There is much that should be in Labour's constitution but which isn't. Where is the mention of socialism or the redistribution of power and wealth for instance?'[90] A group of MPs and trade union leaders also wrote an open letter to the *Guardian*, urging the party to 'seize the opportunity' to enshrine a commitment to full employment in the new constitution.[91]

This attitude was also present among the members who responded positively to the consultation exercise. Some felt that, although they were happy to change Clause IV in principle, the new wording did not inspire them. When asked to identify anything that had been missed out, one said 'A feeling of crusade' and another, 'Some recognition that there is a spiritual, even idealist element: "the brotherhood of man"' and called for the party to 'Remember Rabbie Burns!'[92] Others made suggestions for the new constitution which could not have been further from the intentions of the leadership. One respondent wanted it to include the words 'From each according to ability, to each according to need.' Another felt that the new statement should emphasise that 'Individual freedom is largely illusory. We should aim to emancipate classes / categories of people.' In response to a question on how best to promote a mixed economy, he suggested that the party needed to 'Come up with an even better way of democratically controlling all leading firms. State clearly that the market mechanism is an outright failure.'[93] A third respondent recommended an 'apparent wealth tax' (to apply to housing, yachts, expensive cars etc); an opposition to company cars; worker representation on the boards of all major companies and an 85% top-rate tax bracket for salaries above £150,000 (including shares) so as to 'Challenge those in management & directorships to leave their employment or companies.' He also suggested that there should be a requirement that 'those persons responsible for managing the state-controlled public utilities (Post Office, rail, NHS etc) be shown in their dedication not only competent but socialists too!!'[94]

Similar attitudes were reflected in the parliamentary party. Despite the overwhelming support for the revision of Clause IV, a survey of Labour MPs carried out before the 1997 election found that 68% regarded 'public ownership [as] ... crucial to the achievement of social justice'. After the election, 48% of the much larger, and younger, PLP remained dedicated to the principle of state ownership of major public services.[95] As Edmund Dell notes, this 'was still a large percentage in a party that had begun to describe itself as New Labour. It demonstrated the extent to which New Labour was a camouflage for deep-seated instincts that Blair had not yet charmed away.'[96] While these MPs might have been happy to change Clause IV and to embrace a new, softer wording, they remained committed to the principles which underpinned it: exactly the opposite dynamic to that portrayed by Blair. It was this practical dedication to socialism that Blair and his allies could not – or perhaps wilfully *would not* – understand. They could not accept that the opponents of the reform were following their own request for the party to 'say what we mean and mean what we say'; that it was their *meanings*, rather than just their methods of discourse which differed. By reducing their argument to one that *only* traded in history, symbolism and emotion, Blair was able to neutralise his opponents and to ignore their desire to discuss the ideological direction of the party.

Which history?

The debate on Composite 57 was paired with that on Composite 56, a motion 'congratulat[ing] the Co-operative movement on the 150th anniversary of the founding of the Rochdale Pioneers Co-operative Society'.[97] Indeed most of the speakers in the debate referred to both motions. Many of those who rejected Composite 57 were very happy to sing the praises of Composite 56. Not one person spoke against it. It seemed to have no controversial content, nothing with which a member of the labour movement could possibly disagree. It therefore became something of a touchstone; a way of signalling one's commitment to socialist principles and to the movement's historic roots at the same time as denying the appeal to act on those principles and roots in the modern day. However, it is not as simple as that. In addition to offering congratulations, Composite 56 also called for action from the Labour Party on a number of key policies, including a Co-operatives Act; statutory recognition of housing co-operatives; legislation recognising and protecting voluntary, mutual and self-help groups 'as a separate and distinct sector of the economy'; a commitment to fostering co-operative principles in future policy; and the creation of regional co-operative development agencies.[98]

Why then was the discussion (it doesn't really warrant the term 'debate') over this motion so anodyne, compared to the fierce controversy aroused by Composite 57? There are two possible answers. The clue to the first is in the deliberately contemporary language of the motion, which recognised that the Co-operative Party was 'now revitalised with new vision and new direction'.[99] It disguised an appeal to old principles as a step forward into a world of regional government and the social economy. The seconder of the motion made the distinction between this approach and that of Composite 57 very clear:

> the scale and emphasis of the Co-op has grown and changed so much since those days that it has had to modernise and change [,] to expand to remain successful, keeping alive its retail outlets and jobs. So, too, we in the Labour Party have had to change and modernise, but we will

never lose our principles and values. Later on we will debate Clause IV. This, too, needs modernising, as it uses only the language of the Scargillsaurus.[100]

However, this answer is not satisfactory because, as we have already noted, the defenders of Clause IV also insisted upon the relevance of Clause IV to the modern world – to multi-national corporations, globalisation and devolution.[101] The second answer lies in the particular cluster of roots to which Composite 56 appealed. Larry Witty emphasised the need for a plural notion of public ownership 'which is the centre of [Labour's] industrial policy today [and] reflected in the co-operative ideals in Composite 56'.[102] This is precisely the heritage which Blair, Gould *et al.* were keen to resurrect.

A new identity

As we have seen, this narrative of a pre-1918 progressive alliance had long underpinned social democratic thought and was revived by the architects of New Labour via the work of David Marquand as the SDP dream fell apart. However, a similar narrative had already been used by SDP members to orient their practical alliance and eventual merger with the Liberals. This was a further shift in identity which required careful negotiation. The Gang of Four each had very different positions on the Liberal Party, ranging from Roy Jenkins who, as we have already noted, saw himself as a small 'l' liberal and was keen to merge as quickly as possible, to David Owen who was fundamentally opposed to the whole idea and did not join the merged party but continued to lead a rump SDP. The merger process was prolonged and fraught. Many members and commentators stressed the different histories and political cultures of the two parties; activists on each side feared that their distinctive identity would be diluted in the new party.[103] The idea of a historical progressive alliance was a means of maintaining their political identity for proponents of merger in both parties.

The Liberal leadership made concerted efforts to present the Alliance as a continuation of Liberal history. In his speech at the re-opening of the renovated National Liberal Club in the midst of the merger negotiations, David Steel quoted Gladstone's regret that the Liberal Party had sometimes 'fallen behind in the point of unity of action'. Steel then used this piece of Liberal history to call for 'unity of action' between Liberals and Social Democrats, describing the Alliance as 'the heir in contemporary politics of the Gladstonian

Party of justice and freedom'. Steel did not hesitate to claim the direct authority of Gladstone in his reiteration of the progressive alignment thesis:

> I believe that Mr Gladstone and our great Liberal predecessors would be urging us on to unity now. They would be delighted to see the great streams of social liberalism, divided temporarily in the first half of this century by the emergent Labour Party, now coming together in the full flood of a new party of conscience of reform.[104]

This narrative of a shared historic mission, based on a radical, progressive alliance, was fixed in the founding document of the new party, the Joint Policy Statement drafted by the six alliance negotiators and released on 22 January 1988. It emphasised that the new party would 'not start from a blank page' because their shared 'taproots go deep'. Both parties could 'take pride in our record of promoting social progress and radical reform in Britain' and should now focus on the need to 'rekindle' their shared traditions.[105] The implication of these statements was that by merging as the Liberal Democrats, the progressive alignment would be re-formed, thus effectively undoing seventy years of unnecessary and unfruitful division. A 2002 Liberal Democrat policy paper also sought to reaffirm this legacy, arguing that those Liberals who joined Labour in the years after the First World War 'did not regard themselves as changing their political beliefs; they simply saw Labour as the stronger vehicle for reform'. Moreover, it was 'the political descendants of these people who largely provided the social democratic ethos and approach of the post-war Labour governments', left to form the SDP and then to merge with the Liberal Party.[106]

Yet the Labour Party itself remained divided between left and right, between 'traditionalists' and 'modernisers'. It was not until 1997 that the progressive alignment narrative was able (temporarily) to unite Labour and the Liberal Democrats in a Joint Cabinet Committee on constitutional reform. While this period of at least tacit unity soon dissolved, the idea of an alliance has continued to haunt the political conversation. In 2004 Gordon Brown called for a 'progressive consensus' in his keynote speech to Labour pressure group Compass and later attempted to bring it about by inviting Shirley Williams and Paddy Ashdown to be involved in his 'government of all the talents'.[107] Both turned down this offer, preferring to maintain their Liberal Democrat loyalties. After the 2010 General Election delivered a hung parliament, progressives briefly rallied to the idea of a Lib-Lab alliance at the head of a 'rainbow coalition' including greens and nationalists. This seemed to offer not merely a palatable coalition, but also a 'historic' chance to create a progressive alliance between Liberals and Social Democrats, 'a new and radical settlement' built on shared 'heritage and aspirations'.[108] While the electoral arithmetic was against this coalition, the idea of a progressive alliance also failed to resonate with the public. It was seen as a self-serving attempt for Labour to remain in power and branded a 'coalition of losers'. In the event, it was David Cameron who was able to present himself as the true 'heir to Blair', by sitting Liberal Democrats at his cabinet table in a way Blair only teasingly imagined.

However, as indicated in Chapter 2, the Liberal Democrat Party has yet to resolve the questions arising from its complicated inheritances. The traces of division between the social and classical liberal wings of the party have become more pronounced in recent years. Even before the coalition with the Conservatives forced Liberal Democrats to re-examine their political positioning, tensions were obvious. In 2004 a group of prominent Liberal Democrats, including both of the 2007 leadership candidates, Nick Clegg and Chris Huhne, published a text which claimed to be 'Reclaiming Liberalism'. It was entitled *The Orange Book*, in a clear refutation of the path taken by the party following the new Liberals' 'Yellow Book' (*Britain's Industrial Future*) of 1928. This was in turn answered by *Reinventing the State: Social Liberalism for the 21st Century*, published in 2007 by a group associated with the left of the party. Although some of the 'Orange Bookers' did contribute chapters to *Reinventing the State*, it was clear that tensions between the difference wings of the party remained. This was particularly apparent at the 2007 Party Conference, during a high-profile debate over taxation. The former camp argued for lower taxation to allow citizens to help themselves through the recession; their opponents felt that now, more than ever, it was necessary to support a strong state funded through redistributive taxation. The debate on the conference floor was markedly rooted in the party's history, with Gladstone and Cobden invoked by 'classical Liberals' and Lloyd George, Hobhouse, Keynes and Beveridge by 'social Liberals'. As these names suggest, the tension within the party is not as straightforward as former-SDP versus former-Liberal: *The Orange Book* had a foreword by then party leader and former SDP (and briefly Labour) member, Charles Kennedy and *Reinventing the State* was co-edited by Duncan Brack, who came to the party from the Liberals. In fact, the division could be seen to stem from a much older, Liberal debate over the role of the state. In seeking to resolve the 'progressive dilemma' the social democrats have (largely) joined with the self-proclaimed heirs of the Edwardian New Liberals. Their relationship to classical liberalism remains ambiguous at best.

Conclusion

The SDP could be seen as having been thrust into a novel stance in order to attempt a return to the values of the recent past. To them it was the Militant left which provided the unacceptable break with Labour's history, who practised 'new style politics'.[109] The idea of the progressive alliance was a means of maintaining a sense of personal continuity as they left Labour and eventually merged with the Liberal Party. Their vision of Labour's past however, remained strongly aligned with Gaitskellite revisionism. This was a live and positive legacy, proof that their own position belonged firmly within the mainstream of the party – even if it had been sidelined by recent events. For them, history was a form of identity affirmation, even as they sought to break free of its constraints. The idea of the progressive consensus became a way of maintaining their fidelity to Labour's past, at the same time as critiquing the path the Labour Party had taken since 1918.

This narrative was taken up by New Labour but more as a rhetorical strategy than an urgent attempt to establish personal and political continuity. In his bid to appear '"modern", "up-to-date", "*au fait*"' (in the prophetic words of Henry Drucker), Blair used Labour's traditional temporal positioning in order to portray his opponents as simply nostalgic for a dead past.[110] However, he did not jettison the past completely; instead he retold it. This was historical revisionism, not a complete rejection of the past. As suggested in earlier chapters, this respect for the past – or rather *a* past – was actually more 'in harmony with the dominant time-perspective of our age' than the relentless modernism which Drucker described.[111] The argument that the progressive consensus was an older and *therefore* more accurate narrative was used to validate the positioning of New Labour. Moreover, the experiences of the 1970s and early 1980s, which led to the SDP's radical break with their party, were now incorporated into a new historical narrative by which they became the foundational narrative of the future. No longer looking forward in order to go back, Labour's right wing were now prepared (occasionally and briefly) to look back in order to stride forward. Even the history of the party's most traumatic times became a celebratory narrative of, in Gould's words 'how the modernisers saved the Labour party'.

Notes

1 Black, *The Political Culture of the Left*, p. 135.
2 C.A.R. Crosland, *The Future of Socialism* (London: Jonathan Cape, 1956), p. 97.
3 See Bevir, *New Labour*; James Cronin, *New Labour's Pasts: the Labour Party and its Discontents* (Harlow: Longman, 2004); Fielding, *The Labour Party*; Steven Fielding, 'New Labour and the past', in Tanner *et al.* (eds), *Labour's First Century*, pp. 367–91; Tudor Jones, *Remaking the Labour Party: From Gaitskell to Blair* (London and New York: Routledge, 2006) and Eric Shaw, *Losing Labour's Soul: New Labour and the Blair governments, 1997–2007* (London: Routledge, 2007).
4 Nick Randall, 'Time and British politics: memory, the present and teleology in the politics of New Labour', *British Politics*, 4:2 (2009), 217.
5 Peter Mandelson and Roger Liddle, *The Blair Revolution: Can New Labour Deliver?* (London and Boston: Faber and Faber, 1996), p. vii.
6 Oliver Daddow, 'Playing games with history: Tony Blair's European policy in the press', *British Journal of Politics and International Relations*, 9 (2007), 591.
7 Freeden, 'True blood or false genealogy', 151. Original emphasis.
8 However, the 1998 Special Issue of *Marxism Today* made it clear that Blair should not be seen as a simple inheritor of their political stance and that he had abandoned their hopes of a radical socialist future. See particularly Stuart Hall, 'The great moving nowhere show', *Marxism Today*, Special Issue, November/December 1998, pp. 9–14.
9 It also referenced the party's similarly optimistic 'New Britain' manifesto of 1964.
10 Bevir, *New Labour*.
11 Roy Jenkins speaking at the inaugural meeting of the SDP Lawyers' Association, Lincoln's Inn, 29 April 1981. Quoted in Ian Bradley, *Breaking the Mould? The Birth and Prospects of the Social Democratic Party* (Oxford: Robertson, 1981), p. 28; William Rodgers, 'Government under stress: Britain's Winter of Discontent 1979', *Political Quarterly*, 55:2, (1984), 171.
12 UCL, HG, GP: C194. NEC, 'General Election 1959: report of Election Sub-Committee', 28 October 1959.
13 Michael Kenny and Martin J. Smith, 'Discourses of modernization: Gaitskell, Blair and the reform of Clause IV', in Charles Pattie *et al.* (eds), *British Elections and Parties Review*, vol. 7 (London: Frank Cass, 1997), pp. 110–26.
14 NEC, 'General Election 1959: report of Election Sub-Committee'. Original emphasis.
15 UCL, HG, C212, press release of Hugh Gaitskell's speech in Nottingham, 13 February 1960, issued by Labour Party East Midlands Regional Office; 'New ideas wanted from the Left, says Mr. Gaitskell – why no thanks for these ten?', *Tribune*, 19 February 1960, p. 5.
16 UCL, HG, C212, letter from Hugh Gaitskell to Sam Watson, 3 March 1960. Original emphasis.
17 William Rodgers, 'The SDP and Liberal Party in alliance', *Political Quarterly*, 54:4 (1983), 355.

18 Rodgers, 'Government under stress', 179.
19 Albert Sloman Library, University of Essex (hereafter ASL), Lord Rodgers of Quarrybank, SDP Papers (hereafter ASL, WRSDP), box 2, folder c, Rodgers' speech at the Annual Dinner of the Abertillery Constituency Labour Party, 30 November 1979.
20 See for instance, Lawrence, 'Labour: the myths it has lived by'.
21 *Labour Victory*, Conference Special, no. 17 (London, 1981), p. 3.
22 Roy Hattersley, *Who Goes Home? Scenes From a Political Life* (London: Little, Brown and Company, 1995), pp. 233, 235.
23 ASL, WRSDP, 2: c, 'Who are the guilty men?' [1983?]. Original emphases.
24 ASL, Lord Alec McGivan, SDP Papers (hereafter AMSDP), II, 13, letter to Shirley Williams, 8 February 1981.
25 ASL, WRSDP, 2: c, Rodgers' inaugural speech to the Campaign for Labour Victory, 19 February 1977.
26 Ibid.
27 Ibid.
28 LHASC, Dianne Hayter, Additional Papers (uncatalogued), Box 2, press release of Rodgers speaking in Stockton-on-Tees, 28 August 1975.
29 ASL, WRSDP, 2: b, Bob Mclennan's speech to his CLP, February 1981.
30 ASL, AMSDP, II: 13, 25 January 1981.
31 ASL, WRSDP, 3, 14 April 1981. Emphasis added.
32 ASL, WRSDP, 3, letters from Bill Rodgers to a number of MPs, 12 February 1981; ASL, WRSDP, 2: b, letter from Bill Rodgers to David Basnett, 5 March 1981.
33 Roy Jenkins, *A Life at the Centre* (London: Macmillan 1991), p. 513.
34 Roy Jenkins, *The British Liberal Tradition: From Gladstone to Young Churchill, Asquith and Lloyd George – Is Blair Their Heir?* (Toronto, Buffalo and London: University of Toronto Press, 2001), p. 13.
35 David Owen, *Time to Declare* (London: Michael Joseph, 1991), p. 500.
36 Ibid., p. 496.
37 ASL, WRSDP, 3, letter to *Huddersfield Examiner*, 22 June 1981.
38 ASL, AMSDP, II: 13, letter to David Owen, 27 January 1981.
39 Rodgers, William, 'What happened to the SDP, and what could still happen?', *London Review of Books*, 7 February 1991. Emphasis added.
40 Philip Gould, *The Unfinished Revolution: How the Modernisers Saved the Labour Party* (London: Abacus, 1999), p. 33. Emphasis added.
41 'Testament to equality and democracy', *Tribune*, 4 November 1994, p. 4.
42 Fielding, 'New Labour and the past', p. 383.
43 Letter from Colin Penfold, Powys, *Guardian*, 29 April 1995, p. 26.
44 Constituency delegate, *Special Conference Report* (Labour Party, 29 April 1995), p. 297.
45 Patrick Wintour, 'Prescott calms ruffled left', *Guardian*, 8 October 1994, p. 1.
46 Editorial, *Tribune*, 18 November 1994, p. 2.
47 Steven Fielding and Declan McHugh, '*The Progressive Dilemma* and the social democratic perspective', in John Callaghan, Steven Fielding and Steve Ludlam (eds), *Interpreting the Labour Party: Approaches to Labour Politics and History* (Manchester: Manchester University Press, 2003), 138.
48 David Marquand, 'Inquest on a movement: Labour's defeat and its

consequences', *Encounter* (July 1979), 8–18; David Marquand, *The Progressive Dilemma: From Lloyd George to Blair* (London: Phoenix, 1999).

49 Owen, *Time to Declare*, p. 483.

50 Gould, *The Unfinished Revolution*.

51 Tony Blair, *Let us face the future*, 1945 Anniversary Lecture (London: The Fabian Society, 1995), p. 4.

52 Ibid., p. 12.

53 Ibid., p. 4.

54 LHASC, MF.L31.1.4, letter from Blair to Foot, 28 July 1982.

55 Labour Party: *Annual Conference Report* (Labour Party, 1994), p. 198.

56 Hugo Young, 'Genuine acclaim; simple truths', *Guardian*, 5 October 1994, pp. 1, 22.

57 LHASC, Labour Party Papers, Clause IV Consultation (hereafter LP Clause IV Consultation). It should also be noted that a third respondent agreed with the initial statement but later wrote 'Clause IV has stood the test of time unlike this questionaire [*sic*] – Leave it alone.'

58 *Special Conference Report* , 1995, p. 299.

59 LP Clause IV Consultation.

60 Ibid.

61 Patrick Seyd and Paul Whiteley, *New Labour's Grassroots: The Transformation of Labour Party Membership* (Basingstoke: Palgrave Macmillan, 2002), pp. 155, 42–43.

62 LP Clause IV Consultation.

63 Quoted by Patrick Wintour and Stephen Bates, 'Benn urges the left to rebel on Clause 4', *Guardian*, 22 February 1995, p. 6.

64 Quoted by Erlend Clouston, 'Blair triumph in Scottish Clause 4 vote', *Guardian*, 11 March 1995, p. 1.

65 Patrick Wintour, 'Labour women vote strongly in favour of the new Clause 4', *Guardian*, 3 April 1995, p. 2.

66 Martin Wainwright, '"New Labour" Mandelson blenches at common ownership of chips as Scargill extols Marks and Spencers', *Guardian*, 28 March 1995, p. 6.

67 Martin Kettle, 'Laying Labour's ghost with a liberal dose', *Guardian*, 11 March 1995, p. 25.

68 *Tribune*, 23 December, 1994, p. 8.

69 Alice Mahon MP, 'Standing the test of time', *Tribune*, 16 December 1994, p. 4.

70 Peter Robbins, *Guardian*, 10 October 1994, p. 21.

71 Labour Party, *Conference Arrangements Committee Report* (Labour Party, 1994), p. 32.

72 Ibid.

73 Labour Party, *Conference Arrangements Committee Report* (Labour Party, 1993), p. 37. Emphases added.

74 Patrick Wintour, 'Vote for the past defies leader', *Guardian*, 7 October 1994, p. 7.

75 Michael White, 'Party may still be in turmoil but with a crucial difference', *Guardian*, 8 October 1994, p. 8.

76 Labour Party, *Annual Conference Report* (Labour Party, 1993), pp. 271–7.
77 Quoted in White, 'Party may still be in turmoil', p. 8.
78 *Annual Conference Report*, 1994, p. 192.
79 Jim Mearns, 'Back from breaking point', *Tribune*, 4 November 1994, p. 7.
80 Patrick Wintour, 'Prescott calms ruffled left', *Guardian*, 8 October 1994, p. 1.
81 Alastair Campbell, *The Blair Years: Extracts from the Alastair Campbell Diaries* (London: Hutchinson, 2007), p. 16.
82 Giles Radice quoted by Michael White, 'Blair defines the new Labour', *Guardian*, 5 October 1994, p. 1.
83 Ben Lucas, 'The principles of renewal', *Tribune*, 2 December 1994, p. 6.
84 Greg Pope, 'Saying what we mean, meaning what we say', *Tribune*, 28 October 1994, p. 7.
85 Quoted by Michael White, 'Cliffhanger Clause 4 win boosts Blair', *Guardian*, 11 March 1995, p. 8.
86 Roger Lyons, leader of MSF, quoted by Patrick Wintour and Keith Harper, 'Unions favour redrawing of constitution', *Guardian*, 5 October 1994, p. 9.
87 Michael Meacher, quoted by Patrick Wintour and Keith Harper, 'Unions favour redrawing of constitution', *Guardian*, 5 October 1994, p. 9.
88 LP Clause IV Consultation. Original emphasis.
89 *Annual Conference Report*, 1994, p. 195.
90 Editorial, *Tribune*, 14 October 1994, p. 2.
91 *Guardian*, 6 March 1995, p. 21.
92 LP Clause IV Consultation.
93 Ibid.
94 Ibid.
95 Michael Kenny and Martin J. Smith, '(Mis)understanding Blair', in *Political Quarterly*, 68:3 220–30; Peter Riddell, *The Times*, 28 April 1998. Both quoted in Edmund Dell, *A Strange Eventful History: Democratic Socialism in Britain* (London: HarperCollins, 2000), p. 544.
96 Ibid.
97 *Conference Arrangements*, 1994, p. 32.
98 Ibid.
99 Ibid.
100 *Annual Conference Report*, 1994, pp. 191–2.
101 For a discussion of the Co-op's own struggle to modernise see Black, *Redefining British Politics*, pp. 46–74. The role of Crosland in this process is particularly noteworthy.
102 Ibid., p. 198.
103 For a full discussion see Ivor Crewe and Anthony King, *SDP: The Birth, Life and Death of the Social Democratic Party* (Oxford and New York: Oxford University Press, 1997). The pages of *Liberal News* and *The Social Democrat* are also rich sources of information.
104 David Steel, quoted in Catherine Sample, 'NLC begins the new century with £1m refit', *Liberal News*, no. 1857, 17 July 1987, p. 3.
105 'A Democracy of Conscience', printed in *Liberal News*, no. 1882, 22 January 1988, pp. 4–5.
106 *It's About Freedom*, The Report of the Liberal Democrat Working Group, Policy Paper 50 (June 2002), p. 11.

107 See Martin Bright, 'Reclaim our radicalism, says Brown', *Observer*, 24 October 2004. Available at: www.guardian.co.uk/politics/2004/oct/24 /uk.labour. Accessed 03.07.2009; 'Shirley Williams offered advisory role', 28 June 2007: www.politics.co.uk/news/party-politics/shirley-williams-offered-advisory-role-$475416.htm. Accessed 03.07.2009.
108 Neal Lawson and Richard Grayson, 'Lib and Lab: a dream team', *Guardian: Comment is Free*, 9 May 2010. Available at: www.guardian.co.uk/comment-isfree/2010/may/09/labour-liberal-democrats-progressive-alliance. Accessed 08.06.2010.
109 LHASC, Dianne Hayter, Additional Papers (uncatalogued), Box 2, press release of Rodgers speaking in Stockton-on-Tees, 28 August 1975.
110 Drucker, *Doctrine and Ethos*, p. 35.
111 Ibid.

5
New times, new politics: the collapse of the CPGB's historical narrative

Of all the political traditions examined here, Marxism has the closest connection with the practice of history, its political analysis being explicitly based on a theory of historical development. Indeed, the divisions within both the party itself and the wider Marxist community, which stretched from 1956 right through until 1991, were often framed around questions of historical interpretation. The Communist Party Historians' Group boasted a number of renowned historians and was one of the party's key contributions to wider intellectual debate. However, the historians' ability to analyse the history of either the party itself or of the labour movement in the twentieth century was extremely restricted by political considerations. One of the consolations of the weakening of the Soviet Union was the ability to subject its history to critical historical analysis. In losing the Marxist future, the historians gained access to its past.

The events of 1989–91 created a historical and mnemonic crisis for members of the Communist Party of Great Britain (CPGB) who struggled to reconcile their past identities with their present situation. Unlike the outward-facing revisionism of other political parties, this was an intensely personal affair. The solution for many was to emphasise the need to find new ways to progress socialist aims, without relying on a discredited grand narrative. In contrast, other communist parties, such as the Communist Party of Britain (CPB), which had been established (or 're-established') in 1988, fared rather better. By adhering to the international party line of renewal and continued struggle, the party was able to hold its narrative together, condemning the excesses of totalitarian regimes, while reaffirming the need for international class struggle.

The small size and intense commitment of the CPGB meant that it developed an unusually strong mnemonic culture. The party functioned as a repository for personal, familial and collective memories of struggle, exclusion and comradeship. Raphael Samuel has described the way in which 'To be a Communist was to have a complete social identity' and how the party's activities 'might be seen retrospectively as a way of practising togetherness', notwithstanding the political urgency accorded to them at the time.[1] Robyn Fivush has detailed the extent to which the stories we tell ourselves about our own history and our sense of self are constructed through narrative discourse within the family.[2] Within the CPGB 'family' these narratives were strong enough to infuse all other potential narratives. Phil Cohen's collection of testimonies from former 'communist children' makes clear the extent to which communist identity was tied up with a sense of 'difference' – of holidays spent in Eastern Europe rather than Blackpool, of weekends delivering copies of the *Daily Worker*, of the imperative to challenge school orthodoxies. Parents were busy with party business, and career opportunities disappeared, along with non-party friends.[3] A worldview was constructed not only through the immediate memory work of families and close friendship groups but also through broader, historical narratives of the past – of party, national and international progress and history.

Moreover, Marxism is a peculiarly *historical* ideology, its political analysis being explicitly based on a theory of historical development. For communists, the past was more than a political prop; it was a political force. The CPGB therefore provides an interesting example of the complicated interaction between memory and history. It is clear that there was a tension between the ideal of objective *history* and the need for the communist historians to provide the party with a politically usable *past* – a framework for celebratory collective memories. The ability of even internationally renowned Marxist historians to analyse the history of either the party itself or of the labour movement in the twentieth century, was extremely restricted. Yet more than any other political ideology, communism was predicated upon objective, *scientific*, historical analysis. The political constraints upon such history were therefore particularly damaging.

These tensions became especially apparent in 1956, following Khrushchev's revelations after the death of Stalin and the Soviet invasion of Hungary. It is significant that the party's historians were at the forefront of internal dissent. Over the next three decades, as the divisions within the party deepened, it is unsurprising to find those historians who remained within the party firmly attached to its

Eurocommunist wing. The Gramscian turn away from teleology and certainty and towards a recognition of the particularities and contingencies of lived experience both reflected and shaped the concerns of academic history in this period. For Marxists, in Britain as elsewhere, political revisionism went hand in hand with historical revisionism.

This dual aspect of revisionism marks out the CPGB from other British political parties which have similarly undergone periods of political revisionism. As will be seen below, the CPGB revisionists grouped around *Marxism Today* argued that it was necessary to adapt their ideology to fit present social reality. This has close parallels with debates within the Labour Party in both the 1950s/1960s and 1980s/1990s. But the two parties' attitudes to history were very different. Blair (unlike Gaitskell and Crosland) sought to bolster the revisionists' case by tying it to an alternative interpretation of the Party's past which emphasised the co-operative movement and alliance with new liberalism.[4] This was history in the service of the present. The CPGB's historical revisionism was not intended to justify future changes; changes were made necessary because of a new perspective on the past. More fundamentally, this historical knowledge necessitated a new attitude to both history and politics, one that was characterised by pluralism, openness and contingency.

The particular focus is the final four years of the CPGB's existence. The long-term divisions within the party came to a head in 1988, with the expulsion of leading left-wingers and the formation of the rival Communist Party of Britain. The possible futures of British communism were therefore already in doubt when the USSR collapsed. As we will see, the members (and particularly the leaders) of the CPGB reacted very differently to those of the CPB and an earlier breakaway party, the New Communist Party (formed in 1977). While members of these latter groups were able to maintain both their existing communist identities and their visions of the future, the CPGB disbanded. The loss of the social framework of the CPGB was disorienting for members; the destruction of the collective narrative of communist identity was arguably worse. While many party members made attempts to find inspiration in alternative radical histories, it was by concentrating on the needs of the present and future that they were able to reconcile their past identities with their present situation. They stressed the need to find new ways to progress socialist aims, without relying on a discredited grand narrative of historical development.

Communist history

The Communist Party Historians' Group, established in 1946, was one of the party's key contributions to wider intellectual debate, particularly through the seminal journal *Past and Present*, founded in 1952. The group continued to meet until 1992, when it renamed itself the Socialist History Society, but it lost valuable members in 1956 and its reputation dimmed thereafter. Although Steve Parsons has shown that the 1956 membership exodus was not restricted to intellectuals,[5] it is clear that the Historians' Group had a particularly strong reaction to Krushchev's revelations, quickly forming 'the nucleus of vocal opposition to the Party line'.[6] Almost all of its members left the party; most spectacular were the resignations (under threat of expulsion) of John Saville and E.P. Thompson who had founded a journal, *The Reasoner*, in order to discuss the revelations and (a few months later) the invasion of Hungary. Saville explained that they were both 'emotionally, politically and morally shocked at the reve-lations of what Stalinism really meant' and that 'as Communists and historians we saw clearly that we were obliged to analyse seriously the causes of the crimes which in the past we had defended or apol-ogised for'.[7] The idea that this was their obligation *as historians* is key. Eric Hobsbawm, who famously stayed within the party, made the same point: 'what had been done under Stalin and why it had been concealed was literally a question about history'.[8] Yet, as Perry Anderson has remarked, Hobsbawm's complaint that 'We were not told the truth about something which had to affect the very nature of a communist's belief' showed rather a disconnect between 'militant and historian' – in the case of the Soviet past, it was 'not independ-ent sources critically checked, but the word of authority [which] was expected to deliver the truth'.[9]

Hobsbawm was the first to admit that his (and the other British Marxist historians') approach to the party's history, and even to the twentieth-century history of the labour movement, was very different from their approach to other historical subjects. They were under 'constraint', particularly with regard to 'some notoriously tricky problems' in the party's history. Even on the occasions when they attempted to write such a history – particularly in 1952/3 – they found that 'The gap between what historians thought it necessary to write and what was regarded as officially possible and desirable to write at this stage – or even much later – proved too large.'[10] Hobsbawm also quotes an unnamed colleague's comment at the Historians' Group meeting on 8 April 1956: 'We have accepted Soviet articles on contemporary history in a way we did not for earlier centuries. We stopped being historians as regards the history of the CPSU [Communist Party of the Soviet Union] or current affairs.'[11]

This lack of critical engagement was a serious weakness in a party which placed so much emphasis on a rigorous analysis of the past. Not only were Stalin's distortions of history and historical sources a moral offence, but they also attacked the very notion of a 'scientific' history, based on deductions from empirical research. As Johnstone pointed out in 1979, 'As materialists our starting point must be reality.' The position of the CPSU, in which facts were selected in 'the service of the prevailing political line', made it impossible to learn from mistakes or to draw correct conclusions from the study of history. In support of his position, Johnstone quoted Marx – 'Is it not the first task of the scientific researcher to go directly to the truth without looking to the right or to the left?' – and Lenin – 'We need full and true information and truth should not depend on the question of whom it should serve' – noting laconically that this letter of Lenin's was itself suppressed until after the XXth Congress of 1956.[12]

It is striking that in a movement with so many first-rate historians, Martin Jacques was able to comment that 'Now I think it is fair to say that, not least in Britain, the development of Communist history has not had a very good record.' It was, he felt, 'essentially narrative, descriptive and often celebratory'.[13] This was not for want of trying. In the aftermath of the 1956 revelations, the Historians' Group 'demanded a serious history of the CP'. This led – by Hobsbawm's account – to 'frustrated meetings' with the party leadership who would only countenance a celebratory history – 'a record of battles fought, heroic deeds, sacrifices for the cause, red banners waved'.[14] In a 1979 article for Our History Journal, Monty Johnstone highlighted the disjunction between 'the demand for an objective evaluation of our past' as raised by 1956 and the central party's view of history, as shown in a 1937 statement from the Secretariat, which spoke of 'the urgent need for a history of the British Communist Party, in view of the increasing number of new members coming into the Party, as well as the increasing interest on all sides in the Communist Party'. This was unlikely to be the 'frank and balanced account' the Historians' Group had called for.[15]

1989

Like 1956, the events of 1989–91 could be seen as a *historical* crisis, calling into question both past and future. As an editorial in the Historians' Group's *Our History Journal* put it:

> It can be seen that our understanding of our history is very much conditioned by our expectations about the shape of the future and looks radically different after 1989 from what it did before. The past is not what it used to be.[16]

Our History Journal immediately announced that the next issue would be devoted to 'A review of the processes since the Russian Revolution which have led up to the present state of affairs.' This would 'aim especially to disentangle aspects of development which were intrinsic to the nature of the Soviet Union and its allied regimes from occasions where other decisions might have produced very different outcomes'. The editors also could not resist noting that 'The orientation of this journal for the last several years, to concentrate on the history of the international communist movement and to face its most discreditable aspects has been amply vindicated, for they have proved in the event to be very consequential.'[17]

Nineteen months after that editorial was published, the CPGB ceased to exist and its resources were used to establish a pluralist think-tank called Democratic Left. Francis Beckett has argued that the dissolution of the CPGB was not a consequence of the fall of the USSR, saying that 'Actually at the end of its life, the Party which had sometimes been slavishly obedient to Moscow was surprisingly little affected by what was happening there.'[18] Whilst it is true that the party was tearing itself apart long before 1989, the sources show that party members (and even somewhat distant left-wing intellectuals) were deeply shaken by the news from Eastern Europe and from China and that they were forced into re-examining – and in many cases repudiating – the collective narrative structure upon which their personal identities were founded. Although the debate over the party's redraft of the *British Road to Socialism* had begun in 1988, it was the shocks of the following year which turned it into the *Manifesto for New Times*. Moreover, the longer-term divisions within the party were themselves a direct legacy of the revelations of 1956. Indeed, as the lines between Eurocommunists and traditionalists hardened, the latter were nicknamed 'tankies' in reference to the Soviet tanks which had rolled into Hungary. It is telling that the two breakaway communist parties reacted to the events of 1989 very differently from the CPGB.

The New Communist Party was established in 1977 and the Communist Party of Britain in 1988. Both of these parties claimed continuity with the founding ideals of the CPGB, in their opposition to the revisionist tendencies of the current leadership. The founders of the NCP claimed that 'The old party had ceased to be revolutionary and was no longer part of the mainstream of world revolution. Thus, after 57 years, Communists in Britain had to begin again.' They drew an explicit parallel with the original formation 'with Lenin's help' of the CPGB in 1920:

> The formation of both parties were [sic] important milestones in the history of the working class movement. Both events were motivated by the same aspirations – the need to break with the reformist and social democratic traditions of our labour movement and to unite with all peoples struggling for socialism.[19]

> Today, the banner of those earlier communist fighters is again taken up. The fight has begun once more.[20]

The Communist Party of Britain took this line even further, treating the new party as a 're-establishment' of the old which had effectively ceased to exist as a communist party. As Tony Chater put it in the first debate of the Re-establishment Congress, 'We are not creating a new Party. We are re-establishing the Party on the basis of its' [sic] rules and programme.'[21] The first party card was presented to Andrew Rothstein, who had been a delegate at the 1920 Unity Conference which voted to establish the CPGB. In his acceptance speech he reassured his comrades that 'the spirit of July 31, 1920 is in this hall today' and also said that 'For several years we've been without a Communist Party at the time when Thatcher has been renewing the capitalist offensive against the working class.'[22]

Crisis? Or no crisis?

The differing reactions of the three parties to the events of 1989 depended upon their respective interpretations of the history of the Soviet Union. The NCP saw nothing to regret in that history until the arrival of Gorbachev, whose policies it presented as a counter-revolution. According to this interpretation, it was not communism which was in crisis, but the capitalism which Gobachev had introduced to the USSR. No historical rethinking was therefore required. It was simply necessary to return to the previous state of affairs. Thus, in a letter to the *Morning Star* which was much criticised by CPB members, Eric Trevett, the General Secretary of the NCP 'welcomed' the Soviet coup of August 1991 which not only 'vindicated' the position of the NCP but, he hoped, would also lead to a 'restoration of pride in the Soviet people's achievements and their heroic potential'. Under its new leadership the Soviet Union would now be able to 'once again take its rightful place in the vanguard of progressive humanity in the struggle and achievement of peace, national liberation and Socialism'.[23]

The CPB's position was more nuanced. For all that it was attacked by the CPGB as a 'Stalinist' party, its analysis of events was largely based on adherence to the CPSU line, which involved rejecting Stalin's rule as counter-revolutionary and embracing *perestroika* as an important step towards reviving the socialism of the early years of the USSR and as a necessary stage on the way to full communism. While the horrors of the past were admitted and regretted, this continued belief in a Marxist–Leninist future served to insulate members from the need for serious historical revisionism. The distortions of the Stalinist era could be rejected while the overall historical trajectory of communism in practice was retained and defended. The CPB's revived Young Communist League approvingly published extracts from the Platform of the CPSU agreed in 1990 'as a guide' to the correct interpretation of *perestrokia*. In its words:

> It is [as] dangerous to idealise the past and refuse to learn the complete and grim truth about the tragic aspects of our history, as it is to try to obliterate everything that is truly great and valuable in our historical legacy. The continuity of the Soviet people's labour efforts and struggle must not be interrupted.[24]

A different response again could be seen among Trotskyists. For members of the Socialist Workers Party (SWP), this was a vindication of their view that 'the regimes in the East had nothing to do with socialism'.[25] The events were interpreted in classically Marxist terms as a consequence of the 'state capitalist regimes' becoming 'an impediment to the development of the productive forces, the most important productive force being the workers themselves'. The outcome would therefore be the beginning of 'the epoch of social revolution'.[26] The destruction of the USSR offered both hope that Europe could now be 'remade from below by the masses themselves'[27] and evidence that following Trotsky had been the correct historical course:

> Ideas cannot be smashed by tanks, by force alone. The ideas of Trotsky can be very much like a stream. The stream disappears from sight and then reappears miles later. The stream hadn't dried up, it was just obscured from our sight below the surface.

The same applies to ideas. As Trotsky wrote in 1939, 'the vengeance of history is much more terrible than the vengeance of the most powerful General Secretary'. He has been proved right. Trotsky is smiling and Stalin is dead.[28]

Unsurprisingly, it was in the CPGB where the real crisis of historical narrative took place. As an article in *Socialist Worker Review* put it, 'Because the CP leaders have always seen "socialism" in Eastern Europe – and still do – the crumbling of those regimes must drag down the whole socialist project with them. Everything in the socialist tradition is to be thrown away.'[29] As a first step, the CPGB leadership – and much of the membership – sought to dissociate itself from Soviet communism in all its guises, in the hope that an indigenous tradition could be salvaged. This went as far as suggesting that their support for the October Revolution had been misguided. In her report to the Executive Committee, the CPGB General Secretary, Nina Temple, argued that the circumstances of the CPGB's foundation had tied it to a form of communism that was fundamentally flawed. Although the party had 'moved on' from its origins as 'a Leninist party in the wake of the Bolshevik revolution', this had been only 'a partial and incomplete moving on. As the edifice that was Eastern Europe collapses we have one foot in the rubble.'[30] The fall of the USSR had 'made the world quite literally a different place. A place in which every previous assumption must be reconsidered, especially by us who call ourselves communists.'[31]

The CPGB leadership put out a relentless message of novelty, change and innovation. A promotional sheet encouraged members to 'Keep in touch, be part of it, make it happen!'[32] The appetite for change was combined with a taste for iconoclasm. An earlier press release, with the title '70 Yrs [*sic*] of history "up for grabs"' had boasted that 'Up for grabs at the weekend's Executive Committee meeting will be one of the sacred tenets of communist thinking – INTERNATIONALISM.' Temple had commented on this that 'The internationalism of the 1990s will be as much informed by Greenpeace and Oxfam, as communism *once was* by Marx and Engels.'[33] Temple's message of change was tempered by her insistence that it was only by transforming that the party could preserve its values and traditions. It needed to look back into its own past, to the indigenous English communism championed by the Marxist historians and also outwards to the new Europe:

Can we be part of a new movement that reclaims the best of our traditions, going right back to the Levellers and William Morris? Can we

> play our part in the new dynamic in Europe, overcoming the divisions
> between socialists and communists? [...]
>
> We can be part of the last breath of the old or the first breath of the
> new.[34]

This focus on the realities of the present and possibilities of the future
was not only brought about by the events of 1989. The *Marxism Today*
approach had long been based on the need to be *timely*, to base
communist politics on analyses of society as it was, not as it had
been. The *Marxism Today* authors stressed that this reorientation did
not mean relinquishing the radical socialist future. It was by
'Submit[ting] everything to the discipline of present reality' that this
future could be brought about.[35] In the words of Stuart Hall, 'we can
only renew the project of the left by precisely occupying *the same
world* that Thatcherism does, and building from that a *different* form
of society'.[36] An acceptance of the present was the key to reaching the
future.

But in the years after 1989 the realities of the present did not offer
much fertile soil for communism. At the most basic level, any
political strategy now had to be rethought, reworked. If communism
had failed, how much of Marxism and Marxist historical theory
could be salvaged? In addition, these internal discussions were
taking place against the background noise of the new right's
triumphant declaration of the 'end of history'. Much later, Willie
Thompson was to publish *What Happened to History?* in which he
suggested that the 'near-total defeat' of the left in 1989–91 had
ushered in the 'conceptually flawed and empirically vacuous' project
of deconstructionism. The teleological narrative of Marxism 'has to
be rejected along with all teleologies'.[37] The problem was finding
something with which it could be replaced.

Identity politics

The members of the CPGB, however, did not unanimously follow the
leadership's line. Inevitably the splits of the previous twelve years had
not been clear-cut and some of those who agreed with the positions of
either the NCP or CPB remained within the CPGB. For instance, in
1989 it was still possible to find CPGB members who backed the
Chinese government against the Tiananmen Square protesters. One
such member wrote to Temple to express 'regret' that she had criticised the Chinese government, 'who have educated the students
ignorant enough to foul the city centres'. This member attacked the
victims of Tiananmen Square for their actions, saying that they 'should

show their gratitude for the privileges bestowed on them by returning to work in industries and thereby help in improvements of conditions for the helpless'.[38] Yet for the most part, CPGB members' reactions were more nuanced. While they might not have been as supportive of the CPSU as the CPB or as uncritical of Stalin as the NCP, they cannot be dismissed as purely anti-Soviet liberals. These were people who had remained in the party through 1956 and 1968. They might have had long-standing intentions of changing the party, of revising its line, but for the most part they continued to self-identify as communists even as they argued that the historical experience of communism had served to discredit and misrepresent that creed.

The most common reaction was negotiation, an attempt to preserve some of the dignity of the past at the same time as accepting the need for a new future. Members acknowledged that there had been 'mistakes' but insisted that 'the CPSU record over these 70 years contains a great deal to be proud of as well as some grounds for shame and condemnation'.[39] Another of Temple's correspondents reminded her that the Soviet Union had 'been surrounded by hostile states' and so 'had to take harsh methods to protect the young Socialist society'. But, he assured her, 'if it had not been for Joe Stalin, you and I might not be alive right now'.[40] A third noted that 'Anyone who believed that Socialism can be built without dreadful mistakes, including wrongful deaths must have done very very little thinking about human nature.'[41]

Unsurprisingly, we see a resistance to the leadership's unrelenting drive for change among a membership made up of those who had stayed with the party until the bitter end. In part, their political identities were founded upon that decision to stay in the party; it became a matter of 'pride'.[42] Many members insisted that Marxism was more relevant than ever in the late twentieth century when 'The contrasts between rich and poor in developed societies and between rich and poor countries is increasing. The environment is threatened and radicalism and reactionary nationalism is increasing.'[43] We have already seen Temple's claim that the 'internationalism of the 1990s will be as much informed by Greenpeace and Oxfam, *as communism once was* by Marx and Engels'.[44] But not everyone accepted that this had to be a choice. Instead they stressed the continued relevance of Marx to the problems of the present. One 79-year-old member told how in preparing a speech for a local Greenpeace meeting he 'was struck by the relevance of what I learned 50–60 years ago from Marx'. It wasn't that he was behind the times, just that he couldn't accept 'the total rejection of Marxism'[45]

The emphasis on the challenges of the present moment (and the imagined future) is a key feature of all the party's debates at this time. The editors of the second issue of the *Socialist History Journal* commented that 'It is scarcely imaginable that the *objectives* of the communist movement will not continue to dominate the human agenda, no matter how rightly and vehemently its methods and political structures may be repudiated.'[46] Even in his merciless analysis of the failures of Bolshevism, Willie Thompson clung to the challenges of the present as a way of explaining, if not excusing, the past:

> The events of the past year ... mark a historical terminus ... The human deprivation, ignorance and wretchedness which called the project into being are still as much present as they ever were, and having once been set on foot it is impossible to abandon. The historic mistake was in believing that the communist movement represented the project's final and definitive incarnation: the response now of the women and men who constitute its fragments is to work out what can meaningfully replace it.[47]

In both academic texts and party members' correspondence, the question of the future of Marxism was debated.[48] Whilst most contributors to the discussions accepted that 'the project of 1917 has reached its terminus and ... there is no foreseeable revival',[49] many held out hope that Marxism could be salvaged from the wreckage. As Perry Anderson argued in 1992, socialism had not been given a 'fair trial'.[50] Monty Johnstone similarly felt that Marx's 'long-term objective of a democratic communist society' had 'never yet [been] tried' and remained 'worth working for'.[51]

However, the November 1991 editorial of the CPGB's *Our History Journal* was doubtful about the prospects of rescuing Marxism from the legacy of the CPSU, which it described as 'a parasitic excrescence on society'. By this account, Stalin was not an aberration, rather he 'acquired absolute power by exploiting the contradictions and deadlock in which the communist movement was enmeshed by the 1920s'. Even an international revolution in the years after 1917 could not have avoided the fundamental problem of how to organise production without market forces to regulate demand. The editors pointed out that 'the theoretical underpinning' for solving this issue 'has barely started and will require the work of decades if not generations'.[52]

Such despair at the task ahead was not unusual. Sebastian Berg has shown that 'despite their critical distance' from the party, left-wing intellectuals felt a profound political, intellectual and emotional loss in 1989.[53] As his selections from *New Left Review* show, these feelings were certainly not predicated on an unthinking acceptance of the USSR, but they were associated with a sense of despair that 'the whole idea of socialism as a systemic alternative to capitalism was in danger':

> It is true that I was heavily critical of the Soviet Union, but the angry little boy who pummels his father's chest will not be glad if the old man collapses. As long as the Soviet Union seemed safe, it seemed safe for me to be anti-Soviet. Now that it begins, disobligingly to crumble, I feel impotently protective toward it.[54]

> Ten years of defeat for almost all egalitarian and collectivist endeavours has caused many of us on the left to fall into chronic mutual abuse, to fall upon our own swords, or to fall – some never to rise again – onto the analytic couch.[55]

> As the light of socialist hopes and aspirations fades, and the need for clear vision and historical perspective grows, we might look to the owl of Minerva, trusting she will neither be dazzled by the fires of capitalist celebration (or crisis?) nor succumb to the absolute darkness of despair.[565]

In this 'climate of loss and suffering', the crucial task was 'the theoretical re-foundation and re-conceptualisation of their own politics', beginning with re-evaluating the works of Marx. As Berg shows, responses to this task ranged 'from a wholehearted defence of Marxism as a complete system of thinking to its transformation into a vague Marxian, messianic-utopian "spirit"' – as with Derrida's *Spectres of Marx*.[57] It is significant that such agonised responses came from the New Left as well as from the CPGB; 1989 was, in many ways, a crisis of 'progressive', revisionist Marxism. The CPB, NCP and SWP remained insulated by their differing interpretations of the past and alternate visions of the future.

Taking responsibility for the past

The same work of re-evaluating, re-positioning and rescuing was going on within the party itself. This debate was about the past at least as much as it was about the future; it was the re-examination of the past which necessitated a revision of the present strategy. During the party's 'transformation' process (as it became known), Mark Perryman sent a sheet of rough notes to party leader Nina Temple. He began by saying 'I've been thinking about 5 crucial areas for next stage of CPGB'; at number one was 'Coming to terms, taking responsibility for, and understanding our history and tradition'.[58]

One of the most dramatic expressions of this process came from party member Margaret Peck. In October 1989 she and her husband, John, had written an article for *News and Views* enthusing about a recent trip to the GDR. Although they mentioned their concerns for democracy, the tone of the article was highly optimistic, praising the low rents and plentiful food. They also rejected any suggestion that East Germany was a police state, supporting their claims with anecdotes about the helpful, non-intrusive police they had encountered during their two weeks in the country.[59] By March 1990 Peck had cause to revise her opinions. She wrote a moving letter to *News and Views* admitting that she now felt 'deeply ashamed about an article John and I wrote on our return from East Germany'. Crucially, Peck attacked the stories that British party members had told themselves. 'Yes,' she wrote, 'it is easy to say we were against such and such':

> We are saying now that we opposed Soviet intervention in Czechoslovakia and Afghanistan and were for Solidarity in Poland. But did we actually protest strongly or march against these suppressions? No, we did not. If fact, anybody who did take part publicly in solidarity with the Poles was strongly criticised.

Peck's letter insisted that members incorporate the full story of Soviet communism into their personal and collective memories; not to dilute, excuse or bury it but to carry the truth with them and to bear responsibility for it.

As we have seen, attempts were made firmly to separate the CPGB from the CPSU, in the hope of saving the narrative of the former. Suggestions were made that the party should revive an indigenous English socialist tradition or even an older native 'communism' claiming the Diggers as ancestors.[60] Implicit in these arguments was the idea that the CPGB could somehow dissociate itself from the regimes in Eastern Europe and China, pointing out that 'In Great Britain the Communists have nothing to be ashamed of ... no crimes were committed' and 'A selfless struggle has been conducted which had many historical links with struggles over centuries for democracy and human rights as well as political rights.'[61] This was not a new strategy. Historians including A.L. Morton and Christopher Hill had long sought to demonstrate the native English roots of communism and in the summer of 1936 the party had staged a 'March of History', intended to 'wash away all the stupid and lying statements that Communism is "foreign," "alien," "un-English"' and instead to demonstrate that 'communism springs from England's very soil, from its glorious progressive traditions'.[62] But this was no longer enough. Neither Margaret Peck nor Willie Thompson would allow themselves to seek solace in these kinds of platitudes:

> We are the same as communist parties in eastern Europe. The only difference is that we have had (luckily for the people of this country) no power.[63]

> The non-ruling CPs, though exempt for [sic] responsibility for the crimes and shortcomings of their counterparts in the bloc and often worthy in their criticisms and condemnations, have nevertheless continued to define themselves as part of the same tradition. The British Party, for example, sent a delegation to the Romanian CP congress in 1989 and accepted reciprocal greetings at its own.[64]

Still communist?

The uprooting of the past brought into question the present identity of party members. They struggled to balance their hopes for the future with their obligation to the past. The name of the party was a key part of this balancing act. Those who stayed in the party had to address the disjunction between their own understanding of communism – the ideology to which they had dedicated their lives – and the wider public understanding. For instance, Howie Martin had joined the party in 1944, aged nineteen; he was clear that he would 'always consider [him]self to be a Communist' but acknowledged that the word's meaning had shifted and that the party would have to shift with it: 'To the majority of British people especially young people' communism now 'means Stalin, Ceausescu, the Berlin Wall, the utter collapse of economies in Eastern Europe'. He was, he concluded, 'for a change of name'.[65]

Yet for many members, the change of name was not simply outward-facing strategic change; it was an intensely personal rene-gotiation of self-identity. And this was a gradual process. Some of those who had been against change in 1989 revised their positions in August 1991, following the attempted Soviet coup. In a letter to *Changes* Arthur Mendelsohn explained that before the coup he 'favoured retaining either "communist" or "socialist" in our title – no longer! Our congress must make a decisive break and must carry the majority of members to support the change.'[66] Similarly, George Barnsby told *Changes* that although he had voted for the name 'Communist Federation' in the newspaper's survey, he now believed 'that a complete break with former practices can only come about from those who are prepared to break with the name'.[67] Another longstanding member wrote to Temple on 22 July 1990, telling her that although he had previously been totally opposed to any change in the identity of the party ('When I heard of anyone thinking of name change, I stated do that and I'm off'), again the events in Eastern Europe had changed his mind. His response was nuanced, at first seeming to stick by his original principles, in spite of their corruption by others, but then questioning that response himself:

> Gordon [MacLennan, former General Secretary] was so right, when he claimed these people have tarnished the name of socialism, now Nina *what you and I have always believed in was and is right.* But today, I would see little point in going on the knocker and say good moring [*sic*] I'm a communist, I have come to offer you a better standard of living. They would laugh at us, or to mean it right, they wouldn't want to hear what we have to say.
>
> It may be dishonest to believe in the same things, say the same things, but call it by a different name. *But I don't think we are saying the same things any more, we have new policies, and we need a new name to go with it.*[68]

Opinions on the name of the party were much divided. A survey carried out by *Changes* in October 1991 showed that the largest proportion of respondents (73 of 161) favoured the name proposed by the leadership, 'Democratic Left'. However, as Dave Priscott pointed out in a letter to the Executive Committee, the other votes were split between many competing options. In total, 53% of members wanted to keep the word 'communist' somewhere in the title and 21% wanted the word 'socialist', compared to only 22% who were in favour of neither.[69] It is not surprising that the proposed name change was so contentious. As David Kertzer has shown in relation to the Italian PCI, this was so painful because it was not only the name of the party, but also that of its members: no longer would they be 'communists', except in their own estimation.[70] Whilst some members like Howie Martin were able to reconcile their own identity as communists with the need to change the name of the party, others were not prepared to make this leap.

One 'foundation member' wrote to Nina Temple saying that he was totally opposed to the name change because 'it is a disservice to the services and sacrifices of comrades in the party and others who gave their all to the working class'. He highlighted the particular contributions made by those who fought against fascism in the 1920s and 1930s and emphasised that 'They were not the cause of giving the word Communism a dirty name.'[71] Another felt that 'For the CPGB to abandon the name communist and with it, Marx, Engels, Lenin, Stalin, Dimitrov, Pollitt – to mention a few of the many previously honoured names – would be an entirely retrograde step.'[72]

This debate was particularly poignant because it took place against the backdrop of the seventieth anniversary of the founding of the CPGB. The mid-November 1989 issue of *News and Views* featured an anniversary cover. Inside, two small articles noted respectively that next year's membership cards would have a seventieth anniversary logo and that a commemorative calendar would be available. The calendar featured photographs 'Charting the Party's history and involvement from the first Unity Convention, through the General Strike and the Hunger Marches' right up to 'the miners' strike, the People's March for Jobs and the fight against Poll Tax'.[73] This was the last issue of *News and Views* before the 41st Congress at which the *Manifesto for New Times* was adopted. It is worth noting that this calendar was not mentioned in either the December or January issues. It seems that commemoration was offered as a necessary ritual, part of the mnemonic structure of the CPGB, rather than through any particular sense of its continued importance. Yet this half-hearted approach to the past was not shared by all the members. A recurring fear was that by changing (or disbanding) the party, communists would be betraying their ancestors and denying their sacrifices and achievements. One 1991 letter to *Changes* urged fellow members to 'save the CP against those who are hell bent on the elimination of 70 yrs [*sic*] of struggle'.[74]

Again, there is a clear contrast between the CPGB and the CPB on this issue. The latter party published a celebratory seventieth anniversary history of 'Britain's Communist Party', running from the party's foundation in 1920, through the fights against fascism in the interwar years to the present day. This was an opportunity to assert their unchanging identity as proud communists, regardless of the party's tumultuous recent history. While the international situation was entirely ignored, two of the nine chapters were devoted to the divisions within the CPGB. The first of these was entitled 'The Party and the Paper Attacked' and detailed the revisionists' 'step-by-step coup to take over the party'.[75] The final chapter, 'Towards Re-establishment' stated that 'The CPB is now clearly the inheritor of the traditions of the 70 years of struggle of the Communist Party of Britain' and rejoiced that it was 'now set to resume the long and difficult march to socialism in Britain'.[76] The narrative ended with a statement of continuity:

Seven decades of capitalism and imperialism, of exploitation, oppression and war, have confirmed the justice and necessity of our cause.

Britain's communists have played their role in battling to overcome capitalism's problems at home. We have also mobilised solidarity with national liberation struggles and against imperialist wars, including the Gulf war.

After 70 fighting years, we are prouder than ever to say:
JOIN THE PARTY OF STRUGGLE AND SOCIALISM. BUILD THE COMMUNIST PARTY OF BRITAIN.[77]

The collapse of narrative

Many CPGB members found the process of transforming the party as unsettling as the traumatic events which had inspired it. A report from the London District Secretariat described the 'considerable anxiety and uncertainty in the Party about our role and future' and called for an immediate debate because, as they said, 'We are losing members *now* through their sadness and despair about the party and communism.'[78] The first focus for unease was the process of drafting the *Facing up to the Future* (FUTTF) document. This was intended to be the redraft of the *British Road to Socialism* agreed at the 40th Congress in 1988 but in the wake of the events in Eastern Europe, it became the basis for the *Manifesto for New Times* (MNT), which was adopted at the 41st Congress. This process provoked a heated debate in the CPGB newspapers. For instance, Bill Wildish wrote to *News and Views* saying he was 'confused by the exact status of the document' and concerned that it would be adopted at Congress 'precisely because there is nothing else on offer'.[79]

Some members expressed a fear that they were losing ownership of the party and its processes; they were 'baffled and bewildered' as one letter to Nina Temple put it.[80] The leadership seemed to be rushing ahead into a future they hadn't asked for and couldn't control. One member complained that having voted for the 'twin-track' option at the previous Congress, 'when the Democratic Left constitution arrived it was a "single-track" document, and the Communist Party had disappeared'.[81] Another characterised the available options as 'Which form of dissolution do we most prefer?'[82] In July 1991 Lambeth Branch passed a resolution condemning the 'unequal treatment' given by the Executive Committee (EC) to the Draft Constitution, which was published in 'readable type and attractive layout as against the existing Party Rules printed incomplete and in type so minuscule as to make them difficult to read without a magnifying glass (which was not supplied)'.[83]

Distrust of Temple was an important element in the debate. Her election as General Secretary in January 1990 epitomised the spirit of reform. Born – appropriately enough – in 1956, Temple had long been at the forefront of attempts to reform the party and came to personify its modern, feminist, green values. On her election, she immediately removed the bust of Marx which had always sat in the General Secretary's office.[84] The decision to call the new version of the *British Road to Socialism* a Manifesto, rather than a Strategy, is also significant.[85] The title *Manifesto for New Times* could not have been more explicit in its intention. She even described it as 'very different from the original Communist Manifesto', leaving no doubt that it was intended as a replacement, not an addition. The only similarity she admitted was that 'both share a rejection of capitalism's inequality and exploitation'.[86] Despite the step-by-step approach of the leadership, the adoption of MNT was a clear move towards the dissolution of the party.

The debates over the possible futures of socialism focused not only on the contents of the reformers' strategies, but also on their modes of expression. The debates over MNT and FUTTF showed that it wasn't just the narrative which had changed; it was the mode of storytelling itself. A central line of criticism was that the new documents were un-Marxist in their style and thinking as well as in their conclusions. Rigorous dialectical analysis was out; soft-focus consumer politics were in. As Francis King put it, FUTTF was 'vague verbiage – meaningless chatter about "new agendas", "modernisation" and so on'.[87] Similarly, Jim Tait commented:

> Words are important things ... The past five editions of the British Road to Socialism all used words that they said were programmes for a revolutionary transformation of society from capitalism to socialism.
>
> From my observations of 'Facing up to the Future' the word revolution appears twice and never ever in relation to Socialism.
>
> ... Neither in solitary words nor organised concepts is there any semblance of a revolutionary strategy for socialism in the document.[88]

Where 'revolution' did appear in FUTTF it referred to technological revolution and a hoped-for cultural revolution in male behaviour. The following July, a letter from David Allen noted that MNT overused the words 'progressive' and 'popular'. He felt that they had become 'Eurocommunist newspeak, as much part of our language as "worker" and "the state" are for Trotskyists.'[89] To use the language of Laclau and Mouffe (so popular among the reformers), such terms had become empty signifiers. They came to represent all that was positive and acceptable; to signify an entire system of meaning. All that was not 'progressive' was necessarily negative – no distinctions or differences were permitted.

'Nothing to lose but our certainties'

The extent to which the old forms of expression broke down in 1989/90 can be seen in an extraordinary series of minutes and letters generated by a CPGB working group established to plan a series of 'education' meetings. The nine members of the group found themselves unable to agree on the contents of the meetings, or even on a basic approach to them. As one member of the group put it: 'The Party remains divided between those who seek to retain out-moded "Marxist education" and those who recognise that profound changes must be catered for.'[90] There was a sense that they were arguing over the very nature of communism: its past and its future. This was understandably painful and contentious. After one meeting, one member of the group wrote to another, 'Not for some years have I been present at a meeting which generated so much indignation and resentment.'[91]

One of the most fundamental disagreements was over the format of the talks: should one speaker give a lecture on a subject, or should two or more speakers provide alternative viewpoints?[92] This seemingly organisational matter had important philosophical implications. Could the CPGB any longer claim to speak with one voice? Did it have any right to give lectures on the correct position? Questions were also raised over the contents of the proposed meetings. The original plan was to look at subjects like class, imperialism and revolution, dealing with the future of the party only at the end of the series of meetings. This was vigorously opposed by one elderly member of the group who felt that 'The explanations given by CP literature and speakers in the past cannot even begin to provide what is needed today' and insisted that the subjects needed to be far more 'tentative'. She went on to argue that the party needed to break out of the Marxist historical framework and open itself to the possibilities of the future:

> I am absolutely against the proposed form of six talks, however they are presented – with two speakers or with any number. It is the approach that is wrong – nothing but a trip down memory lane.
>
> We have nothing to lose but our old certainties – which have turned out to have been not as certain as we thought. We have a world of exciting new possibilities to win. We may win or we may not, but if we

don't accept the challenge we shall certainly dwindle away into the past and not count for anything in the future.[93]

The final titles were indeed 'tentative'; question marks abounded: 'Socialism – the Death of a System?'; 'Capitalism Triumphant?'. This is an important episode as it shows how deeply the crisis had penetrated the mindset of the party. It was no longer acceptable to impart information or philosophy; instead it was time to ask questions and to admit doubts. Instead of being based on the certainties of the past, the CP narrative was now open to the unpredictable possibilities of the future. History was no longer a fixed narrative, it was an unfolding process.

New histories?

The collapse of the Soviet bloc provided not only the political space but also the archival materials for truly analytical histories of the CPGB to be produced. A key event was the publication in 1990 of the transcript of the leadership's debates over the onset of war in 1939, after many years of speculation about their contents. In 1979 the History Group had held a conference on the 1939 change of line and requested a copy of the stenogram of the debate from the Institute of Marxism–Leninism but 'drew a blank'. It was only in October 1987, with the changes resulting from Gorbachev's leadership, that a further request 'received a sympathetic response' and in 1989 the document was received by the British party.[94] It was, according to Kevin Morgan, an 'exhilarating' discovery which allowed the individual personalities to speak 'like an old sepia photograph [which] suddenly becomes voluble and argumentative'.[95] This was particularly exciting for Morgan who had been frustrated by the 'curiously impersonal' tone of the official histories and by the striking lack of biographical material on party figures: 'Such were the Communist Party's loyalties and collective discipline that, even long after the event … [n]ot only memoirs, obituaries and funeral odes, but periodicals, speeches, even the interviews given years later to oral historians, usually adhered to a convention of collective responsibility.'[96]

The historical work of CP members did not stop with the dissolution of the party. The final issue of *Our History Journal* noted 'the firm intention of both the Historians' Group and the editor to continue publishing' not least because 'the requirement to explore and analyse socialist history has never been more urgently felt'.[97] Publication resumed under the new name of *Socialist History Journal* and every attempt at continuity was made. The publication schedule was not interrupted and the first two issues of *Socialist History Journal* even continued the numbering of *Our History Journal*, appearing as numbers 19 and 20. It was not until 1993, when the new publication merged with *Our History*, that a new numbering system was adopted. Throughout this time, the *Journal* had continued to publish scholarly work on historical subjects, alongside analyses of the global crisis.[98]

Analyses of the party also began to appear rather quickly, including Willie Thompson's *The Good Old Cause* in 1992 and Andrews, Fishman and Morgan's *Opening the Books* in 1995.[99] The work of writing the now 'unofficial' history of the party also continued with John Callaghan's *Cold War: Crisis and Conflict* appearing in 2003 and the final volume, Geoff Andrews' *Endgames and New Times*, appearing in 2004.[100] As publishers Lawrence and Wishart explain in the description of Callaghan's book, these final volumes benefit from 'much better access to archives and the views of former party members' and are also 'written from a more critical position than previous titles in the series'.[101]

The parallel tasks of analysing and preserving the past can be seen in a Socialist History Society newsletter from November 1993, which both notified members of a forthcoming conference entitled 'What Went Wrong in the USSR and Eastern Europe?' and also asked them to consider coming forward for an oral history project, being undertaken with the CP Archive and Manchester University, 'building an archive of memoirs of CP members from all eras of the Party's history'.[102]

The expected progress of history had been disrupted, and so had its narrative, its certainties, its *shape*. Eric Hobsbawm's plans for *Age of Extremes* underwent a dramatic shift. Rather than the 'diptych' of 'Age of Catastrophe' and 'Golden Age', proposed to his publisher as late as 1988, Hobsbawm ended up writing a triptych with the years from 1973 re-cast as 'landslide':

> What had changed was not the facts of world history since 1973 as I knew them, but the sudden conjunction of events in both East and West since 1989 which almost forced me to see the past twenty years in a new perspective.[103]

Even this about-turn was not drastic enough for some. Perry Anderson has suggested that Hobsbawm's picture of the post-war 'Golden Age' does not fit the evidence of violence and misery in those years, but is governed by his commitment to the central historical role of the 'initially gradual, and then hurtling descent of the Soviet experiment'.[104] Along with many others, Anderson himself insisted that understanding the true nature of the past was a precondition for the 'refoundation of the socialist project' and far more important than 'mere repudiations'. He found comfort in Robin Blackburn's *After the Fall* which showed that 'Serious reflection on the political and intellectual legacy of the modern socialist movement ... reveals many riches that were forgotten as well as roads that were mistaken.'[105]

In 1978 Martin Jacques had suggested that an honest, evaluative history of the party would have the benefit of giving coherence to 'what would otherwise be ... a disparate set of experiences and outlooks, traditions and ideologies, that exist within the Party'. It would be a positive experience, allowing members 'to understand that the Party actually has been through many changes and developments and shifts and ... to understand it in terms of that process and not in any way to despise it'.[106] Thirteen years later, the final edition of *Marxism Today* (except for the special 1998 issue) attempted what could be seen as a version of that task. It combined articles on the party's troubled past with those on the political struggles still ahead. In typical *Marxism Today* style, the serious sat alongside the playful; the centrefold of the magazine was a boardgame entitled 'Moscow Gold', featuring such nuggets as 'The Party is Over. Advance to the End of History (you can't miss it)' and 'Perestroika Prospect. Become a Designer Socialist Overnight. Advance to Mandelson Rise'. The rules also declared that 'To avoid competition there will be no winners. You have nothing to lose but your principles.'[107] This self-aware parody was a clear attempt to absorb the collapse of the CPGB into a new narrative structure.

The task of constructing a new narrative identity on both a personal and collective level necessarily involved gallows humour, just as it involved emotional repudiations of the past, denials of reality and claims to have issued warnings long ago. The New Times rhetoric of innovative, post-party, post-materialist 'new' politics provided an alternative identity for those who wanted it. This offered an opportunity to be in tune with the times, to be on the side of history. Others began the work of unpicking and analysing the past because, as Willie Thompson argued, 'if there is to be any rebirth of the left in Britain or beyond, it surely has to start from a sober understanding, free from sentiment or nostalgia, of the reasons why history has proved – so far – not to be on our side'.[108]

A further level of analysis was concerned with what history would make of the communist experiment. How would it be treated by future historians? This was the 'crucial question' according to the editors of the *Socialist History Journal*: 'whether this failed enterprise, which has dominated, either positively or negatively, the history of the twentieth century, will ultimately serve as an inspiration to the future or as a dreadful warning'.[109] As early as 1992, Perry Anderson was trying to predict the 'possible futures' of socialism within the pages of history. Would it be regarded by future historians as akin to Jesuit experiments with egalitarian living in seventeenth- and eighteenth-century Paraguay? Would it be able to perpetuate its message even as the movement fell by the wayside like the Levellers? Or would the fate of communism be more similar to Jacobinism or Liberalism? Would the CPGB's future be 'Oblivion, transvaluation, mutation, redemption'?[110] While Britain's communists had to resign themselves to no longer being at the vanguard of historical development, no longer *making history*, they could console themselves with the task of historical analysis. As Eric Hobsbawm put it, 'there is nothing which can sharpen the historian's mind like defeat'.[111]

Notes

1 Raphael Samuel, *The Lost World of British Communism* (London: Verso, 2006), p. 13.
2 Robyn Fivush, 'Remembering and reminiscing: how individual lives are constructed in family narratives', *Memory Studies*, 1:1 (2008), 49–58.
3 Phil Cohen (ed.), *Children of the Revolution* (London: Lawrence & Wishart, 1997)
4 See Tony Blair, *Let us Face the Future*.
5 Steve Parsons, 'What happened inside the CPGB', in *Our History: The Communist Party and 1956*, Speeches at the Conference, pamphlet 88 (Socialist History Society, February 1993), p. 26.
6 E.J. Hobsbawm, *Interesting Times* (New York and London: The New Press, 2002), p. 206.
7 John Saville, 'The XXth Congress and the British Communist Party' in *Socialist Register* (1976), 7–8.
8 Hobsbawm, *Interesting Times*, p. 207.
9 Perry Anderson, *Spectrum* (London: Verso, 2005), p. 284.
10 Eric Hobsbawm, 'The Historians' Group of the Communist Party', in Maurice Cornforth (ed.), *Rebels and their Causes: Essays in Honour of A. L. Morton* (London: Lawrence and Wishart, 1978), pp. 28–9.
11 Ibid., p. 41.
12 Monty Johnstone, 'What kind of Communist Party history?', *Our History Journal*, 4 (February 1979), 7.
13 Martin Jacques, 'Why study the history of the CP?', *Our History Journal*, 2 (July 1978), 6.

14 Hobsbawm, *Interesting Times*, p. 209.

15 Johnstone, 'What kind of Communist Party history?', 5.

16 Editorial, *Our History Journal*, 16 (November 1990), p. 1

17 Editorial, *Our History Journal*, 15 (April 1990), 1.

18 Francis Beckett, *Enemy Within: The Rise and Fall of the British Communist Party* (London: John Murray, 1995), p. 212.

19 New Communist Party, *The Case for the New Communist Party* (London: The New Communist Party, undated [1977?]), p. 3.

20 Ibid., p. 9.

21 Tony Chater introducing the First Debate at the *Communist Party of Britain, Re-establishment Congress* (London: Communist Party of Britain, 1988), London, 23/24 April 1988, p. 4.

22 Andrew Rothstein, receiving the first party card in Ibid., pp. 16–17.

23 Eric Trevett, Letters, *Morning Star*, Thursday 22 August 1991, p. 5.

24 'CPSU June '90 Congress Platform', reprinted as part of Kenny Coyle, 'What do we mean by socialism?', *Young Communist*, 7 (undated [1990?]), 10.

25 Editorial, 'Rulers in retreat', *Socialist Worker Review*, 126 (December 1989), 3.

26 Tony Cliff, 'Earthquake in the east', *Socialist Worker Review*, 126 (December 1989), 11, 14.

27 Alex Callinicos, 'Horrible heritage', *Socialist Worker Review*, 126 (December 1989), 17.

28 Cliff, 'Earthquake in the east', 14.

29 Duncan Blackie, 'End of the road?', *Socialist Worker Review*, 127 (January 1990), 14.

30 Temple, '*New* times, *new* politics'.

31 Ibid.

32 CP/CENT/EC/24/08, flyer, 'Party in new times' (undated [January 1990?]).

33 CP/CENT/EC/24/09, draft press release: '70 yrs of history "up for grabs"', 6 March 1990. Emphasis added.

34 Temple, '*New* times, *new* politics'.

35 Hall, *The Hard Road to Renewal*, p. 14.

36 Ibid., p. 15. Original emphases.

37 Willie Thompson, *What Happened to History?* (London: Pluto Press, 2000), pp. 54, 182, 144.

38 LHASC, CP/CENT/SEC/14/05, letter to Nina Temple (hereafter NT), 27 July 1990.

39 LHASC, CP/CENT/SEC/14/06, letter to NT, 25 April 1990

40 LHASC, CP/CENT/SEC/14/06, letter to NT, 2 April 1990.

41 LHASC, CP/CENT/SEC/14/05, letter to NT, 19 August 1990.

42 Hobsbawm, *Interesting Times*, p. 218.

43 LHASC, CP/CENT/SEC/14/06, notes on discussion of Harlow Branch CP, sent to NT, March 1990.

44 LHASC, CP/CENT/EC/24/09, draft press release: '70 yrs of history "up for grabs"', 6 March 1990. Emphasis added.

45 LHASC, CP/CENT/SEC/14/06, letter to NT, 24 April 1991.

46 Willie Thompson, David Parker and Mike Waite, Editorial, 'What was communism?', *Socialist History Journal*, 2 (Autumn 1993), 4. Original emphasis.

47 Willie Thompson, 'History's last word? The Communist Party in dissolution', *Our History Journal*, 16 (November 1990), 7.

48 For instance, Derrida's *Spectres of Marx: The State of the Debt, the Work of Mourning and the New International* (New York and London: Routledge, 1994, tr. Peggy Kamuf) was based on his plenary speech to a conference entitled 'Whither Marxism? Global crises in international perspective' held at the Center for Ideas and Society, University of California, Riverside, 22 and 23 April 1993.

49 Thompson, Parker, Waite, 'What was communism?', 2.

50 Perry Anderson, *A Zone of Engagement* (London and New York: Verso, 1992), pp. 360–1.

51 Nina Temple *et al.*, 'Assessments – what was communism?', *Socialist History Journal*, 2 (Autumn 1993), 8.

52 Editorial, 'Back to the drawing board?', *Our History Journal*, 18 (November 1991), 1–3.

53 Sebastian Berg, 'Intellectual radicalism after 1989: theoretical and political discussions in a British and an American journal', *Socialist History*, 30 (2007), 44.

54 A. Cohen, 'The future of a disillusion', *New Left Review*, 190 (1991), 10. Quoted in ibid., p. 46.

55 Lynne Segal, 'Whose left? Socialism, feminism and the future', *New Left Review*, 185 (1991), 82–3. Quoted in ibid.

56 Göran Therborn, 'The life and times of socialism', *New Left Review*, 194 (1992), 17. Quoted in Ibid.

57 Berg, 'Intellectual radicalism', 46–7.

58 LHASC, CP/CENT/SEC/14/05. Original emphasis. The other four areas were students; marginal constituencies and tactical voting; internal organisation; and experimenting and funding [?] new forms [of democracy?]. Uncertainty due to handwriting.

59 *News and Views*, no. 49, October 1989, pp. 8–9. Wrongly labelled as issue 48 on cover.

60 See for example LHASC, CP/CENT/SEC/14/06, letter to NT, 26 June 1990.

61 LHASC, CP/CENT/SEC/14/06, 'The Future of the CPGB', Bradford Branch, 11 January 1990.

62 *Daily Worker*, 23 September 1936, p. 4.

63 *News and Views*, no. 55, March 1990, p. 17.

64 Thompson, 'History's last word? The Communist Party in dissolution', p. 7.

65 Howie Martin, *Changes*, no. 24, 28 Sept–11 Oct 1991, p. 5.

66 Arthur Mendelsohn, *Changes*, no. 24, 28 Sept–11 Oct 1991, p. 6.

67 George Barnsby, *Changes*, no. 23, 14–27 Sept 1991, p. 6.

68 LHASC, CP/CENT/SEC/14/06, letter to NT, 22 July 1990. Emphases added.

69 LHASC, CP/CENT/EC/25/12, Dave Priscott to EC, 26 October 1991.

70 D.I. Kertzer, *Politics and Symbols: The Italian Communist Party and the Fall of Communism* (New Haven and London: Yale University Press, 1996).

71 LHASC, CP/CENT/SEC/14/06, letter to NT, 7 June 1990.

72 Michael Balchin, *Changes*, no. 23, 14–27 September 1991, p. 4.

73 *News and Views*, no. 51, Mid-Nov 1989, inside cover.

74 Cathie McMahon, *Changes*, no. 24, 28 Sept–11 Oct 1991, p. 5.

75 Joe Berry, *70 Years of Struggle: Britain's Communist Party, 1920–1990* (London: The Communist Party of Great Britain, 1991), p. 18.

76 Ibid., p. 22.

77 Ibid., p. 22. Original emphasis.

78 LHASC, CP/CENT/EC/24/08, report of London District Communist Party to the Political Committee and the Executive Committee, 4 January 1990. Original emphasis.

79 Bill Wildish, *News and Views*, no. 46, Sept 1989 p. 12.

80 LHASC, CP/CENT/SEC/14/06 letter to NT, 2 April 1990.

81 Edith Constable, *Changes*, no. 21, 3–16 Aug 1991, p. 1.

82 Steve Johnson, *News and Views*, no. 55, March 1990, p. 27.

83 LHASC, CP/CENT/EC/25/10, letter to EC, 10 July 1991. The criticism was accepted by NT who promised to resolve it before the Congress.

84 Beckett, *Enemy Within*, p. 214.

85 In May 1989 the EC minutes record 17 votes in favour of the title *Manifesto for New Times* over *Strategy for New Times*. The votes against and abstentions are not given: LHASC, CP/CENT/EC/24/04.

86 Temple, '*New* times, *new* politics'.

87 Francis King, *News and Views*, no. 39, Feb 1989, p. 13.

88 Jim Tait, *News and Views*, no. 37, Jan 1989, p. 13. In FUTTF, the word 'revolution' is used in the context of technological revolution and a hoped-for cultural revolution in male behaviour.

89 David Allen, *News and Views*, no. 44, July 1989, p. 12.

90 LHASC, CP/CENT/SEC/14/06, letter from Frank Stone to NT, 30 June 1990.

91 LHASC, CP/CENT/SEC/14/06, letter from Pat Allen to Pat Turnbull, 8 July 1991.

92 LHASC, CP/CENT/SEC/14/06, minutes of the Working Group on Education, 15 and 29 July 1991.

93 LHASC, CP/CENT/SEC/14/06, Vivien Pixner's notes, read out at meeting of the Working Group on Education, 1 July 1991.

94 Monty Johnstone, 'Introduction', in Francis King and George Matthews (eds), *About Turn: The British Communist Party and the Second World War: The Verbatim Record of the Central Committee Meetings of 25 September and 2–3 October 1939* (London: Lawrence & Wishart, 1990).

95 Kevin Morgan, 'The CPGB and the Comintern Archives', *Socialist History Journal*, 2 (Autumn 1993), 10.

96 Kevin Morgan, 'Parts of people and communist lives', in John McIlroy, Kevin Morgan and Alan Campbell (eds), *Party People, Communist Lives: Explorations in Biography* (London: Lawrence & Wishart, 2001), pp. 12–14.

97 Editorial, 'back to the drawing board', *Our History Journal*, 3.

98 See for instance, Stephen Roberts, 'Thomas Cooper: a Victorian working-class writer', *Our History Journal*, 16 (November 1990), 12–25; Rodney Hilton, 'Class analysis of feudal society', *Our History Journal*, 17 (May 1991), 33–7.

99 Willie Thompson, *The Good Old Cause: British Communism 1920–1991* (London: Pluto Press, 1992); Geoff Andrews, Nina Fishman and Kevin

Morgan (eds), *Opening the Books: Essays on the Social and Cultural History of British Communism* (London: Pluto Press, 1995).

100 John Callaghan, *Cold War: Crisis and Conflict* (London: Lawrence and Wishart, 2003); Geoff Andrews, *Endgames and New Times: The Final Years of British Communism 1964–1991* (London: Lawrence and Wishart, 2004).

101 www.lwbooks.co.uk/books/archive/coldwar_crisis_conflict.html. Accessed 18.09.2010.

102 Socialist History Society Newsletter, November 1993.

103 Eric Hobsbawm, *On History* (London: Abacus, 1998), p. 313.

104 Anderson, *Spectrum*, pp. 302, 314.

105 Anderson, *A Zone of Engagement*, p. 362.

106 Jacques, 'Why study the history of the CP?', 8.

107 Chris Granlund, 'Moscow Gold: you bought the magazine, now play the game', *Marxism Today*, December 1991, pp. 32–3.

108 Willie Thompson, 'End of our history? The terminus of the CPGB', *Socialist History Journal*, 19 (May 1992), 6.

109 Thompson, Parker, Waite, Editorial, 'What was communism?', 3.

110 Anderson, *A Zone of Engagement*, p. 375.

111 Hobsbawm, *On History*, p. 317.

Conclusions

History is a fundamental part of political positioning, whether as conservative inheritance, radical obligation, affirming grand narrative, lost 'golden age' or the backdrop against which revisionism can take place. As has been suggested in this study, these different ideological approaches have converged on a rather functional approach to political history, in which particular interpretations of the past are used to provide legitimacy for particular courses of action, to orient identity and to supply lessons for the present. The past is an ever-present rhetorical device, used both within and between parties in order to hold opponents accountable for their own (or their predecessors') actions and to claim legitimacy on the basis of past records.

However, it is the overall sense of history as a *process* which really serves to confer authority on political activity, above and beyond these uses of specific narratives of the past. Political actors have a strong sense of themselves as *part* of history and this lends a particular strength to their calls to seize the moment and take action. Even in positioning their actions as a break in the ongoing narrative, party political actors have tended, paradoxically, to present this as the return to a different narrative based on a more accurate interpretation of the past.

Whereas left-wing commentators, such as Ralph Miliband, have long suggested that Labour has been absorbed into a parliamentary narrative at odds with the experience of its supporters, the argument of this book has been that this temporal positioning is in tune with wider cultural trends. Since the mid-1970s, commentators have noted a growth in public nostalgia, whereby 'pastness' has come to denote 'authenticity'. This is mirrored by the political use of the past as a marker of sincerity, integrity and commitment. The flipside of this nostalgia is that the past is constructed as *past*. While a connection with one's roots may be desirable, it must be balanced by an avoidance of anachronism. To be perceived as 'stuck in the past' is a political liability. The result of these combined trends has been the closing down of the past as a political force; instead it has been repackaged as 'heritage' and celebrated for its very pastness. While the details of party political historical narratives may resonate only within a rather closed (if cross-partisan) circle of interested participants, a wider sense of parliamentary politics as both historic and historical does persist.

At the start of this book, it was suggested that parliamentary politics encourages a sense of lived continuity with the past. Moreover, the *appearance* of continuity is itself a source of authority and legitimation. This could be seen as an example of the aesthetic of pastness, which Fredric Jameson discussed in the early 1990s. Jameson suggested that postmodernity is characterised by a-historicity, in which an authentic relationship to the past has been replaced by affective, personal encounters with pastness, which creates a 'whole new emotional groundtone' of 'intensities'.[1] He felt that 'nostalgia films' and historical novels operate 'a new connotation of "pastness" and pseudohistorical depth, in which the history of aesthetic styles displaces "real" history'.[2] In the case of political parties, this aesthetic is reinforced by the political system itself. From the archaic rituals of parliament, to the 'continuity effect' of long-standing political parties, the aesthetic of pastness underpins the political system. However, this is increasingly becoming the pastness of the 'beachcomber' and the 'antiquarian', derided by John Casey.[3] Classical conservative and socialist understandings of the political past emphasised its capacity to make demands upon the present, from Casey's 'customs and pieties' to Raphael Samuel's radical 'history from below'. Both of these traditions were able to offer powerful critiques of the present, yet both have now been sidelined in favour of a present-focused view of the past as heritage, which can be embraced or rejected as politically expedient. A past which can be picked up and put down at will, venerated then forgotten about, does not retain any of this power. It is a political prop, not a political force.

This temporal attitude is above all presentist. While the ubiquitous contemporary belief in political progress and social improvement signifies a shift from conservative pessimism, it remains rather distant from the utopian aspects of socialism. This is not a mindset which advocates progress towards a particular imagined endpoint. Instead it is focused on the particular moment of the present, portrayed as the edge of the horizon, staring into an unknown future. Although the emphasis on parliament as a means of incremental progress has affinities with the Whig interpretation of history, this is not a teleological 'grand narrative' approach to history. It is characterised by an openness to the future and a willingness to reinterpret the past. Yet these reinterpretations involve a certain sleight of hand. While it has recently become common for politicians and commentators to borrow from the language of cultural theory in emphasising the need for parties to construct 'narratives',[4] the belief in a stable and knowable past, able to provide both models and warnings, remains remarkably consistent. Political actors, from Conservative right to Marxist left, display a marked suspicion of epistemic doubt.

We have seen that in the debates over the National Curriculum for History, postmodernism tended to be grouped together with left-wing historical revisionism: both posed a threat to established, conservative narratives of British history and nationhood. However, the history of the left was still based on a knowable, usable past, in which it was possible to show how, when and why traditions had been invented and nationalisms forged. This was simply a different usable past from that favoured by conservatives, which told different stories for different purposes. In fact, postmodernism was just as problematic for Marxist historians as for conservatives. The problem, as Harvey Kaye outlined, was that in rejecting a teleological, ordered, comprehensible view of history, postmodernists were unable to conceive of a way of improving the world, 'of making *new* history, let alone new *forms* of history'.[5] Kaye, writing in 1991, saw the new right and postmodern left arriving at a similar end point; both 'deny reason to hope that the future could actually be different from the present'.[6] However, it is not only end-of-history and post-history thinkers who are unable to conceive of new political futures. This is the consequence of presentist parliamentary politics as described throughout this book. We have seen Martin L. Davies' argument that the historicised mindset sets the present within the frameworks of the past, making it always 'the same old thing'. More than this, it also imagines the future in the same way. Making history is therefore seen as making *more of the same*. Claims to be 'historic' should be understood as attempts to be set within an orderly line of similarly historic actions reaching from the known past into the projected future.

Moreover, while it is clear that political actors are determined that their actions be interpreted 'correctly' by future historians, there is also a sense of fatalism, almost of melancholy, about these efforts which betrays the knowledge that no single 'truth' exists – or at least that it cannot be captured by history. As Margaret Thatcher reflected when she donated her papers to the Churchill Archive Centre, 'even the fullest written record in my experience never conveys the essence of a crisis ... the mood of the moment is lost. Tension and trouble ... are efficiently smoothed away by the note-takers.'[7] This is not the creation of a historic mythologised self (that was done through her political practice). The papers represent what is left when that has myth been analysed – historicised – away.[8] However, Thatcher continued,

> I would caution against politicians and historians imagining that a knowledge of the facts and access to past experience alone provides the answers to the most important questions. Convictions drawn from outside politics are also required in order to take the right political decisions. Our beliefs, and indeed our instincts, must anchor us firmly, if we are not to capsize in the daily storms of office. There is more to leadership than enlightened pragmatism – but perhaps the papers in the Churchill Archives Centre will suggest that too.[9]

Thatcher seems here to view the past as the source only of 'enlightened pragmatism' based upon the 'lessons of history'. While this is valuable, she counsels, it can only take us so far. The image of the politician rooted in a present moment is clear. This kind of presentist politics sees the past, on the one hand, as both knowable and comparable to the present – the source of lessons and examples. On the other, it is treated as distant, tame, even somewhat exotic, to be admired or rejected, investigated or invoked. Labour's 2006 centenary celebrations, for instance, managed to generate interest in the party's past and served as a focus for demonstrating continuity and solidarity. They did not, however, leave 'a lasting impression' on the party. The aspect of ongoing historical political education which Dianne Hayter had advocated 'soon became just a means of promoting best practice in electioneering'.[10] Active, living memory is a political liability, able to provoke unpredictable emotions or uncontrollable judgements; a historicised past can be invoked and then forgotten.

It is not, however, so easy to close down the recent past. Simplistic historical analogies between, for instance, the spending cuts pursued by the Conservative–Liberal Democrat coalition and those of Thatcher's governments can be seen as part of a political game, which revels in self-referential cries of repetition. Yet the legacies of both Thatcherism and New Labour still define the political present.

Their policies continue to shape the political, social and economic landscape in which their successors operate; they limit both what it is practically possible to do and what it is possible to imagine doing. Whether we think of this in terms of 'path dependence' (preferred by institutionalist political scientists) or 'tradition' (preferred by interpretivists), it is clear that the past – or at least ideas about the past – matter.

Moreover, ideas about *history* also matter. Politicians' self-image as part of an unfolding historical narrative inevitably influences their actions in the present. In his first Prime Minister's Questions as Conservative leader, David Cameron taunted Blair, 'I want to talk about the future. He was the future once.'[11] This statement is a perfect expression of the presentist political position: it privileges an idea of the future defined not in terms of a particular vision but as simple chronological progression. It also displays a clear confidence that not only parliamentary politics, but also individual politicians, are the very stuff of history: past, present and future.

Notes

1 Fredric Jameson, *Postmodernism, or the Cultural Logic of Late Capitalism* (London and New York: Verso, 1991), p. 6.

2 Ibid., p. 20.

3 Casey, 'Tradition and authority', p. 85.

4 See for instance, Peter Hain, 'Gordon, you are without a narrative', *Independent on Sunday*, 8 March 2009. Available at: www.independent.co.uk/opinion /commentators/peter-hain-gordon-you-are-without-a-narrative-1639663.html. Accessed 23.10.2009.

5 Harvey J. Kaye, *The Powers of the Past: Reflections on the Crisis and the Promise of History* (New York and London: Harvester Wheatsheaf, 1991), p. 148. Original emphasis.

6 Ibid.

7 Margaret Thatcher, speaking at the opening of the new wing of the Churchill Archives Centre, 30 October 2002. Available at: www.margaretthatcher .org/speeches/displaydocument.asp?docid=109441. Accessed 26.11.2009.

8 I have explored the 'reality effect' of archives in Emily Robinson, 'Authenticity in the archive: historical encounters with "pastness"', in Rune Graulund (ed.), *Desperately Seeking Authenticity: Interdisciplinary Approaches* (Copenhagen: Copenhagen Doctoral School, 2010), pp. 13–28.

9 Thatcher opening new wing of the Churchill Archives Centre.

10 Dianne Hayter, 'Practioners: the PLP 1906–2006', 162, 161.

11 David Cameron, House of Commons PMQs, 7 December 2005, Column 861.

Bibliography

Archive Collections

Albert Sloman Library, University of Essex
Lord Alec McGivan, SDP papers
Lord Rodgers of Quarrybank, SDP papers

Bishopsgate Institute, London
The Raphael Samuel Archive

Conservative Party Archive, Bodleian Library, Oxford
Conservative Central Office, Papers
Conservative Research Department, Papers

Labour History Archive and Study Centre, People's History Museum, Manchester
Communist Party of Great Britain, Papers
Michael Foot, Papers
Dianne Hayter, Additional Papers (uncatalogued)
Labour Party, Papers
Labour Party Manifesto Group, Papers
LPGS Collection, Arts for Labour, Papers (uncatalogued)

Liddell Hart Centre for Military Archives, Kings College London
Sir Arthur Wynne Morgan Bryant, Papers

London Metropolitan Archives
Festival of Labour, Papers

London School of Economics
Liberal Party, Papers

Marx Memorial Library
Communist Party of Britain, Papers
New Communist Party, Papers

University College London
Hugh Gaitskell, Papers

Political reports, minutes and manifestos

Communist Party of Britain, *Re-establishment Congress Report*, 1988
Communist Party of Britain, *41st Congress Report: Branches, Districts & National Committees: Resolutions*, 1991
Communist Party of Great Britain, *Manifesto for New Times: A Communist Party Strategy for the 1990s, London: Marxism Today*, 1989
Hansard, *Parliamentary Debates, Commons*, various, 1953–2001
Labour Party, *Annual Conference Report*, 1993
Labour Party, *Conference Arrangements Committee Report*, 1993
Labour Party, *Annual Conference Report*, 1994
Labour Party, *Conference Arrangements Committee Report*, 1994
Labour Party, *Special Conference Report*, April 1995
Labour Party, *Minutes of 1906 Centenary Fringe Meeting*, Blackpool, 28 September 2005
National Union of Conservative and Unionist Associations, *Conference Minutes*, 1946

Interviews

Stephen Bird
Duncan Brack
Nigel Cochrane
Penelope J. Corfield
Iain Dale
Sue Donnelly
John Grigg
Dianne Hayter
Graham Lippiatt
Jeremy McIlwaine
Joan O'Pray
Tessa and Derek Phillips
Jeanne and Dave Rathbone
Anne Reyersbach
Andrew Riley

Helen Roberts
Greg Rosen
Sheridan Westlake

Newspapers, magazines and newsletters

Changes
Daily Telegraph
Daily Worker
Guardian
Independent
Independent on Sunday
Labour Heritage Bulletin
Labour Heritage Women's Research Committee Bulletin
Labour Victory
Liberal News
London Review of Books
Marxism Today
Morning Star
News and Views
New Statesman and Society
Observer
The Social Democrat
Socialist History Society Newsletter
The Spectator
Sunday Telegraph
The Times
Tribune
West Somerset Post
Young Communist

Websites

BBC News: http://news.bbc.co.uk
Civitas: www.civitas.org.uk/blog
Climate Rush: www.climaterush.co.uk/index.html
Communist Party Archive: www.communistpartyarchive.org.uk
Daniel Hannan, blog: http://blogs.telegraph.co.uk/daniel_hannan/blog
Labour Heritage: www.labourheritage.com/
Labour History Group: www.labourhistory.org.uk
Lawrence and Wishart: www.lwbooks.co.uk

Levellers' Day: www.levellers.org.uk/levellersdayhistory.htm
Liberal Democrat History Group: www.liberalhistory.org.uk
Making History: www.history.ac.uk/makinghistory
Margaret Thatcher Foundation: www.margaretthatcher.org/
North West Labour History Group: www.workershistory.org
Politics.co.uk: www.politics.co.uk
Progress: http://theprogressive.typepad.com
University of York, 'Dictionary of Labour Biography': www.york
.ac.uk/depts/poli/centres/labour.htm

Television, video and radio

Adam, Sharon (dir.), *Dear Diary*, BBC, 2010
Curtis, Adam (dir.), *The Living Dead, 3: The Attic*, BBC, 1995
Marchant, Mike (dir.), *Red Battersea: One Hundred Years of Labour* (Battersea Labour Party, 2008)
The Coal Board's Butchery, Miners' Campaign Tape Project / NUM, 1984
Walden, Brian, *Weekend World*, London Weekend Television, 16 January 1983. Transcript available at: www.margaretthatcher.org/speeches/displaydocument.asp?docid=105087. Accessed 09.10.2009

Speeches, lectures and addresses

Biffen, The Rt Hon John, MP, *Forward from Conviction*, The Second Disraeli Lecture, St Stephen's Constitutional Club, 14 October 1986, CPC pamphlet no. 0510–764 (London: Conservative Political Centre, 1986)
Blair, Tony, 'Let us face the future', 1945 Anniversary Lecture (London: The Fabian Society, 1995)
—— speech to Labour Party Conference, 28 September 1999. Available at: http://news.bbc.co.uk/1/hi/uk_politics/460009.stm. Accessed 23.10.2009
Brown, Gordon, speaking to the Major Economies Forum, 19 September 2009. Available at: www.number10.gov.uk/Page21030. Accessed 23.10.2009
Butler, Rt Hon R.A., 'Address to the Annual Conference of the Conservative Teachers' Association, Caxton Hall, Westminster, 13 March, 1948', *The Right Angle: Journal of the Conservative and Unionist Teachers' Association*, 1:1 (June 1948), 7–13
Cameron, David, New Year Message 2009/10. Available at: http://conservativehome.blogs.com/thetorydiary/2009/09/do-

you-receive-conservativehomes-daily-email.html. Accessed 05.01.2010

—— Rose Garden Press Conference, 10 Downing Street, 12 May 2010

Castle, Barbara, Presidential Address to Labour Party Annual Conference, Saturday 28 November 1959, available in UCL Library Services, Special Collections, Gaitskell Papers: C194

Clegg, Nick, Hugo Young Lecture, London, 23 November 2010

Clywd, Ann, Labour Party Centenary Conference, Blackpool, 12 February 2006

Cranbourne, Robert, *Allegiance: The nation State, Parliament and Prosperity*, Politeia Address Series, no. 7 (London: Politeia, 1999)

Gaitskell, Hugh, speech in Nottingham, 13 February 1960, Press Release issued by Labour Party East Midlands Regional Office, UCL Library Services, Special Collections, Gaitskell Papers: C212

Hague, William, speaking at the dinner to celebrate the twentieth anniversary of Thatcher's election as Prime Minister, 20 April 1999. Available at: www.guardian.co.uk/politics/1999/apr/20/conservatives1. Accessed 26.11.2009

Harris, Robin, *The Conservative Community: The Roots of Thatcherism – and its fFuture*, CPS Winter Address, St Stephen's Constitutional Club, 7 December 1989 (London: Centre for Policy Studies, 1989)

Jenkins, Roy, *The British Liberal Tradition: From Gladstone to Young Churchill, Asquith and Lloyd George – is Blair Their Heir?* 4th Annual Senator Keith Davey lecture, Victoria University, University of Toronto, 2000 (Toronto, Buffalo and London: University of Toronto Press, 2001)

Johnson, Paul, *The Spring Address: What is a Conservative?* (London: Centre for Policy Studies, May 1996)

Lawson, Nigel, MP, *The New Conservatism*, a talk given to the Bow Group, 4 August 1980 (London: Centre for Policy Studies, 1980)

Lilley, Peter, Butler Memorial Lecture, Carlton Club, 20 April 1999. Available at: www.peterlilley.co.uk/text/article.aspx?id=12&ref=859. Accessed 26.11.2009

Linsted, Hugh, MP, 'Education and politics', Extracts from an address given at a meeting of the London Teachers' Association, *The Right Angle*, 2:3 (Summer 1950), 5–7

Moore, Charles, *How to be British*, Annual Centre for Policy Studies lecture, Blackpool, 12 October 1995 (London: Centre for Policy Studies, 1995)

Osborne, George, 'Progressive reform in an age of austerity', speech to Demos, 11 August 2009. Available at: www.demos.co.uk/press_releases/george-osborne-progressive-reform-in-an-age-of-austerity. Accessed 06.09.2010

O'Sullivan, John, *Conservatism, Democracy and National Identity*, the third Keith Joseph Memorial Lecture, 16 February 1999 (London: Centre for Policy Studies, 1999)

Portillo, Michael, *The Ghost of Toryism Past: The Spirit of Conservatism Future*, CPS meeting at Party Conference, 9 October 1997 (London: Centre for Policy Studies, 1997)

Queen's Speech, 15 May 1979, Parliamentary Debates, Commons, vol. 967 cols 47–51. Available at: http://hansard.millbanksystems .com/commons/1979/may/15/queens-speech. Accessed 17.01.2010

Ramsden, John, *Britain is a Conservative Country that Occasionally Votes Labour: Conservative Success in Post-war Britain*, Swinton Lecture, Churchill College, Cambridge, 4 July 1997, CPC Pamphlet no. 916 (London: Conservative Political Centre, 1997)

Rodgers, Bill, speaking in Stockton-on-Tees, 28 August 1975. Press release in Labour History Archive and Study Centre, Dianne Hayter, Additional Papers (uncatalogued), Box 2

—— inaugural speech to the Campaign for Labour Victory, 19 February 1977. Transcript in Lord Rodgers of Quarrybank, SDP Papers, Albert Sloman Library, box 2, folder c

—— speech at the Annual Dinner of the Abertillery Constituency Labour Party, 30 November 1979. Transcript in Lord Rodgers of Quarrybank, SDP Papers, Albert Sloman Library, box 2, folder c

St John-Stevas, Norman, speaking at the launch of the Conservative Education Campaign, 'Values '78'. Conservative Party Archive, Bodleian Library, E2 News release: 63/78, CRD 4/5/49, Conservative Opposition Speeches 1974–May 1979

Thatcher, Margaret, speech accepting the Conservative leadership, Grosvenor Square, 20 February 1975. Available at: www.margaret-thatcher.org/speeches/displaydocument.asp?docid=102629. Accessed 04.01.2010

—— *Dimensions of Conservatism*, Iain Macleod Memorial Lecture, delivered to the Greater London Young Conservatives, 4 July 1977. Available at: www.margaretthatcher.org/speeches/display document.asp?docid=103411. Accessed 09.10.2009

—— speech to Conservative Rally at Blenheim Palace, Woodstock, Oxfordshire, 16 July 1977. Available at: www.margaretthatcher.org /speeches/displaydocument.asp?docid=103420. Accessed 09.10.2009

—— speech to International Democrat Union Conference in Tokyo, 22 September 1989. Available at: www.margaretthatcher.org/speeches /displaydocument.asp?docid=107773. Accessed 23.10.2009

—— speaking at 10 Downing Street, 9 May 1990. Available at: www.margaretthatcher.org/speeches/displaydocument.asp?

docid=108085. Accessed 23.10.2009

—— *Liberty and Limited Government*, the Keith Joseph Memorial Lecture, SBC Warburg, Swiss Bank House, London, 11 January 1996 (London: Centre for Policy Studies, 1996)

—— speaking at the opening of the new wing of the Churchill Archives Centre, 30 October 2002. Available at: www.margaret-thatcher.org / speeches / displaydocument.asp?docid=109441. Accessed 26.11.2009

Utley, T.E., CBE, *One Nation: 100 Years On*, lecture to CPC at Blackpool, 14 October 1981, CPC pamphlet no. 511–521–680 (London: Conservative Political Centre, 1981)

Willetts, David, MP, *Who Do We Think We Are?* Speech to Centre for Policy Studies meeting at Conservative Party Conference, 8 October 1998 (London: Centre for Policy Studies, 1998)

Books, pamphlets, chapters, articles and theses

Addison, Paul, *The Road to 1945: British Politics and the Second World War* (London: Pimlico, 1994)

Allmendinger, Philip and Thomas, Huw (eds), *Urban Planning and the New Right* (London: Routledge, 1998)

Amery, Colin and Cruickshank, Dan, *The Rape of Britain* (London: Elek, 1975)

Anderson, Perry, *A Zone of Engagement* (New York and London: Verso, 1992)

—— *Spectrum* (London: Verso, 2005)

Andrews, Geoff, *Endgames and New Times: The Final Years of British Communism 1964–1991* (London: Lawrence and Wishart, 2004)

Andrews, Geoff, Fishman, Nina and Morgan, Kevin (eds), *Opening the Books: Essays on the Social and Cultural History of British Communism* (London: Pluto Press, 1995)

Bale, Tim, *The Conservative Party: From Thatcher to Cameron* (Cambridge and Malden, MA: Polity, 2010)

Beckett, Francis, *Enemy Within: The Rise and Fall of the British Communist Party* (London: John Murray, 1995)

Bellamy, Joyce M. and Saville, John (eds), *Dictionary of Labour Biography* vol. I (London and Basingstoke: The Macmillan Press, 1972)

Benjamin, Walter, 'Theses on the philosophy of history', in Walter Benjamin, *Illuminations*, tr. Harry Zorn (London: Pimlico 1999 [1955]), pp. 245–55

Berg, Sebastian, 'Intellectual radicalism after 1989: theoretical and political discussions in a British and an American journal', *Socialist History*, 30 (2007), 43–59

Berkeley, Humphrey, 'Activities in teachers' training colleges', *The Right Angle*, 1:4 (Summer 1949), 10

Berry, Joe, *70 Years of Struggle: Britain's Communist Party, 1920–1990* (London: The Communist Party of Great Britain, 1991)

Bevan, Aneurin, *In Place of Fear* (London, Melbourne and New York: Quartet Books, 1998 [1952])

Bevir, Mark, *New Labour: A Critique* (Abingdon and New York: Routledge, 2005)

Black, Lawrence, *The Political Culture of the Left in Affluent Britain: 1951–64* (Basingstoke: Palgrave Macmillan, 2002)

—— *Redefining British Politics: Culture, Consumerism and Participation, 1954–70* (Basingstoke, Palgrave Macmillan, 2010)

Blackie, Duncan, 'End of the road?', *Socialist Worker Review*, 127 (January 1990), 14–15

Blair, Tony, *The Third Way: New Politics for the New Century* (London: Fabian Society, 1998)

Blunkett, David, *Politics and Progress: Renewing Democracy and a Civil Society* (London: Demos, 2001)

Bonnett, Alastair, *Left in the Past: Radicalism and the Politics of Nostalgia* (London: Continuum, 2010)

Boym, Svetlana, *The Future of Nostalgia* (New York: Basic Books, 2001)

Brack, Duncan, 'What influences Liberal Democrats?', in *Liberal Democrat History Group Newsletter*, no. 8 (September 1995), pp. 1–3

—— (ed.), *Dictionary of Liberal Biography* (London: Politico's, 1998)

Brack, Duncan, Grayson, Richard and Howarth, David (eds), *Reinventing the State: Social Liberalism for the 21st Century* (London: Politico's, 2007)

Bradley, Ian, *Breaking the Mould? The Birth and Prospects of the Social Democratic Party* (Oxford: Robertson, 1981)

Bragg, Billy, *The Progressive Patriot: A Search for Belonging* (London: Bantam Press, 2006)

Bryant, Arthur, *A History of Britain and the British People, Vol. 2, Freedom's Own Island: The British Oceanic Expansion* (London: Grafton Books, 1987)

Burton, Muriel, *100 Years of Liberalism: General Elections in Mid & North Oxfordshire* (Mid-Oxon Liberal Association, June 1977)

Butterfield, Herbert, *The Whig Interpretation of History* (Harmondsworth: Penguin, 1973 [1931])

Calder, Angus, *The People's War: Britain 1939–1945* (London: Pimlico, 1992 [1969])

Callaghan, John, *Cold War: Crisis and Conflict* (London: Lawrence and Wishart, 2003)

Callaghan, John, Fielding, Steven and Ludlam, Steve (eds), *Interpreting the Labour Party: Approaches to Labour Politics and History* (Manchester: Manchester University Press, 2003)

Callinicos, Alex, 'Horrible heritage', *Socialist Worker Review*, 126 (December 1989), 17

Campbell, Alastair, *The Blair Years: Extracts from the Alastair Campbell Diaries* (London: Hutchinson, 2007)

Campbell, John, *Nye Bevan: A Biography* (London: Hodder and Stoughton, 1994 [first published as *Nye Bevan and the Mirage of British Socialism*, Weidenfeld & Nicolson, 1987])

Carroll, W.S., *92 Years: A Chronicle of the Richmond and Barnes Conservative Association, 1880–1972* (Surrey: Thameside Property Trust, 1972)

Casey, John, 'Tradition and authority', in Maurice Cowling (ed.), *Conservative Essays* (London: Cassell, 1978), pp. 82–100

Charmley, John, interviewed by Szamuely, Helen, 'A Conservative historian speaks ...', *Conservative History Journal*, 5 (Autumn 2005), 2–6

—— *A History of Conservative Politics since 1830* (Basingstoke: Palgrave Macmillan, 2008)

Chase, Malcolm and Shaw, Christopher, 'The dimensions of nostalgia', in Christopher Shaw and Malcolm Chase (eds), *The Imagined Past: History and Nostalgia* (Manchester and New York, Manchester University Press, 1989), pp. 1–17

Cliff, Tony, 'Earthquake in the east', *Socialist Worker Review*, 126 (December 1989), 11–14

Cohen, Anthony P., *The Symbolic Construction of Community* (London and New York: Routledge, 2004)

Cohen, Phil (ed.), *Children of the Revolution* (London: Lawrence & Wishart, 1997)

Collette, Christine, 'Editorial', in *Labour Heritage Women's Research Committee Bulletin*, 2 (London: The Labour Party, Labour Heritage, Spring 1987), p. 2

Connerton, Paul, *How Societies Remember* (Cambridge: Cambridge University Press, 1989)

Conservative and Unionist Central Office, *The Young Britons Organisation*, Organisation Series, no. 11 (London: Conservative and Unionist Central Office, May 1949)

—— *Our Party: Blueprint for Change: A Consultation Paper for Reform of the Conservative Party* (London: CCO, 1997)

Cooke, Alistair B. (ed.), *The Conservative Party: Seven Historical Studies, 1860s to the 1990s*, CPC Pamphlet no. 914 (London: Conservative Political Centre, 1997)

Cormack, Patrick, *Heritage in Danger* (London: New English Library, 1976)

Cornforth, Maurice (ed.), *Rebels and their Causes: Essays in Honour of A. L. Morton* (London: Lawrence and Wishart, 1978)

Cornwell, John (ed.), *Tomb of the Unknown Alderman and Other Tales from the Town Hall* (Sheffield: J.C. Cornwell, 2006)

Cowling, Maurice, 'The present situation', in Maurice Cowling (ed.), *Conservative Essays* (London: Cassell, 1978), pp. 1–24

—— (ed.), *Conservative Essays* (London: Cassell, 1978)

—— *Mill and Liberalism* (Cambridge: Cambridge University Press, 1990 [1963])

Craig, F.W.S., *British Parliamentary Election Results, 1950–1970* (Chichester: Political Reference Publications, 1971)

Crewe, Ivor and King, Anthony, SDP: *The Birth, Life and Death of the Social Democratic Party* (Oxford and New York: Oxford University Press, 1997)

Cronin, James, *New Labour's Pasts: The Labour Party and its Discontents* (Harlow: Longman, 2004)

Crosland, C.A.R., *The Future of Socialism* (London: Jonathan Cape, 1956)

Crossman, Richard, *Labour in the Affluent Society*, Fabian Tract 325 (London: Fabian Society, 1960)

Daddow, Oliver, 'Playing games with history: Tony Blair's European policy in the press', *British Journal of Politics and International Relations*, 9 (2007), 582–98

Davies, Martin L., *Historics: Why History Dominates Contemporary Society* (Abingdon: Routledge, 2006)

Davis, J.C., *Fear, Myth and History: The Ranters and the Historians* (Cambridge: Cambridge University Press, 1986)

de Groot, Jerome, *Consuming History* (London: Routledge, 2008)

Delafons, John, *Politics and Preservation: A Policy History of the Built Heritage 1992–1996* (London: E & F.N. Spon, 1997)

Dell, Edmund, *A Strange Eventful History: Democratic Socialism in Britain* (London: HarperCollins, 2000)

Derrida, Jacques, *Spectres of Marx: The State of the Debt, The Work of Mourning and The New International*, tr. Peggy Kamuf (New York and London: Routledge, 1994)

Deuchar, Stewart (ed.), *What is Wrong with our Schools?* (York: Campaign for Real Education, no. 4, 1987)

—— The New History: A Critique (York: Campaign for Real Education, 1989)

Drucker, H.M., Doctrine and Ethos in the Labour Party (London: George Allen & Unwin, 1979)

Eccleshall, Robert, 'Party ideology and national decline', in Richard English and Michael Kenny (eds), Rethinking British Decline (Basingstoke: Macmillan Press Ltd, 2000), pp. 155–83

English, Richard and Kenny, Michael (eds), Rethinking British Decline (Basingstoke: Macmillan Press Ltd, 2000)

Favretto, Ilaria, 'British political parties' archives: an exemplary case', Journal of the Society of Archivists, 18:2 (1997), 205–13

Feiling, Keith, A History of the Tory Party 1640–1714 (Oxford: Clarendon Press, 1924)

—— What is Conservatism? (London: Faber & Faber, 1930)

Fergusson, Adam, The Sack of Bath: A Record and an Indictment (Salisbury: Compton Russell, 1973)

Fielding, Steven, 'New Labour and the past', in Duncan Tanner et al. (eds), Labour's First Century (Cambridge: Cambridge University Press, 2000), pp. 367–91

—— The Labour Party: Continuity and Change in the Making of New Labour (Basingstoke: Palgrave Macmillan, 2003)

Fielding, Steven and McHugh, Declan, 'The Progressive Dilemma and the social democratic perspective', in John Callaghan, Steven Fielding and Steve Ludlam (eds), Interpreting the Labour Party: Approaches to Labour Politics and History (Manchester: Manchester University Press, 2003), pp. 134–49

Fivush, Robyn, 'Remembering and reminiscing: how individual lives are constructed in family narratives', Memory Studies, 1:1 (2008), 49–58

Flinn, Andrew, 'Community histories, community archives: some opportunities and challenges', Journal of the Society of Archivists, 28:2 (October 2007), 151–76

Freeden, Michael, 'True blood or false genealogy: New Labour and British social democratic thought', in Andrew Gamble and Tony Wright (eds), The New Social Democracy (Oxford: The Political Quarterly Publishing Co. Ltd, 1999), pp.151–65

—— (ed.), Reassessing Political Ideologies: The Durability of Dissent (London and New York: Routledge, 2001)

Freeman, Anthony, 'Which history?', in Nick Seaton (ed.), Conference 1990: Which History? Whose Values? What Culture? Illiteracy, Inspectors and Primary School Matters, no. 5 (York: Campaign for Real Education, March 1990), pp. 4–8

Frow, Edmund and Frow, Ruth, 'Origins of the Working Class Movement Library: travels with a caravan', *History Workshop Journal*, 2. Reprinted in Michael Herbert and Eric Taplin (eds), *Born with a Book in his Hand: A Tribute to Edmund Frow, 1906–1997* (Salford: North West Labour History Group, 1998), pp. 27–32

Gamble, Andrew, *The Conservative Nation* (London: Routledge & Kegan Paul Ltd, 1974)

—— and Wright, Tony (eds), *The New Social Democracy* (Oxford: The Political Quarterly Publishing Co. Ltd, 1999)

Gaus, Gerald F., 'Ideological dominance through philosophical confusion: liberalism in the twentieth century', in Michael Freeden (ed.), *Reassessing Political Ideologies: The Durability of Dissent* (London and New York: Routledge, 2001), pp.13–34

Gilmour, Ian, *Inside Right: A Study of Conservatism* (London: Hutchinson, 1977)

Glazer, Peter, *Radical Nostalgia: Spanish Civil War Commemoration in America* (Rochester, NY: University of Rochester Press, 2005)

Golding, Janet A.C., 'An end to sweating? Liverpool's sweated workers and legislation 1870–1914', *Journal of the North West Labour History Group*, 21 (1996/97), 3–29

Gould, Philip, *The Unfinished Revolution: How the Modernisers Saved the Labour Party* (London: Abacus, 1999)

Green, E.H.H., *Ideologies of Conservatism: Conservative Political Ideas in the Twentieth Century* (Oxford: Oxford University Press, 2002)

—— *Thatcher* (London: Hodder Arnold, 2006)

Griffiths, Clare, 'Remembering Tolpuddle: rural history and commemoration in the inter-war labour movement', *History Workshop Journal*, 44 (1997), 145–69

Hague, The Rt Hon William, MP, *A Fresh Future for the Conservative Party* (London: Conservative Central Office, July 1997)

—— *William Pitt the Younger* (London: HarperCollins, 2004)

Hall, Stuart, 'The great moving right show', *Marxism Today*, December 1978. Reprinted in Stuart Hall, *The Hard Road to Renewal* (London and New York: Verso in association with *Marxism Today*, 1988), pp. 39–56

—— *The Hard Road to Renewal* (London and New York: Verso in association with *Marxism Today*, 1988)

Hamilton, Carolyn *et al.* (eds), *Refiguring the Archive* (Cape Town: David Philip Publishers, 2002; Dordrecht: Kluwer Academic Publishers, 2002)

Harrington, Michael, 'A Conservative ideology?', *Swinton Journal*, 19:2 (Summer 1973), 27–33

Hattersley, Roy, *Who Goes Home? Scenes from a Political Life* (London: Little, Brown and Company, 1995)

Haworth, Alan and Hayter, Dianne (eds), *Men Who Made Labour* (Abingdon: Routledge, 2006)

Hayter, Dianne, 'The fightback of the traditional right in the Labour party, 1979–1987', PhD thesis (University of London, 2004)

—— *Fightback!: Labour's Traditional Right in the 1970s and 1980s* (Manchester: Manchester University Press, 2005)

—— 'Practioners: The PLP 1906–2006', *Parliamentary Affairs*, 60:1 (2007), 153–63

Hayward, Rhodri, *Resisting History: Religious Transcendence and the Invention of the Unconscious* (Manchester: Manchester University Press; New York: Palgrave, 2007)

Heffer, Simon, *Nor Shall My Sword: The Reinvention of England* (Weidenfeld & Nicolson, 1999)

Henderson, Rt Hon Arthur, MP, 'Introductory: Labour as it is to-day', in Herbert Tracey (ed.), *The Book of the Labour Party: Its History, Growth, Policy and Leaders* (London: Caxton Publishing Company, 1925), pp. 8–34

Herbert, Michael and Taplin, Eric (eds), *Born with a Book in his Hand: A Tribute to Edmund Frow, 1906–1997* (Salford: North West Labour History Group, 1998)

Hewison, Robert, *The Heritage Industry: Britain in a Climate of Decline* (London: Methuen, 1987)

—— *Culture and Consensus: England, Art and Politics since 1940*, revised edn (London: Methuen, 1997)

Hillgate Group, *The Reform of British Education: From Principles to Practice* (London: Claridge, 1987)

Hilton, Rodney, 'Class analysis of feudal society', *Our History Journal*, 17 (May 1991), 33–7

Hobbes, Thomas, *Leviathan*, ed. Richard Tuck (Cambridge: Cambridge University Press, 1996)

Hobsbawm, E.J., 'The social functions of the past: some questions', *Past and Present*, 55 (1972), 3–17

—— 'The Historians' Group of the Communist Party', in Maurice Cornforth (ed.), *Rebels and their Causes: Essays in Honour of A. L. Morton* (London: Lawrence and Wishart, 1978), pp. 21–47

—— *On History* (London: Abacus, 1998)

—— *Interesting Times* (New York and London: The New Press, 2002)

Hogg, Quintin, *The Case for Conservatism* (Middlesex: Penguin, 1947)

Howard, Michael, 'Foreword', in Anthony Seldon and Peter Snowdon, *The Conservative Party: An Illustrated History* (Stroud:

Sutton Publishing, 2004), pp. vii–viii

Jacques, Martin, 'Why study the history of the CP?', *Our History Journal*, 2 (July 1978), 5–8

Jameson, Fredric, 'Marxism and historicism', *New Literary History*, 11:1 (Autumn 1979), 41–73.

—— *Postmodernism, or the Cultural Logic of Late Capitalism* (London and New York: Verso, 1991)

Jarvis, Mark, *Conservative Governments, Morality and Social Change in Affluent Britain, 1957–64* (Manchester: Manchester University Press, 2005)

Jenkins, Hugh (ed.), *Rank and File* (London: Croom Helm, 1980)

Jenkins, Roy, *A Life at the Centre* (London: Macmillan, 1991)

Johnstone, Monty, 'What kind of Communist Party history?', *Our History Journal*, 4 (February 1979), 5–9

—— 'Introduction', in Francis King and George Matthews (eds), *About Turn: The British Communist Party and the Second World War: The Verbatim Record of the Central Committee Meetings of 25 September and 2–3 October 1939* (London: Lawrence & Wishart, 1990), pp. 13–49

Jones, Tudor, *Remaking the Labour Party: From Gaitskell to Blair* (London and New York: Routledge, 1996)

Katz, Richard S. and Mair, Peter, 'Changing models of party organization and party democracy: the emergence of the cartel party', *Party Politics*, 1:1 (January 1995), 5–28

Kaye, Harvey J., *The Powers of the Past: Reflections on the Crisis and the Promise of History* (New York and London: Harvester Wheatsheaf, 1991)

Kelly, Veronica, 'Little Moscow and Moscow Row', *Labour Heritage Bulletin* (Autumn 2008), 1–5

Kenny, Michael and Smith, Martin J., '(Mis)understanding Blair', in *Political Quarterly*, 68:3 (1997), 220–30

—— 'Discourses of modernization: Gaitskell, Blair and the reform of Clause IV', in Charles Pattie *et al.* (eds), *British Elections and Parties Review*, vol. 7 (London: Frank Cass, 1997), pp. 110–26

Kertzer, D.I., *Ritual, Politics and Power* (New Haven: Yale University Press, 1988)

—— *Politics and Symbols: The Italian Communist Party and the Fall of Communism* (New Haven and London: Yale University Press, 1996)

King, Francis and Matthews, George (eds), *About Turn: The British Communist Party and the Second World War: The Verbatim Record of the Central Committee Meetings of 25 September and 2–3 October 1939* (London: Lawrence & Wishart, 1990)

Kingsford, Peter, 'A worm's eye view of the General Strike', *Labour Heritage Bulletin* (Spring 2007), 12–13

Kirchheimer, Otto, 'The transformation of the western European party systems', in Joseph LaPalombara and Myron Weiner (eds), *Political Parties and Political Development* (Princeton: Princeton University Press, 1966), pp. 177–200

Larkham, Peter J. and Barrett, Heather, 'Conservation of the built environment under the Conservatives', in Philip Allmendinger and Huw Thomas (eds), *Urban Planning and the New Right* (London: Routledge, 1998), pp. 53–86

Lawlor, Sheila, *The National Curriculum, CPS Response to Proposed Draft Order for History* (London: Centre for Policy Studies, February 1991)

Lawrence, Jon, 'Labour: the myths it has lived by', in Duncan Tanner *et al.* (eds), *Labour's First Century* (Cambridge: Cambridge University Press, 2000), pp. 341–66

—— *Electing our Masters: The Hustings in British Politics from Hogarth to Blair* (Oxford: Oxford University Press, 2009)

Liberal Democrat Party, *It's About Freedom*, The Report of the Liberal Democrat Working Group, Policy Paper 50, June 2002

Liberator, *Liberator Songbook*, Fifteenth edition (London: Liberator, 2004)

—— *Liberator Songbook*, Nineteenth edition (London: Liberator, 2008)

Lowenthal, David, 'Nostalgia tells it like it wasn't', in Christopher Shaw and Malcolm Chase (eds), *The Imagined Past: History and Nostalgia* (Manchester and New York, Manchester University Press, 1989), pp. 18–32

Mandelson, Peter and Liddle, Roger, *The Blair Revolution: Can New Labour Deliver?* (London and Boston: Faber & Faber, 1996)

Mandler, Peter, *History and National Life* (London: Profile Books, 2002)

Marquand, David, 'Inquest on a movement: Labour's defeat and its consequences', *Encounter* (July 1979), 8–18

—— *The Progressive Dilemma: From Lloyd George to Blair* (London: William Heinemann, 1991). Revised Second Edition (London: Phoenix, 1999)

Marshall, H.E., *Our Island Story* (London: Civitas, 2007 [1905])

Marshall, Paul and Laws, David (eds), *The Orange Book: Reclaiming Liberalism* (London: Profile, 2004)

Mathew, Don, *From Two Boys and a Dog to Political Power: The Labour Party in the Lowestoft Constituency 1918–1945* (Lowestoft: Lowestoft Constituency Labour Party, 1979)

Mbembe, Achille, 'The power of the archive and its limits', in Carolyn Hamilton *et al.* (eds), *Refiguring the Archive* (Cape Town: David Philip Publishers, 2002; Dordrecht, Kluwer Academic Publishers, 2002), pp. 19–26

McIlroy, John, 'The Society for the Study of Labour History, 1956–1985: its origins and its heyday', in John McIlroy *et al.* (eds), *Making History: Organizations of Labour Historians in Britain Since 1960: Labour History Review Fiftieth Anniversary Supplement*, April 2010, pp. 19–112

McIlroy, John, Morgan, Kevin and Campbell, Alan (eds), *Party People, Communist Lives: Explorations in Biography* (London: Lawrence & Wishart, 2001)

Morgan, Kevin, 'The CPGB and the Comintern archives', *Socialist History Journal*, 2 (Autumn 1993), 9–29

—— 'Parts of people and communist lives', in John McIlroy, Kevin Morgan and Alan Campbell (eds), *Party People, Communist Lives: Explorations in Biography* (London: Lawrence & Wishart, 2001), pp. 9–28

Morrison, Alasdair, 'The historic basis of conservatism', *Swinton Journal*, 15:1 (Spring 1969), 22–9

New Communist Party, *The Case for the New Communist Party* (London: The New Communist Party, undated [1977?])

Nora, Pierre (ed.), *Realms of Memory: Rethinking the French Past, vol. I, Conflicts and Divisions* (New York: Columbia University Press, 1996), English language edn edited by Lawrence D. Kritzman, tr. Arthur Goldhammer [*Les Lieux de Mémoire*, Editions Gallimard, 1992]

'No Turning Back' Group of Conservative MPs, *Save Our Schools* (London: Conservative Political Centre, July 1986)

O'Keefe, Dennis (ed.), *The Wayward Curriculum* (Exeter: Social Affairs Unit, 1986)

O'Sullivan, John, 'The direction of conservatism', *Swinton Journal*, 16:4 (Spring 1970), 30–6

Owen, David, *Time to Declare* (London: Michael Joseph, 1991)

Parsons, Steve, 'What happened inside the CPGB', *Our History: The Communist Party and 1956: Speeches at the Conference*, pamphlet 88 (Socialist History Society, February 1993), pp. 24–38

Partington, Geoffrey, 'History: re-written to ideological conviction', in Dennis O'Keefe (ed.), *The Wayward Curriculum* (Exeter: Social Affairs Unit, 1986), pp. 63–81

Pimlott, Ben, 'Foreword', in Duncan Brack (ed.), *Dictionary of Liberal Biography* (London: Politico's, 1998), pp. x–xi

Plumb, J.H., *The Death of the Past* (Basingstoke: Palgrave Macmillan, 2003 [1969])

Powell, Enoch, *Wrestling with the Angel* (London: Sheldon Press, 1977)

Randall, Nick, 'Time and British politics: memory, the present and teleology in the politics of New Labour', *British Politics*, 4:2 (2009), 188–216

Renton, Dave, 'The historian as outsider: writing public history from within and without a group', *Journal of the North West Labour History Group*, 25 (2000/01), 48–54

Roberts, Stephen, 'Thomas Cooper: a Victorian working-class writer', *Our History Journal*, 16 (November 1990), 12–25

Robinson, Emily, 'Authenticity in the archive: historical encounters with "pastness"', in Rune Graulund (ed.), *Desperately Seeking Authenticity: Interdisciplinary Approaches* (Copenhagen: Copenhagen Doctoral School, 2010), pp. 13–28

Rodgers, William, 'The SDP and Liberal Party in alliance', *Political Quarterly*, 54:4 (October–December 1983), 354–62

—— 'Government under stress: Britain's Winter of Discontent 1979', *Political Quarterly*, 55:2 (April–June 1984), 171–9

Rosen, Greg (ed.), *Dictionary of Labour Biography* (London: Politico's, 2001)

Salber Philips, Mark, 'On the advantage and disadvantage of sentimental history for life', *History Workshop Journal*, 65 (2008), 49–64

Samuel, Raphael, *Theatres of Memory, Vol. I: Past and Present in Contemporary Culture* (London and New York: Verso, 1994)

—— *Island Stories: Unravelling Britain: Theatres of Memory, Vol. II*, ed. by Alison Light with Sally Alexander and Gareth Stedman Jones (London and New York: Verso, 1998)

—— *The Lost World of British Communism* (London: Verso, 2006)

Samuel, Raphael and Thompson, Paul (eds), *The Myths we Live By* (London and New York: Routledge, 1990)

Saville, John, 'Introduction', in Joyce M. Bellamy and John Saville (eds), *Dictionary of Labour Biography* vol. I (London and Basingstoke: The Macmillan Press, 1972), pp. ix–xiii

—— 'The XXth Congress and the British Communist Party', *Socialist Register* (1976), 1–23

SDP / Liberal Joint Policy Statement, 'A democracy of conscience', printed in *Liberal News*, no. 1882 (22 January 1988), pp. 4–5

Seaton, Nick (ed.), *Conference 1990: Which History? Whose Values? What Culture? Illiteracy, Inspectors and Primary School Matters*, no. 5 (York: Campaign for Real Education, March 1990)

Seldon, Anthony and Snowdon, Peter, *The Conservative Party: An Illustrated History* (Stroud: Sutton Publishing, 2004)

Seyd, Patrick and Whiteley, Paul, *New Labour's Grassroots: The Transformation of Labour Party Membership* (Basingstoke: Palgrave Macmillan, 2002)

Shaw, Christopher and Chase, Malcolm (eds), *The Imagined Past: History and Nostalgia* (Manchester and New York: Manchester University Press, 1989)

Shaw, Eric, *Losing Labour's Soul: New Labour and the Blair Governments 1997–2007* (London: Routledge, 2007)

Sherlock, Neil and Lawson, Neal, 'Whatever happened to the progressive century?', *Political Quarterly*, 78:1 (January–March 2007), 175–81

Smith, Bonnie G., *The Gender of History: Men, Women, and Historical Practice* (Cambridge, MA and London: Harvard University Press, 1998)

Soffer, Reba N., *History, Historians, and Conservatism in Britain and America: The Great War to Thatcher and Reagan* (Oxford: Oxford University Press, 2009)

Stanley, Jo, 'Liverpool's women dockers', *Journal of the North West Labour History Group*, 25 (2000/01), 2–14

Stapleton, Julia, *Sir Arthur Bryant and National Life in Twentieth-Century Britain* (Oxford: Lexington Books, 2005)

Tabili, Laura, 'Labour migration, racial foundation and class identity. Some reflections on the British case', *Journal of the North West Labour History Group*, 20 (1995/96), 16–35

Tanner, Duncan *et al.* (eds), *Labour's First Century* (Manchester: Manchester University Press, 2007)

Taylor, Barbara, 'Heroic families and utopian Histories', Historein, 3 (2001), 59–74.

Temple, Nina, '*New* times, *new* politics', Report to CPGB Executive Committee, January 1990.

—— *et al.*, 'Assessments – what was communism?', *Socialist History Journal*, 2 (Autumn 1993), 6–8

Thatcher, Margaret, *The Downing Street Years* (London: HarperCollins, 1993)

Thomas, Hugh, *History, Capitalism and Freedom* (London: Centre for Policy Studies, 1979)

Thompson, Willie, 'History's last word? The Communist Party in dissolution', *Our History Journal*, 16 (November 1990), 2–8

—— 'End of our history? The terminus of the CPGB', *Socialist History Journal*, 19 (May 1992), 3–6

—— *The Good Old Cause: British Communism 1920–1991* (London: Pluto Press, 1992)

—— *What Happened to History?* (London: Pluto Press, 2000)

Thompson, Willie, Parker, David and Waite, Mike, Editorial, 'What was communism?', *Socialist History Journal*, 2 (Autumn 1993), 1–5

Tracey, Herbert (ed.), *The Book of the Labour Party: Its History, Growth, Policy and Leaders* (London: Caxton Publishing Company, 1925)

Trouillot, Michel-Rolph, *Silencing the Past: Power and the Production of History* (Boston: Beacon Press, 1995)

Vernon, James, *Politics and the People: A Study in English Political Culture, c.1815–1867* (Cambridge: Cambridge University Press, 1993)

Vincent, John, *The Seven Voices of Conservatism*, CPC pamphlet no. 0510/821 (London: Conservative Political Centre, February 1991)

Walton, Molly, Foreword to *Colne Valley Labour Party, 1891–1991: Souvenir Centenary History* (Colne Valley Constituency Labour Party, July 1991), p. i

White, Hayden, *Metahistory: The Historical Imagination in Nineteenth-century Europe* (Baltimore: The Johns Hopkins University Press, 1973), pp. 22–9

White, Stuart (ed.), *New Labour: The Progressive Future?* (Basingstoke: Palgrave, 2001)

Willetts, David, MP with Forsdyke, Richard, *After the Landslide: Learning the Lessons from 1906 and 1945* (London: Centre for Policy Studies, September 1999)

Wincott, Daniel, 'Thatcher: ideological or pragmatic?', *Contemporary British History*, 4:2 (November 1990), 26–8

Woodward, Alan, 'Know your enemy', *The Right Angle*, 1:3 (Spring 1949), 15–16

Wright, Patrick, *On Living in an Old Country: The National Past in Contemporary Britain* (Oxford: Oxford University Press, 2008 [Verso, 1991])

Index

Note: 'n' after a page reference indicates the number of a note on that page

1688 *see* commemoration

archives
    access to 50, 173–4
    disregard for 52–6
    importance of, increasing 48
    limitations of 51–2, 184
    obsession with 47–8
    of political parties 7, 11, 48–59, 72,
        81
    and research 12, 51, 54, 56–7, 61,
        173–4
    and shaping history 51–3
    see also Communist Party of Great
        Britain; Conservative Party;
        Labour Party; Liberal
        Democrat Party; Liberal Party;
        Marxist history; Social
        Democratic Party; Thatcher,
        Margaret
Association of Conservative and
    Unionist Teachers *see*
    Conservative Party
Attlee, Clement 50, 127, 129, 134,
    135, 138, 140
authenticity
    as cultural value 4, 181
    of historical evidence 22–3
    of living witnesses 63–5
    past, association with 122, 181
    as political response 22–3
    of self-identity 5–6
    see also heritage; past; pastness

Battersea Labour Party
    and archives 55
    and Burns, John 66
    centenary history project 7, 56,
        65–6, 69, 73, 76, 78
    choir 76
    and Despard, Charlotte 65, 76
    and Ganley, Caroline 65, 73
    Women's Section 65–6
    see also Labour Party
Benn, Tony 35–7, 70–1, 80, 137
Bevan, Aneurin 39, 40, 70–1, 129–30,
    134, 138
Blair, Tony
    and 1945, legacy of 134
    on 'conservatism' 27
    Foot, Michael, letter to 134–5
    and Gaitskell, legacy of 132–3, 155
    and history of Labour Party 124,
        135
    and Labour Party members 137
    and liberalism 124, 134–5, 155
    and New Labour, foundation
        narrative of 122
    and 'progressive alliance' 122, 124,
        134
    on 'progressivism' 27
    and Social Democratic Party,
        legacy of 133
    temporal positioning of 13, 122–4,
        125, 147
    on 'young country', Britain as 114
    see also Clause IV; Labour Party;
        New Labour

Bragg, Billy 15n.5, 37, 76
'breaking the mould'
  Clegg, Nick 10
  Social Democratic Party 9, 10, 125
  Thatcher, Margaret as described
    by Hall, Stuart 9
Brown, Gordon 4, 16n.22, 144
Butler, R.A. 26, 91
Butterfield, Herbert 31–2

Callaghan, James 4, 29, 129–30
Cameron, David 1, 9, 28, 38, 146, 185
  see also Conservative-Liberal
    Democrat coalition;
    Conservative Party; General
    Election (2010)
Casey, John 30–1, 182
Castle, Barbara 27, 127
Charmley, John 89–90, 91, 109
Charter 88 34
Churchill, Winston 38, 71, 72, 80, 92,
    93, 98, 100, 110
classical liberalism see liberalism
Clause IV
  Blair's revision of 12, 134–44
  contemporary politics, relevant to
    138–43
  Defend Clause 4 Campaign 137–8
  Gaitskell's attempted revision of
    126–8
  see also Blair, Tony; Labour Party;
    New Labour
Clegg, Nick 1, 10, 10
  see also Conservative-Liberal
    Democrat coalition; General
    Election (2010); Liberal
    Democrat Party
Colley, Linda 101, 109
commemoration 11
  of 1688, tercentenary 34–6
  of Battersea Labour Party,
    centenary 7, 56, 65–6, 69, 73,
    76, 78
  of Communist Party of Great
    Britain, 70th anniversary

    169–70
  of English Civil War 33, 36–8
  of Labour Party, foundation 41, 56,
    66–7, 76–7, 81, 82
  Levellers' Day 36–8, 73
  of Liberal Party, foundation 81–2
  as political action 73–5
  of Putney Debates, 360th
    anniversary 36, 37
  resistance to 35–6
  of Rochdale Pioneers Co-operative
    Society, foundation 143–4
  of Spanish Civil War 23, 75
  of Tolpuddle Martyrs 22, 37
  see also heritage; 'heritage
    industry'; history; memory
communism
  continuing need for 163–4
  Eurocommunism 155, 171
  and history 153, 154, 156–8,
    169–70, 173–6
  as indigenous British tradition 36,
    161, 166–7
  perceptions of 167–8
  revisionism 155, 159, 165, 169
  as social identity 154, 167–8
  Soviet 14, 153, 154, 156–7, 159–61,
    164–5, 166, 167
  see also Communist Party of
    Britain; Communist Party of
    Great Britain; Marxism;
    Marxist history; New
    Communist Party; socialism;
    Socialist Workers Party; USSR
Communist Party Historians' Group
  see Marxist history
Communist Party of Britain (CPB)
    153, 155, 159, 160, 163, 165,
    169–70
Communist Party of Great Britain
    (CPGB)
  and 1956 14, 156–7, 158
  and 1989 14, 158–9, 161–76
  archive of 49, 52, 174
  British Road to Socialism / Facing

Up to the Future 158, 170
and collective responsibility 173
culture of 154, 173
Democratic Left 158, 168, 170
divisions within 158
'education' meetings, controversy
    over 172–3
foundation of, 70th anniversary
    169–70
history of 154, 156–7, 175
identity, members' crisis of 153–4,
    155, 158, 161, 165, 167–9, 175
Manifesto for New Times 158, 169,
    170
and Marxist history 14
and modernity 162, 171
party name, controversy over
    167–9
and pluralism 155
presentism of 14, 155
as progressive 30
revisionism of 155, 159, 165, 169
'transformation' process 12, 165–6,
    170–2
see also communism; Marxism;
    Marxism Today; Marxist
    history; socialism; Temple,
    Nina; USSR
conservatism 18–21
    and change 25, 28, 88–9, 91, 96–7,
        99
    and continuity 25–6, 28, 98, 109
    and duty to future 24, 93, 111, 128
    and duty to past 18, 24, 31, 42
    'forces of' 27
    and historical process 19–20, 97
    and ideology 69, 104–5
    in Labour Party 27, 127
    and liberalism 30–1, 97–100, 108–9
    and losing causes 26
    and Marxism 30–1, 100–1, 108–9
    and nostalgia 18, 24
    'one nation' 90, 92, 95–6
    and progressivism 19–21, 28, 99,
        111

strands within 94–9
and time 18–20
see also conservative history;
    Conservative Party; new right;
    Toryism; tradition
conservative history 19
    Conservative Party history,
        interpretations of 90, 96–100
    and contingency 98, 109
    and liberalism 108–9
    and Marxism 30–1, 108–9
    and the National Curriculum for
        History 106–8
    Whig history, opposition to 31,
        106–7, 108–9
    see also conservatism; Conservative
        History Group; Toryism
Conservative History Group 61, 62,
    66
    see also conservative history;
        Conservative Party
Conservative-Liberal Democrat
    coalition 1, 9, 78, 100, 146
    'progressive', claims to be 20
    and Thatcher governments 10, 184
    see also Cameron, David; Clegg,
        Nick; Conservative Party;
        General Election (2010);
        Liberal Democrat Party
Conservative Party
    and 1906 General Election 91
    and 1945 General Election 91–2
    and 1951 General Election 94
    and 1979 General Election 94
    and 1997 General Election 13, 24,
        72, 89–95, 114–16
    archive of 49–50, 52–3, 54, 59, 72,
        78–9
    Association of Conservative and
        Unionist Teachers 102–3
    Associations 12, 54, 55, 81, 83n.33,
        89–90, 100
    Blueprint for Change 12, 93
    historical figures, admired by
        members 72

history of 32, 59, 72, 90
and history teaching 13, 102–9
local histories of 55, 81, 83n.33
and Marxist history 14
members of 12, 54, 79, 89–90
memorabilia of 78–9
as the national party 2, 12–13, 39,
    59, 69, 92–3, 99
and the national soul, loss of
    connection to 32, 88, 92–3, 99
organisational change 12, 89–90,
    93
and post-war settlement 26
strands within 20
and Thatcher, Margaret 13, 88,
    114–60
Tory Reform Group 28
Young Britons 102–3
see also Cameron, David;
    conservatism; Conservative
    history; Conservative History
    Group; Conservative-Liberal
    Democrat coalition; General
    Election (2010); new right;
    Thatcher, Margaret; Toryism
convergence between parties 11, 18,
    41–2, 47, 61, 79–80, 82, 181
Corfield, Penelope J. 7, 55, 56, 57, 69
Cowling, Maurice 44n.47, 98, 108–9,
    110
Crosland, Tony 27, 123, 128, 134
Crossman, Richard 27, 40, 127

Davies, M.L. 4, 9, 91, 183
Disraeli, Benjamin 28, 90, 95–6
Drucker, Henry 1–2, 32, 42, 147

'end of history' 14, 19, 162, 183
English Civil War see
    commemoration

Foot, Michael 70, 80, 134–5
Freeman, E.A. 6
Frow, Ruth and Eddie 58–9, 67
    see also socialist history

future 19, 20, 41, 137, 138, 158, 185
    fear of 24
    history, written for 56, 64, 83n.33
    history, written in 7, 51, 56, 57–8,
        64, 175–6
    hope for 110–11, 160, 167
    imagined 1–2, 11, 56, 125, 162, 164,
        165, 183
    loss of 11, 14, 88, 111, 153, 165
    obligation to 7, 21, 22, 24, 36, 39,
        56–8, 93, 111, 128, 138, 163–4
    openness to 131, 172–3, 183
    orientation towards 110–11, 123–5
    shaping the 25
    as unknown 6, 125, 132, 182–3
    see also optimism

Gaitskell, Hugh 122, 126–8, 129–30,
    132
General Election (2010) 9
    as 'historic' 9
    and Labour Party 29–30, 145–6
    'progressive', uses of term 20, 28
    see also Conservative-Liberal
        Democrat coalition
Gladstone, William Ewart 72, 81,
    95–6, 99, 144–5, 146
Gould, Philip 123, 132, 134, 144, 147

Hague, William
    and 1997 General Election 89
    and Conservative Party
        organisation 89, 93
    Thatcher's legacy, defence of 94,
        115
    William Pitt the Younger: A
        Biography 80
Hall, Stuart 8, 9, 42
Hayter, Dianne 7, 80
    Fightback! Labour's Traditional Right
        in the 1970s and 1980s 56–7, 123
    and Labour Party centenary 56,
        66–7, 81, 184
    see also Labour Party
Heath, Edward 29, 97

heritage 2
  cultural value of 3–4, 14, 36, 124, 181
  and memorabilia 78–9
  obligation, replacement for 38, 73, 181–2
  and popular culture 3–4
  preservation of 111–12
  and temporal distance 24, 182
  see also commemoration; 'heritage industry'; history; memory; nostalgia; past; 'pastness'
'heritage industry' 4, 112, 113
  see also commemoration; heritage; memory; nostalgia; past; 'pastness'
Hill, Christopher 36, 37, 100, 166
historical process 3, 10, 18–19, 97, 181
  see also teleology
history
  competing visions of 100–4, 106–9
  distortion of 157
  elite / marginalised 3
  and emotion 5, 184
  as gendered 33
  as identity affirmation 2, 4, 6, 23, 32, 101, 107–8, 147
  and ideology 3, 18–19, 32, 60, 154
  judgement of 160–1, 175–6
  learning from 2, 11, 54, 61–2, 80, 181, 184
  legitimating power of 4, 13, 14, 32, 123–4, 181–3
  as linear 14, 20, 26, 108, 183
  making 2, 11, 58, 62, 123, 134, 176, 183
  and memory 47–8, 56–7, 63–5, 154
  and myth 22, 32, 51, 61, 90, 122, 124, 184
  National Curriculum for 104–9, 183
  national / sectional 2–3, 49
  as political force 2, 36
  post-modern 183
  professionalisation of 32–3, 107–8
  and public time 32–3
  as repetition 10
  respect for profession of 7, 56–7
  responsibility for 166–7, 181
  revisionism 124, 155, 183
  'scientific' 157
  shaping of 7–8, 21, 25–6, 48, 51–2, 63, 96, 110, 174
  on the side of 91, 175
  social 40, 67, 103, 107, 112
  teaching of 102–9
  as unfolding process 173, 181, 185
  see also conservative history; 'end of history'; heritage; 'history is past politics'; Marxist history; memory; myth; parliamentary history; past; pastness; political party history; socialist history; Whig history
'history is past politics'
  Festival of Labour 41
  Freeman, E.A. 6
History Workshop see socialist history
Hobsbawm, Eric 23, 100, 156, 157, 174, 176

ideology 5, 47, 69, 70, 72, 75, 95, 104–5, 155, 167
  and history 3, 18–19, 32, 60, 154
individuals, celebration of 66–72

Jameson, Fredric 31, 182
Jenkins, Roy 13, 26, 71, 80, 125, 131

Labour Heritage see socialist history
Labour History Group 39–40, 60–1, 62, 63–5, 66, 67, 68
  see also labour movement, Labour Party, socialist history
labour movement 1, 4, 22, 29, 32, 37–8, 39–40, 41, 58–60, 61, 66, 67, 76, 124, 143, 153, 154, 156, 159
  see also Labour Party; socialist history; tradition

Labour Party
  and 1959 General Election 26,
    126–8
  2000 centenary 56, 81, 82
  2006 centenary 56, 66–7, 76–7, 80,
    81, 184
  archive of 49, 52, 53–5, 58, 59
  Campaign for Labour Victory 129
  'conservatism', accusations of 27,
    127
  Festival of Labour 40–1
  fiftieth jubilee 66
  and General Election (2010) 29–30,
    145–6
  heritage of 4, 39–40, 60
  as a historic movement 1, 41
  individuals, attitude to 66–71
  Lib-Lab Pact 29
  local histories of 67–8, 81, 83n.33
  members, role of 12
  as 'modern' 2, 40–1
  and modernity 26–7, 60, 126–8
  National Executive Committee
    53–4, 57, 60
  as a national party 13, 39–40, 59
  organisational change 12
  and 'progressive alliance'
    narrative 145–6
  Red Flag, singing of 76–7
  and Social Democratic Party 50
  strands within 20, 40, 123, 129–30,
    145–6
  Tribune group 127, 130, 132, 133,
    137, 141
  see also Battersea Labour Party;
    Blair, Tony; Clause IV; General
    Election (2010); Labour
    History Group; labour
    movement; New Labour;
    social democracy; socialism;
    socialist history
Levellers' Day see commemoration
Liberal Democrat History Group
  61–4, 66, 81–2, 71–2
  see also Liberal Democrat Party;

Lloyd George Society
Liberal Democrat Party
  archive of 50–1, 52
  foundation of 145
  Glee Club 75, 77–8
  historical figures, relationship to
    71–2
  Liberal history 50–1, 62–3, 81–2,
    145
  Lloyd George Society 71, 80
  and 'progressive alliance'
    narrative 145–6
  and Social Democratic Party 50–1,
    63, 145
  strands within 20, 146–7
  see also Clegg, Nick; Conservative-
    Liberal Democrat Coalition;
    Liberal Democrat History
    Group; liberalism; Liberal
    Party; social democracy;
    Social Democratic Party
liberalism
  classical 20, 21, 146–7
  and conservatism 30–1, 97–100,
    108–9
  individuals, attitude to 71–2
  language of 98
  in Liberal Democrat Party 146–7
  New 122, 124, 133, 146–7, 155
  social 20, 145–7
  see also Liberal Democrat Party;
    Liberal Party; Lloyd George
    Society; tradition; whiggism;
    Whig history
Liberal Party
  archive of 50–1
  and Conservative Party 100
  Lib-Lab Pact 29
  and Social Democratic Party 50–1,
    71, 144–5
  see also Liberal Democrat Party;
    liberalism; Lloyd George
    Society; Steel, David;
    whiggism
Lib-Lab Pact 29

Lilley, Peter 91, 93, 114–15
Lloyd George, David 50, 71, 72, 134,
    146
Lloyd George Society 71, 80

Macmillan, Harold 26, 28, 40, 96
Major, John 92, 94, 96, 114
Marquand, David 124, 133–4, 144
    see also New Labour 'progressive
        alliance'; Social Democratic
        Party
Marxism
    after 1989 162, 163–5, 172
    and conservatism 30–1, 100–1,
        108–9
    and history 153, 154–5, 156–8,
        173–6
    language of 171–2
    progressive 165, 171–2
    see also communism; Marxist
        history; socialism
Marxism Today 30, 125, 155, 162, 175
Marxist history
    after 1989 173–6
    as alternative narrative of British
        history 36, 154, 166–7
    archives, access to 173
    Communist Party Historians'
        Group 14, 106–7, 153, 154–5,
        156–8, 173–5
    Conservative attacks on 100–4
    and postmodernism 162, 183
    Socialist History Society 60, 156,
        174
    see also communism; Marxism;
        socialist history
memory
    crisis of 153–4, 155
    cross-generational 74–5
    fragility of 57
    and history 47–8, 56–7, 63–5, 79,
        154
    obligations of 184
    performative 73–8
    and place 73

in political parties 5, 47–8, 73–5,
    79–82, 153–4, 166
prosthetic 47
in witness seminars 63–5
see also heritage; 'heritage
    industry'; history; myth;
    nostalgia; past; pastness
Miliband, Ralph 40, 181
miners' strike 35, 73–4, 169
modernity 2, 26–8
    and Communist Party of Great
        Britain 162, 171
    and Labour Party 2, 26–7, 40–1,
        126–8
    and New Labour 19, 27, 114, 125,
        147
    as progressive 42
    and Social Democratic Party 122,
        125, 131–2
    see also future; novelty; optimism
Morris, William 38, 134, 161
Morton, A.L. 36, 37, 166
myth 22, 32, 51, 61, 90, 122, 124, 184

National Curriculum for History 13,
    33, 194–5
    see also Conservative Party, and
        history teaching
national past 4, 32, 33, 69, 70, 100–2,
    105, 107, 111–13, 154
New Communist Party (NCP) 155,
    159–60, 163, 165
New Labour
    and 1945 9, 134
    and co-operative movement 134,
        143–4, 155
    foundation narrative of 57, 123–4,
        147
    heritage, rejection of 53, 60, 122,
        124
    legacy of 184–5
    millennialism of 19
    and modernity 19, 27, 114, 125, 147
    as a national party 14, 92–3
    and 'progressive alliance'

narrative 9, 13–14, 124, 145–6,
147
resistance to 60
and Social Democratic Party 13
temporality of 13–14, 122–4, 125,
147
see also Blair, Tony; Clause IV;
Gould, Philip; Labour Party;
social democracy
New Liberalism see liberalism
new right 8, 20, 25, 98, 183
North West Labour History Group
see socialist history
nostalgia 18, 108, 115, 181
as an accusation 122, 124, 127,
140–1, 143, 147
as connection to past 23
conservative 24, 108
and Labour Party 40–1, 124, 140–1,
143, 147
of Levellers' Day 37–8
as playful 77–9
progressive 11, 23, 24
radical 23
for recent past 37–8
'reflective' 24, 48
and reminiscence 65
'restorative' 24
and socialist history 39
and temporal distance 24, 48, 181
see also heritage; 'heritage
industry'; memory; past;
pastness; pessimism
novelty 8–10, 27–8
and Communist Party of Great
Britain 161
desirability of 2, 13, 14–15, 26–7,
42, 114, 182
and New Labour 13, 114, 122
and Social Democratic Party 13,
122, 125, 131–2
see also future; modernity

optimism 21, 26
and Conservative Party 59

and social democracy 21
see also future; modernity
Osborne, George 1, 28
Owen, David 128, 131, 134, 144

parliamentary history
as 'historic' 6–10, 182–3, 185
as legitimating narrative 3, 6, 8,
183
as marginal interest 82, 182
and socialist history 39–40, 60–1,
67
as Whig history 33, 183
see also history; political party
history; Whig history
party history groups 7, 11, 61–6,
79–80
see also commemoration;
Conservative History Group;
Labour History Group;
Liberal Democrat History
Group; Marxist history;
parliamentary history;
political party history;
socialist history
past
accountability for 35–6, 166–7
as affirmation of the present 2, 42
conservative duty to 2, 18, 31, 42,
182
disregard for 53–4, 61
exoticism of 24, 184
injustices of 21–3, 35–6
as inspiration 21–3, 32, 34, 67, 107,
154, 157
judging the present 30–1, 182
the national 4, 32, 33, 69, 70, 100–2,
105, 107, 111–13, 154
nostalgia as personal connection to
23
obligation to 2, 18, 22–4, 42, 167,
168–9, 181, 182
political power of 2, 36, 38, 42, 109,
154, 182
usable 107, 154, 183

see also heritage; 'heritage industry'; history; memory; nostalgia; pastness
pastness
 aesthetic of 182
 Thatcher, Margaret and 109–14
 see also heritage; 'heritage industry'; history; memory; nostalgia; past
People's March for Jobs 73, 169
pessimism 20–1, 24, 26, 113, 182
Plebs' League *see* socialist history
Plumb, J.H. 32
political party history
 and academic history 7–8, 183
 as identity affirmation 5
 as 'historic' 6, 9–10, 182, 183, 185
 historical records, neglect of 55–6
 lived continuity 5, 182
 as marginal interest 3, 5, 47, 80–2, 182
 Parliament, reinforced by 5, 182
 place, connection to 73–5
 promotion of 54
 see also conservative history; history; Marxist history; memory; party history groups; socialist history; Whig history
post-war settlement 8, 25–6, 94, 98, 115
Powell, Enoch 24, 72, 96, 110
presentism 11, 14, 18, 30–1, 41–2, 53, 56, 110–13, 132, 155, 182–3, 184, 185
progress 14, 21, 26, 30, 36, 39, 42, 123, 154, 182
 'forces of' 27, 31, 42
 language of 28
 see also modernity; optimism; progressivism
'progressive alliance' 28–9, 100
 and Conservative Party 28, 100
 and Labour Party 145–6
 and Liberal Democrat Party 145–6

and New Labour 9, 13, 124, 145–6, 147
and 'progressive dilemma' 133–4
and Social Democratic Party 71
see also Blair, Tony; Marquand, David; progressivism; tradition
'progressive consensus' *see* 'progressive alliance'
progressivism 18–21, 34, 160
 in Communist Party of Great Britain 165, 171–2
 'conservative' 1, 28
 and conservatism 19–21, 28, 101, 111
 and historical process 19–20
 as left-wing 28–9
 as Lib-Lab tradition 1, 20, 28–9
 Marxist 165, 171–2
 as moderation 28–9
 and modernity 28
 'new' 1
 and nostalgia 23, 24
 and obligation 18
 as pluralism 28–30
 political meanings of 20
 as shaping history 25–8
 as social justice 28
 and time 18–20
 see also progress; 'progressive alliance'; social democracy; socialism

re-enactment 73–5
regression 26, 42
ritual 75–6, 169, 182
Rodgers, Bill 128, 129–31, 132

Samuel, Raphael 3, 51, 95, 107, 154, 182
Saville, John 55–6, 156
singing 74–8
social democracy
 within Liberal Democrat Party 20, 146–7

and Marxism 14
as 'modern' 2, 42
and optimism 21
and revisionism 8, 13, 126–9
see also Labour Party; Social
    Democratic Party; socialism;
    tradition
Social Democratic Party (SDP)
archive of 50–1
attacks on 128
and continuity 13, 122, 125,
    128–31, 147
foundation of 13, 124–5
and Gaitskellite revisionism 13,
    128, 147
and Labour Party 13, 125, 128–31,
    147
and liberalism 125, 144–5
and Liberal Party 50–1, 71, 144–5
as loyal to Labour tradition 128–31
novelty of 13; 122, 125, 131–2
and 'progressive alliance'
    narrative 13, 125, 134–5, 144–5,
    147
temporality of 13
see also Jenkins, Roy; Liberal
    Democrat Party; social
    democracy; Owen, David;
    Rodgers, Bill; Williams,
    Shirley
socialism
after 1989 19, 160–1, 163, 164–5,
    168, 165, 173, 176
and Blair, Tony 27, 134–5
in Communist Party of Britain
    169–70
in Communist Party of Great
    Britain 14, 168, 171, 173
and conservatism 92, 97, 99–100
'end of' 19, 165
future, obligation to 22, 36, 39, 58,
    128, 138
in Labour Party 20, 70, 92, 124, 128,
    134, 135, 137, 138–43
and Liberal Party 100

and liberalism 77
and past 21–2
popular 8
and social democracy 21
and Thatcher, Margaret 94, 97
'United Front' against 100
and USSR 160–1, 163, 165
as utopian 182
varieties of 9, 124, 134
see also communism; labour
    movement; Marxism; social
    democracy; socialist history;
    tradition
socialist history 19, 37, 59–60
as alternative narrative of British
    history 2, 58–9, 73
Book of Labour 48, 58, 59, 66–7
Conservative attacks on 100–4
development of 48, 58
Dictionary of Labour Biography 48,
    55–6, 67
and exclusion 39
History Workshop 48
as identity affirmation 107
individuals, attitude to 66–71
Labour Heritage 39, 59–60, 68
North West Labour History Group
    59
and nostalgia 39
and obligation to the past 22–4
Plebs' League 48
Society for the Study of Labour
    History 39, 59
Working Class Movement Library
    48, 58–9, 67
see also Labour History Group;
    labour movement; Labour
    Party; Marxist history;
    socialism
Socialist History Group see Marxist
    History
Socialist Workers Party 160–1, 165
social liberalism see liberalism
Society for the Study of Labour
    History see socialist history

Spanish Civil War *see*
  commemoration
Steel, David 29, 144–5

teleology 31, 109–10, 155, 162, 183
  see also 'end of history'; Marxist
    history; Whig history
Temple, Nina 161, 163, 170–1
Thatcher, Margaret
  and 1688 tercentenary 34–6
  archive of 51–2, 72, 184
  and change 26
  and Churchill 7, 110
  and Conservative Party history 9,
    13, 88, 96, 97–100, 110–1
  Conservative Party members,
    admired by 72, 79
  Friends Of 65, 72
  history, views of 104–5, 109,
    110–11, 184
  legacy of 94, 114–16, 184–5
  and Liberal Party history 9, 96–100
  and National Curriculum for
    History 104–5, 108
  and 'pastness' 109–14
  post-war settlement, challenge to
    26, 98–9
  presentism of 110–13
  as 'progressive' 26, 28
  as radical 28, 98–9
  shape history, desire to 26, 96
  Steel, David, offer from 29
  temporal positioning of 96, 109–14,
    115–16
  and 'Victorian values' 112–3
  see also Conservative Party;
    conservatism
Thompson, E.P. 100, 156
Thompson, Willie 162, 164, 167, 174,
  175
time 2, 5, 14, 18–20, 24, 25, 32–3, 91,
  113, 125
Tolpuddle Martyrs *see*
  commemoration
Toryism 20, 30–1, 97, 98

see also conservatism; tradition
tradition 48, 185
  conservative 9, 30, 109–10, 111
  labour 38, 58–60, 123, 129, 134–5
  liberal 9, 50, 62–3, 71, 77, 100, 125,
    145
  New Liberal 124
  progressive 1, 20, 28–9, 71, 99–100,
    124, 145
  radical liberal 134–5
  social democrat 13, 50, 63, 145, 159
  socialist 77, 131, 132, 134, 161, 166
  Tory 98
  see also heritage; 'heritage
    industry'; history; memory;
    nostalgia; past; ritual; singing

USSR 19, 27, 95, 127, 155, 158–62,
  165, 174
  see also communism; Marxism

Walter, Benjamin 21
Whig history 6, 19, 31–3, 183
  and Butterfield, Herbert 31–2
  conservative historians, rejected
    by 31, 106–7, 108–9
  dominance of 30–2, 42
  and National Curriculum for
    History 106–9
  parliamentary history as 33, 183
  Plumb, JH, attacks on 32
  and Thatcher, Margaret 110–1
  see also liberalism; whiggism
whiggism 26, 30–2, 34–5, 98, 109
  see also liberalism; Whig history
White, Hayden 18–9
Willetts, David 92–3, 94, 100–1, 114
Williams, Shirley 77, 145
Wilson, Harold, 26, 111
Workers Educational Association 36
Working Class Movement Library
  see socialist history

Young Britons *see* Conservative Party

Lightning Source UK Ltd.
Milton Keynes UK
UKOW06f0748220816

281123UK00007B/100/P